Abraham Lincoln–March 6, 1865

WILLIE SPEAKS OUT!

THE PSYCHIC WORLD OF ABRAHAM LINCOLN

CAPTAIN ELLIOTT V. FLECKLES
Chaplain, United States Air Force, Retired

1974
LLEWELLYN PUBLICATIONS
ST. PAUL, MINNESOTA 55165

ISBN 0-87542-233-0
First edition 1974

Library of Congress
CIP *73-23123*

Publisher: LLEWELLYN PUBLICATIONS
Typographer: Imperial Press, Inc., Long Beach, Ca.
Lithographer: R. R. Donnelley & Sons, Co., Chicago, Ill.

PRINTED IN THE UNITED STATES OF AMERICA

To my devoted partner, my 'forgiving Grace'. Her persuasive personality and patience finally made it possible to complete this Lincoln Project and to submit it for publication.

TABLE OF CONTENTS

Abraham Lincoln
by George Henry Story

I am optimist enough to believe in this new age now beginning — The Aquarian Age — the flame of knowledge and enlightenment will spread like wild fire. It will be a poor look-out for the world if I am wrong, for mankind has been headed for destruction and has not missed the goal by much.

Former British Air Marshall Lord Dowding

INTRODUCTION

We are informed that we now live in the Aquarian Age. Lincoln we know was an Aquarian. We are likewise told we are passing through a spiritual evolution or revolution. That was Lincoln, throughout most of his life. He wound up by becoming 'too spiritual to be religious.' That man has a body but is a soul, has yet to dawn upon most of mankind.

Both Abraham Lincoln's friends and enemies (in particular the latter) provide plenty of data concerning the unfoldment of Mr. Lincoln's mystic-psychic life as related to the spiritual. Yet why do Lincoln students, both historians and biographers, invariably leave more or less untouched this side of a great president's private life? The burning of Lincoln's private, personal correspondence by his eldest son Robert has only tended to make the entire question a more burning issue. It has likewise limited, if not prevented, access to first hand Lincoln source material.

To get beyond words like 'occult' or 'parapsychology', a word invented because psychology failed to fulfill its original meaning (science of the soul or psyche), this book under whatever name or sign attempts to illustrate that through Abraham Lincoln, what we call supernatural can become natural and the paranormal can become normal, or a so-called 'miracle' when clearly understood, can cease to be a miracle in the accepted sense, but rather a fulfillment of Divine Law. All of God's children have in some degree certain endowments referred to as 'gifts of the spirit' simply awaiting the chance to be exercised or expressed through Divine Love or the Holy Spirit.

In allowing Mr. Lincoln's favorite son Willie to narrate the entire story from the 'other side,' underscores his father's conviction that there is but ONE LIFE and that LIFE IS ETERNAL. Willie passed over at age eleven. His father soon accepted as a fact of life that Willie was more alive than ever. Personal survival became paramount in the life of this primitive pioneer who was to hold the position of our nation's chief executive during a period when this nation was being torn asunder as never before or since. For lack of formal education Lincoln was able to freely activate his abundant intuitive, instinctive powers, those gifts of the Spirit that we now call ESP or HSP (Higher Sensory Perception) until he experienced the 'Emancipation', first of his inner self and then of the nation.

If Willie were asked to justify his account of his father's psychical life as a means of achieving the spiritual, he might respond in some such manner . . .

. . . Among a great cloud of witnesses on the other side, thoughts rather than words, keep coming. My death occured over 100 years ago. That does not matter. Time and space do not matter. Physics is proving that 'matter does not matter' any more. The American Nobel Prize winner and physicist, DuBoise, states; "There is less and less disposition to deny that there are psychic and spiritual forces as yet latent in human nature, of which we know naught whereunto the future development may reach."[1]

We know that the experimental search for antimatter initiated in 1928 by Paul Dirac, a British physicist, has recently been taken up by two young Russian nuclear physicists, Valentin I. Petrukhin and Valdimir I. Rykalin. The expectation is that a new form of 'useful energy' can ultimately be produced.[1a]

Where we are, time and space do not matter. This is something to remember throughout this story of mine. We are far more aware of what takes place on your planet than you are. Indeed, we know far more about your life than you do about ours.

Pa remained something of a mystery to me, his proud, young son. A distinguished contemporary admitted: "I could never quite fathom his thoughts or be quite sure that I saw the line along which he was working."[2] This gives me some consolation however. It has been possible for me to "fathom out" more of Pa since my death and his. There is less of mystery and more of meaning in the totality and fullness of his life.

One apparent fault among others in this account could be, as indicated, the feeling that some material has been lifted out of context. Whatever the failings, the intent has been to throw fresh light on Lincoln's innermost life. In the cause of accuracy and balance, a wide range of documentary data, as stated, has been drawn from the more intimate, if not reliable sources.

You will also understand and recall that the extensive documentation as applied to Pa's psychic life does *not* come from the same Willie who died at age 11 but rather a Willie who has undergone a metamorphosis, a transformation or transition, which involves growth.

We know that Pa stood his ground when persecution followed his psychic trail. The psychical for him was more than a passing phenomenon. It was, let us not forget, the pathway to the Spiritual. He was prepared to pursue that path, fully aware that in human hands psychical research was and is ever, in danger of defeating itself. This is especially true when psychical research becomes organized. It may thus become a self-perpetuating, ingrown institution doomed to bury the very truth it strives to uncover and explore.

Henry Ward Beecher, one of Pa's many psychic friends, speaks in these terms: "Dead, he (Lincoln) now speaks to men who are willing to hear what before they refused to listen to . . . Is Washington dead? Is any man that was fit to live dead?" Disenthralled of flesh and risen in the unobstructed sphere . . . he (Pa) begins his illimitable work.[3]

This narrative is an introduction and a vindication of Pa's psychical life; born of the Holy Spirit. The reality of this narrative will dawn upon those who are able to explore with Pa. This is the purpose of the Spiritual Frontiers Fellowship now operating *within* the churches. It aims to open the churches to the biblical-psychical so fundamental to all religion. It has Pa's blessings although he is aware that the best way to kill truth is to organize it.

Pa emerged from a background of orthodoxy and dogma to realize how self defeating can be an attempt at establishing a new religion out of an old truth. Pa saw Spiritualism as one of many examples. He had a caution, if not an aversion, toward institutionalized religion in general. It inevitably crucifies the highest and best. Pa in this context became too spiritual to be religious. "Things seen are temporal, things unseen are eternal" — that was Abraham Lincoln.

If the term Spiritualism seems overstressed it is simply because it was so loosely used (if not abused) in Lincoln's day, even as today, so that it becomes practically synonymous in the minds of many with what is called extra sensory or higher sensory. During the Lincoln rebellion, Spiritualism as a religion first became a craze. Then and since it has gone through periods of boom and bust.

Fears vanish when we learn that it is the soul of man which links him with other souls . . . like atoms, like suns, like galaxies our spirits are systems of forces which vibrate continually to each others attractive powers.

Frederic W. H. Meyers
Human Personality and Its Survival After Death

PROLOGUE

Those who find *Willie Speaks Out* disappointing, if not disillusioning, may find some consolation in the comments of Sydney Harris, the well known and respected author and lecturer who confesses: "*Jonathan Livingston Seagull* to me is an utterly synthetic book yet deemed an inspiration by millions of readers."

This book should put at rest the notion that the main, if not the only, evidence now available concerning the séances held in and out of the White House during the Lincoln administration, is derived from a book which bears the sensational title *Was Abraham Lincoln a Spiritualist?* My account of Mr. Lincoln's psychical mystical life, as narrated by his favorite son Willie, is intended to dispel some of the controversy surrounding the publisher of the book as well as the author Nettie Colburn Maynard.

The extensive documentation is designed to show among other things, that there is no book which constitutes *the* one substantial source material for the mystic-psychic Lincoln

This book attempts to explain why so many have so long thought the Maynard book, with a misconceived title by a misunderstood author, has been full of superficial claims.

We shall see that over the years Lincoln students have gone far beyond, and long before the Maynard book, to Lincoln's contemporaries and enemies to come up with conclusions both pro and con, but all testifying to Lincoln's participation in the mystical-psychical life of his times.

There will be those who still contend that any reference to Lincoln's séances or sittings is merely a rehash of the Maynard book and so much bunk!

The title no less than the content of my book may seem obtuse, if not frivilous, to those unable to comprehend the continuity of personality or individuality as well as their unfoldment through eternity, even though this spiritual concept is *basic* to most, if not all religions.

Also, if the 'sixth sense' does not make common sense, then my book, although extensively documented, will remain mere controversial, conjectural claims.

Six men were instrumental in the preparation of this book. All six, like most people, had a sixth sense.

My dad was the first of the six. He was a prolific reader of history and biography, including the Bible. He turned my attention to Abraham Lincoln. After much formal education, and much later in life, my interest in Lincoln was all but lost.

Then came Dr. Ralph Harlow. For over a quarter of a century he devoted his life to his students in the Department of Religion at Smith College. He was always out on the frontiers with his wife Marion and sometimes with men like Sherwood Eddy or Norman Thomas. On his sabbatical leave, he would be in Athens at the American College or Robert's College. The Harlows became our neighbors in Northampton and Martha's Vineyard, Massachusetts. To know Ralph or any one of the other six was to become involved on many fronts; in particular, the frontiers of the spirit. No one of them would consider himself or herself a Lincoln scholar. Most of them, except my father, were students of the sixth sense or the extra-sensory. Some of them were more experienced than others. Among the books Ralph Harlow has written is *A Life After Death,* which recounts his spiritual-psychical life.

Ralph introduced me to Kivie Kaplan and Rev. Arthur Ford. They are both mentioned in Ralph's book. Kivie, a successful business executive, was to become President of the National Association for the Advancement of Colored People.

All three of us, Ralph, Kivie and myself, were to come under the influence of Arthur Ford. Arthur's name has become synonymous nationally with the development of the psychical as applied to the spiritual. Arthur, along with Sherwood Eddy, as mentioned in this book, were the founders of the Spiritual Frontiers Fellowship. It was the Reverend Ford who revived my study of Lincoln. His gift of an elaborate copy of Stefan Lorant's *Lincoln* was an incentive. Most of all, Arthur Ford stimulated a spiritual-psychical approach to the Great Emancipator.

'Guilt by Association' is the title of one section in this book. In or out of the news media, it is as commonplace today as in Lincoln's time. Mr. Lincoln can testify that one of the primary targets in this process is the President of the United States. Mediumship by its very nature is suspect and subjected to abuse. The Reverend Arthur Ford over the years has not been exempt, yet no one more than Ford was aware of the human defects and limitations which enter the psychical as related to the spiritual life. Whatever Ford's faults and failures, of which he confesses to his share, he was nevertheless the founder of a *Fellowship* which continues to spread within the church at home and abroad.

Meantime Ford's batting average remains a challenge to those who have neglected their 'gifts of the spirit'. On more than one occasion Reverend Ford struck out or made a foul play, not to mention the pop flies that were caught. Yet to his own amazement, and that of endless participants and spectators, he has hit many homers, while giving himself little or no credit.

The various charges against Ford and other noted sensitives fade in the background in view of the numberless occasions around the world when he and his guide (Fletcher) worked together among total strangers, individually or in groups. The latter included college students, seminarians and members of the armed forces. And what about the vast crowds on whom he excercised his gifts of the spirit in some public forum or church congregation, anywhere and everywhere, often in the name of The Spiritual Frontiers Fellowship?

Ford was no Lincoln and Lincoln no Ford, yet both were recognized by the great and near great, at home and abroad, and both were subjected to bitter, if not undue, criticism.

Fifth in the line of six men was Rev. George Daisley. George came to this country as a notable British psychic. He was considered by Ford as one of Britain's great mediums. He is deeply spiritual. He has been active since childhood as a sensitive. His whole life has been dedicated to the development of the spiritual-psychical nature in people. On his arrival in this country, he sought to work through the Spiritual Frontiers Fellowship, and has, to some extent. He is the founder of the Hallowed Grounds Fellowship at Santa Barbara, California. A healing center has recently been opened in the outskirts of that city. George, according to my wife's notes, predicted when this Lincoln project would materialize. The preliminary stages had been under way for some years.

The last in line is the main character of this narrative, Abraham Lincoln. He, of all six men, has brought to this book an appreciation of his higher sensory perception. His sixth sense was first and last a spiritual phenomena. My birthday follows by a few days that of Mr. Lincoln. This, we are told, has given to our separate lives a certain 'Aquarian' drive and it comes in for comment during the course of this book.

Innumerable Lincoln collections, private and public, rare and not so rare, have been consulted. To name a few: there is the William Wyles Collection at the University of California at Santa Barbara; the McLellan Collection at Brown University, Providence, Rhode Island; the John Hay Collection at the Illinois State Historical Society Library, Springfield, Illinois; and the Risdon Collection at Occidental College, Los Angeles, California. Then came various collections at the Library of Congress and the National Archives in Washington, D. C. Also the Huntington Library at San Marino, California; the Lincoln Foundation Library at Fort Wayne, Indiana and the Lincoln Book Shop in Chicago, Illinois have all produced some profitable study material. Among the big city public libraries which have made a contribution to this book are those in New York City, Cleveland, Los Angeles, and Chicago. Then came the second-hand book shops such as Acres of Books in Long Beach, California. Thanks to the Long Beach Press-Telegram for the illustration and inscription from their September 28, 1973 edition which relates to the removal of the local library and the temporary removal of the

Lincoln Statue. The old local library contributed much to my work on Lincoln. Also my appreciation to the Library of Congress for their supply of illustrations as well as the Illinois Historical Society, the Chicago Historical Society and of course, the Lincoln Life Foundation at Ft. Wayne Indiana. Some valuable literature was uncovered in the British Museum and London University, as well as the British College of Psychical Science. One of my sons, then on the faculty of the University of Hawaii, made possible access to their library and further data. My youngest and most artistic son, now a teacher, was at the age of 15 very Lincoln conscious. Some of his Lincoln sketches, accomplished as a lad, are included in this book. Born the day before Lincoln's birthday could account for his early psychic awareness.

This narrative as told by Willie could be classified as a combination of history, biography and philosophy. It is primarily an interpretation or an introduction to the spiritual-psychical Lincoln. This presentation of a great American in this manner may constitute, to some, neither bird nor beast, just fowl! Something needs to be said, however, of Abraham Lincoln other than the usual historical-biographical line. Lincoln student, Dr. George Fox once commented: "*The Collected Works* (of Lincoln), wonderful as it is, by its very nature does not permit inclusion of a study of the spiritual content of Lincoln's life — and who can deny that there is a rich spiritual element in his make-up and activities? Much of the knowledge of this phase of his life comes from the very sources which the editors to *The Collected Works* by-passed."[1] From the standpoint of this book, 'the rich, spiritual element' is the mystical-psychical Lincoln.

Lincoln has much to say concerning the revolution in progress in our educational and religious institutions. Much of what he has to say is born of his mystical-psychical nature. It requires no artificial stimulants. If we ask why so much of history has judiciously avoided or prejudiciously treated the psychic, sensitive part of Lincoln, this book has suggestions. One section of this book deals with 'the careful historian' . . . careful to preserve the Lincoln image . . . careful lest the controversial mar his greatness. Few historians or biographers have done a more thorough job on Lincoln than Prof. James G. Randall. He speaks for himself and all Lincoln authors when he warns; "To write of Lincoln's fundamental views requires a good deal of caution. It is the commonest thing to see the mind of Lincoln fitted into a preconceived pattern. Sometimes this is done by an elastic or strained interpretation of what he actually said, sometimes by pure conjecture as to what he would have said or done on a matter far beyond his time. Writers look into the body of Lincoln utterances, or skim the surface, for the most diverse purposes. Obviously not all of the Lincolns we have presented to us can be genuine."[2]

One response to such admonition is 'amen and amen.' It is warning enough to prick the conscience or consciousness of those who attempt a Lincoln book. This writer begs the indulgence of all who would accompany him on this venture into the soul of the psychic-mystic Lincoln. Please, pardon any real or apparent strained interpretation or preconceived pattern. Professor of History Current, University of North Carolina, has alluded to those Lincoln authors who are "more disciplined in their judgments than Nicolay or Hay and more recent biographers."[3] That writer obviously regards himself as one of the 'more disciplined.' But who is to judge another person's judgment as to what is more or less disciplined? This becomes especially true when the subject matter (as in the case of this book) is admittedly controversial. As to this controversial subject matter, we are told; "The trouble is the scholars disagree. They differ at many points in their analysis, both of events and personalities."[4] In the course of time, as this book indicates, this subject matter may become less, rather than more controversial. In contrast to earlier years, for example, it has been my privilege in recent times to 'sit' with some of the great sensitives (mediums) in Great Britain and America.

My years as a school librarian at a conservative New England institution, later as Chaplain in the Army Air Force, followed by more years as Chaplain in the Veterans' neuro-psychiatric hospitals have been conducive to the writing of this book. One of my first attempts as an author dealt with the soul of a neuro-psychiatric patient. My manuscripts, related to the work of Carl

Jung, are quoted several times in this present endeavor.

If the use of quotations in this book appears to be overdone or out of place, my apologies to the reader and the originator of the quotation. A detailed section on footnotes at the rear of this book recognizes by name and number the source of each quotation. In addition, there appears a complete bibliography. As for the appropriate selection of quotations and their proper location in the narrative, there is undoubtedly room for improvement. The news columnist, Sidney Harris, asks; "Which Lincoln do you want to hear?" He dwells on "the evil of taking statements out of context and making a synthetic fabric out of individual strands."[5]

Willie was the alter-ego of his father and like his father he made the most of a brief life on earth. He remained on this level of life just eleven years; long enough to see his 'Pa' move from his home-state capitol to the national capitol. As the story unfolds, Willie becomes increasingly aware of his father's affirmative attitude toward personal survival and spirit communication. From his vantage point in the spirit world, Willie is now able to evaluate the prevalent scientific and spiritual advances toward survival and communication. *Willie Speaks Out* in vain to those who cannot become attuned to the idea of personal survival and spirit communcation, particularly as applied to Abraham Lincoln. Willie is speaking to those who want to hear of the Lincoln whose gifts of the spirit include the psychical and mystical.

Willie would be the first to concede, "the Lincoln seen and the Lincoln interpreted rarely correspond to the Lincoln that was."[6] If anyone, however, is qualified to overcome that handicap, it should be Willie. He now has a perception and a perspective which can penetrate the veil between the here and the hereafter. Moreover, Willie would remind you again the child that was, has matured spiritually and psychically. Thus he observes and bears witness to those aspects of his father's life which made for the Emancipation Proclamation and the personal emancipation of his Pa. Willie takes Lincoln through the stages of his spiritual-psychical unfoldment from his own death to that of his father.

A fair criticism of this interpretation of Lincoln could be the absence of direct data from the hand and heart of Lincoln. Most of the evidence of Lincoln's psychic life is circumstantial, yet substantial. It is substantial if we consider the various sources and independent cross references. One who is skeptical of the psychical in Lincoln writes: "Where there is neither proof nor disproof, they (Lincoln's biographers) accept those reports, however ill-founded, which fit in with their own conceptions of what is truly Lincolnian."[7] The term "ill-founded" can be another value judgment. An aversion to the psychical could account for such terms. Incidentally, some of the more realistic reports and attitudes have been found among Lincoln contemporaries and friends. One Lincoln enthusiast wrote: "I know that the custom among students of Lincoln now is to discount any life of Lincoln that has not been scientifically processed and to throw into the historic rubbish heap the many old biographies of the martyred President by those who knew him or were associated with him, particularly, if many years had passed between his life and that of the narrators. But I submit that the people who know one best are those associated with one a great deal, or who have intimately known him the longest."[8] This book has drawn heavily from those 'associates.'

Nothing could be more rewarding to the author of this book than if it should lead to the discovery of old and original material which might provide new or first-hand information on Lincoln's higher sensory perception. Such added data might open a few closed minds among scholars and teachers. It could alter the curricula in schools and colleges, including Church schools. The place to develop the gifts of the spirit are not merely in the home where they are too often suppressed, but rather in day by day grade school. Mrs. Eloise Shields, Psychologist for the Torrance, California United School District, reports; "The adolescent years between 12 and 18 are a very rich period of ESP and other psychic experiences." She urges parents to allow their children to "talk about them". As higher sensory or extra-sensory perception is becoming an acceptable subject for study, the day will dawn when the mystic-psychic life of world leaders in the Lincoln tradition is recognized as a legitimate part of public education. Then evolution will begin to replace violent revolution.

The mysticism of the orient must come to the rescue of the materialism of the occident and vice versa. This was apparent in Lincoln's life and times, even as it is today. This in part is the thesis of this book. Evolution, unlike revolution, is imperceptible. It is both painful and peaceful.

It takes a Lincoln to suffer the consequences of an activated faith in the unseen forces at work around us and within. We are dealing with a president who spoke and understood the language of a rebellious generation . . . a generation caught in a losing, endless battle between the states. If we feel that the riots and civil strife of our day are extra-ordinary, consider the wholesale slaughter going on within our own borders during Lincoln's administration. The people were yearning for some experience that would allow release from their preoccupation with the destruction of persons and property, of American homes and families. They looked beyond their five senses . . . their finite minds. They wanted something more than the mere assurance that life is continous . . . they wanted to communicate with their loved ones killed or lost in battle.

In this book Lincoln is not interpreted as the Great Emancipator who freed the slaves. That is as misleading to this present day generation of blacks and whites, North and South, as in other generations. In *Willie Speaks Out* we see his Pa as the Great Emancipator of himself and others from the limitations of the physical and the planetary time and space. "In the

Infinite Universe, man may now feel at home for the first time. The worst fear is over; the true security is won. The worst fear was the fear of spiritual extinction or spiritual solitude; the true security is in the telepathic law."[9] The elepathic law includes communication with the spirit world.

The epilogue to this book carries the title *Vindication.* This entire book is intended as an introduction and a vindication of Lincoln, the spiritual psychic and mystic. By virtue of his character and position, Lincoln appears to have side-stepped the 'isms' of his day whether in politics or religion. If there is any justification for an epilogue or *Vindication,* it is to tie up some loose ends and to indicate some of the more distinguished world figures who, like Lincoln, have derived much strength from the mystic and psychic in life. Some times they have done so in secret . . . sometimes not. Many of these people have paid the price of being ahead of their time. Lincoln learned to live with the psychical, the mystical and the critical even as he learned to live with his mental-physical nature. This book indicates a probable correlation between his diverse characteristics.

As this introduction began with six men, let it end with five people, all of whom have been persuasive in the completion of this book. First, two dear ladies Cherille and Grace. Cherille was a devoted wife and mother on this earth plane. Grace has since become a faithful, devoted wife, most patient in my pursuit of Lincoln. Then comes Si Slavin and his wife Jane, our friends and sponsors of Spiritual Research in addition to their active business and professional lives. A most unexpected aide came through a cousin and namesake, William Elliott Martin. To him and his family, I am deeply indebted for their most thoughtful concern. I can only hope for their approval of this Lincoln project.

Willie Speaks Out to every generation and all mankind if they care to listen. That was no less true of his father, Abraham Lincoln. A concomitant theme or learning from Lincoln is that the threat of total annihilation or extinction need no longer trouble us. Not alone creation and recreation go on through eternity . . . so does communication. The personality survives death.

The words 'truth' or 'proof' as used in this book carry no final or fixed implications or conclusions. Lincoln would prefer to think of such words as relative, not absolute! The purpose of this presentation is not to prove anything, but to point out those references, direct and indirect, to Lincoln's psychic-mystic personality born of the Spirit.

In his discovery of self, Lincoln revealed an innate capacity to deal with life and death far beyond any of the prescribed rules laid down by institutional systems, political or religious, military or educational. The rebirth of Lincoln led to the tapping of unknown resources and unused talents in handling affairs of State. Through his son Willie he is telling us that there is far more to life than the here and the now. Much of the story is told in the light of modern science and psychical research.

In no sense can the author claim the gift of automatic writing or mediumship. As for insight and inspiration, that is something else!

William Wallace Lincoln
by Matthew Brady (1861)

Do you ever find yourself talking with the dead? . . . I do. Ever since Willie's death, I catch myself involuntarily talking to him as if he were near me . . . and I feel that he is!

Abraham Lincoln to his Secretary of the Treasury Salmon P. Chase

CHAPTER I
ME, MY DEATH AND MY FAMILY

1
My Gift for Words

My name is William Wallace Lincoln.

I was born December 21, 1850.[1] My home town was Springfield, Illinois. My father's first name was Abraham. Tad, my younger brother, and I called him Pa. Tad pronounced it 'Paw.'[2] Most people thought of me as the counterpart of Pa.

A family friend, Mr. N. P. Willis, wrote that my "leading trait was a fearless, kindly frankness." He added that I was willing that "everything should be as different as it pleased . . . yet I was unmoved in my conscious single-heartedness."[3] If such a description of me is accurate, it confirms in some degree that Pa and I had much in common. It is indeed a profile of Pa.

Tad was more like Ma.

My Pa had many gifts, among them a gift for words. My Pa was unschooled and unlettered, yet in his correspondence, his speeches and his debates, there came through his gift for words, including his gifts of the spirit. This became evident at Cooper Union during his political campaigns, then later at Gettysburg and his second inauguration.

That I had Father's gift for words was first suggested by my correspondence. Two of my childhood letters appeared in print. They were addressed to one of my playmates in Springfield, Henry Remann.[4] Three years elapsed between the letters. One Lincoln biographer, W. A. Evans, was impressed by my "extended vocabulary" and improved style.

The first letter was dated Chicago, June 18, 1859. It was full of me and Father. We had traveled. We had gone to the theatre. Father was great for theatrical plays, mostly comedy. "Me and Father have a nice room together." The letter goes into detail, "We had two little beds. We had two little washbasins." The word 'little' hardly applies to Father. The second letter is dated Washington, D. C., September 30, 1861. At the top I wrote "Executive Mansion." The war fever had spread. "My companions and I are raising a battalion.[5]

Father, in his role as commander-in-chief of the armed forces, did not share my boyhood enthusiasm. I was then almost eleven. Father's aim was to wage peace, not war. In Springfield, somewhat to Pa's dismay, I had been infected by both the war hysteria and politics.

Another paternal literary trait was my propensity for writing poetry. Our Negro maid in the White House, Elizabeth Keckley, referred to me as "a studious boy with literary taste."[6] Upon entering my room, she would find me pencil and paper in hand, with an open book. That also describes Pa much of the time.

At the outbreak of the Civil War, former Senator, Col. Edward D. Baker was killed. It was the 21st day of October, 1861. Pa had great admiration for the Colonel, which I shared. The death of the Colonel, not many months before my death, prompted me to write a poem. It was published in the *National Republican Times.*[7] My poem drew from the editor of the local press the comment; "Quite creditable as a first effort from one so young."[8] Pa named my brother Eddie after Colonel Baker. Eddie's middle name was Baker.[9] Eddie died very young, shortly before I was born. I recall the Colonel taking me in has arms and kissing me. A few months later the Colonel was killed in battle. Tad and I would shout; "Pa says there is a battle in Virginia." It was the Battle of Bull Run fought July 21, 1861. Overcome by curiosity, we would run to a White House window. To us the roar of battle was like the slamming of doors. To Pa it was something else. The doors of hope were slammed shut.[10]

In Springfield when I would lead the kids in a parade, I was called upon to

Springfield 1860
Lincoln with sons Willie and Tad (peeping from behind corner post). Photo by John Adams Whipple.

make a speech. According to one of our young neighbors, I "proudly responded." She commented on my success as a speech-maker.

She further described my attendance at Miss Corcoran's School in Springfield. Here I took "delight in discussing problems of the day with the other boys."[11]

I was to find Washington stimulating, intellectually if not spiritually. It was full of history. We were soon in the thick of it. Our home was the White House. The high and the low, the great and the would-be great knocked at our doors. My Washington diary tells the story. It contains a collection of memoranda; news clippings of daily events. In later years Father was to show it to friends. The accounts of Pa's first inauguration consumed considerable space. The dates, defeats, and deaths of distinguished leaders in numerous battles were recorded. One biographer recounts that "Willie's mind was becoming increasingly mature."

Julia Taft, a young neighbor girl of 16, assisted in the training and education of Tad and myself. She served to prepare us for our school work . . . on week-days and for Sunday. The latter meant far more to me than to Tad.[12] In addition to me and Tad there were the two Taft children, Bud and Holly. Tad became 'unruly ' on occasions.[13]

Mother had been an Episcopalian, but we attended the New York Avenue Presbyterian Church . . . sometimes as a family. Father appreciated the spiritual counsel of the pastor, Dr. Phineas D. Gurley. He was to preside at my funeral.[14] Father was fundamentally religious but not a religious fundamentalist. He was deeply spiritual but not a spiritualist.

2

My Love of Animals

Another characteristic I shared with my father was love of animals. Back in Springfield, when Pa was not riding the circuit (law courts) on horseback, he was attending horse shows and horse races. Now and then he placed a wager. Tad and I, with our neighborhood friends, were invited to these events. This was not Pa's only diversion in those days. He played handball.[1]

A letter signed by Father is dated around May 10, 1861. Pa's script and spelling left something to be desired. It was thought to read, "My boy, William, wishes you to sell a *man* for him." To some this illustrated Pa had a split personality over slavery. A Lincoln scholar finally decided the 'n' was meant to be an 'r.'[2]

In Washington my delight was my pony. In all kinds of weather I was on his back. It weakened my health and contributed to my fatal illness.[3] Between Tad and myself, we had a collection of animals at the Executive Mansion. We had cats, dogs, goats, ponies, and "even a turkey."[4]

In the heat of the war, when Father was frantically chasing between the state department building and the war department, we would run ahead of him "chasing pebbles."[5] We were his one consolation. He decided to get us a goat. Pa had two goats of his own. They would come bounding at the sound of his voice.[6] On Wednesday night, February 10, 1862 a great tragedy occurred. It was just ten days before my death. The White House stables burned to the ground and Tad and I lost our ponies. Tad threw a fit.[7] I did not survive it!

3

Spoiled yet Unspoiled

In his diary, Attorney General Bates wrote of me as being "too much idolized by his parents."[1] Upon my death, Tad became the center of Pa's devotion. Tad lived to be eighteen. He has been described as a "lovable, incorrigible youngster who captured the country's heart."[2] He was tongue tied. If we were spoiled, Pa was largely to blame. Ma was the disciplinarian. Herndon, Pa's law partner, does not exaggerate when he describes the law office as a wreck soon after our arrival. "The boys were absolutely unrestrained . . . if they pulled all the books from the shelves, bent the points of all the pens, overturned ink-stands, scattered law papers over the floor or threw the pencils in the spittoon, it never disturbed the serenity of their father's good nature."[3]

We were spoiled, yet unspoiled. My mother's sister commented that I was "thoughtful and grave beyond my years." She relates that Tad once put on a scene at a guest luncheon in the White House. I sat in silence. To our guest, Congressman Galloway, Father remarked that my silence reminded him of himself. My cousin, Mrs. Grimsley, gives no reason for the disturbance. She was more impressed by Pa's reference to my silence. "I know every step of the process by which that boy arrived at a satisfactory solution of the question before him. It is just by such a slow method I attain results."[4]

Robert, my older brother, was more a Todd, than a Lincoln. Tad was in between. My coming into the world was most welcome; it came so soon after the passing of young Eddie.[5]

Eulogies can be colored. An example is the tribute paid me upon passing. "With all the splendor that was around this little fellow in his new home, he was so bravely and beautifully himself . . . and that only. A wild flower planted from the prairie to the hot-house, he retained his prairie habits, unalterably pure and simple, till he died."[6] The same person, my poet friend Willis, once referred to my "self-possession" upon the arrival of royalty. It was Prince Napoleon, accompained by Secretary of State Seward.

The contrast between the President and his Secretary of State Seward was painful. This was true of other cabinet members like Stanton and Chase. No one compared with Pa.

As the august gentlemen of state entered the White House grounds, according to Mr. Willis, I doffed my cap and bowed, then proceeded "unconcernedly" with my play.[7] Here again, like father like son. A coachman and guardian at the White House gate once observed that "my head leaned toward my left shoulder," as a Lincoln.[8] A comment on my unconcernedness in the presence of royalty, an observation which touched me, read; "It was (in) this mingling of qualities that Willie so resembled his father."[9]

On one occasion, Pa related my dismay when he gave me less spending money than I had expected. It was at his law office in Springfield. I walked out, leaving the money on the table. Said Pa to Herndon, "he will be back." I soon returned and quietly disappeared with the money.[10] Father was to observe that he too, in a crisis, would respond in some such manner.

Our young devoted caretaker and neighbor in Washington was Julia Taft. She embarrassed me when she wrote, "he is a lovable, sweet-tempered boy."[11] That is too much, yet it reminded me of Pa much of the time.

Julia was hard on yound Tad.[12] By nature, Pa could not refrain from intervening when Ma put her foot down. Tad and I begged to attend a reception. Ma insisted we should remain at home. We had messed ourselves with molasses candy. Pa agreed to take care of us if we were allowed to attend the reception. We attended.[13]

Nothing irritated Pa more than public adoration. I sympathized with him. One day, visitors to the Capitol stared at me. I reacted: "Wasn't there ever a President who had children?"[14]

4
My Illness

The reports varied as to the onset of my illness. I was supposed to be in an unbroken "delirium" for five days.[1] Then I was "improved and out of danger."[2] Finally, I was "hopelessly ill."

I brightened up on February 20, 1862. I held my Buddy's (named Bud) hand. On that day, at 5:00 p.m., I expired.[3] It was peaceful.

It had been painful and there was no definite diagnosis. Some called it an "acute malarial infection." The term "bilious fever" was used. To others, it was "typhoid fever."[4]

Morbid public speculation surrounded my death. Privacy is no part of a president's life in or out of the White House. Our family was no exception. It irritated both my parents.

We had lived in the White House less than one year when the Civil War had begun. As the war ended, my younger brother Tad cheered, while my older brother Robert went into seclusion.

Among the factors which contributed to my fatal illness, was the lack of sanitation in the Capitol. During the 1860's it was referred to as a place of "wretched unhealthiness."[5] There were "open sewers and a walled-in filthy city canal." The city garbage was dumped into the water at the foot of 17th Street. This was Washington, our city of national pride and devotion. The streets were either muddy or dusty, depending on the weather. The city had "70 separate and distinct stinks." The pollution of air and water was real. Pa's favorite retreat was the Soldier's Home.[6] During the hot, smelly months Pa would ride the four miles to his retreat on horseback.

A map dated 1865 carries the title, *The Stranger's Guide to Washington.* On the lower right side of the map there is this quote: "Remember, Willie Lincoln probably died of typhoid." There are numerous quotes verifying conditions in Washington.[7] Another element entered into my early demise. It was my "delicate constitution."[8] This could not be said of Pa; his health was poor because he did not care for himself. Tad and I caught the measles soon after our arrival in Washington.[9] A letter, dated July 4, 1860, written from Springfield, is addressed to Dr. A. G. Henry of Oregon and is signed, A. Lincoln. In it, Pa tells of "my hard and tedious spell of Scarlet Fever."[10] Pa was worried. This was no preparation for Washington.

Yet Julia Taft, writing of Tad and me during those days in Washington, pictures us a "two healthy, rollicking Western boys, never accustomed to restraint or notice which their father's exalted position drew."[11]

In the midst of my illness came a White House family crisis. The first official reception had been planned. Invitations were sent to the honored guests. The seriousness of my illness became increasingly evident. On the evening of the reception my condition was critical. To my parents the official reception became a nightmare. For several days previous Pa and Ma had considered calling off the whole affair. "To be or not to be" — that was the question. Plans for the reception proceeded when the White House physician declared, "the boy is out of danger!"[12] Throughout the reception Pa and Ma kept watch over me. Most of the evening Pa seemed to be at my bedside. Senator and Mrs. Orville Browning, close friends, agreed to remain at the White House throughout the day and night.[13] Adding to the confusion was Tad's condition. He was threatened by my illness.[14]

5

Pa Overwhelmed

Pa had secured the services of a nurse, Mrs. Rebecca R. Pomroy. She came through the efforts of Dorothea Dix, superintendent of women's nurses in

Washington. Mrs. Pomroy had been on the staff of the military hospital. As my death drew near, this lady became a source of strength.[1] She had lost several sons and her husband. Her trust in God came to Pa's rescue. His sanity became more secure as death overtook me.[2] Like a child, Pa would cry, "Why, why, why?" Our nurse would lament; "As blow came upon blow and all were taken . . . I could and did submit. Then I was very happy." The agonizing heart of the president was consoled . . . "Your experience helps me bear my affliction."[3]

Mrs. Pomroy remained at the White House after my passing to care for Pa. He was "sick at heart."[4] My death proved to be one of the great inner crises of Pa's whole life.[5] A Lincoln scholar refers to it as the hardest blow Pa ever suffered.[6] Pa had suffered many blows. He was to suffer many more during the war.

Overwhelmed by my death, he walked into the office of his private secretary, Nicolay, and cried; "He is gone, he is gone."[7] Then came the familiar lines, over and over again; "My poor boy. He was too good for this earth. God called him home. I know that he is much better off in Heaven . . . but then I loved him so. It was hard, hard to have him die. He was so young."[8]

Pa and Ma, as we shall see, were to understand that in death I was even closer to them.

Another of Father's secretaries was William Stoddard. He wrote of Pa's initial burst of emotion on the day I passed over to the otherside. Then Stoddard added; "Calmer counsels prevailed. The voice of duty was clearly heard."[9]

Secretary (of State) Seward may have been aware that attention to duty can be "grief's opiate." In the midst of the presidential mourning, he brought up an international problem. England and France might turn against the Union unless something was done about the capture of Mason and Slidell.[10]

In spite of himself, there were days Pa could not leave my corpse alone. He would not let me go! As my body lay in death on my bed, Pa would enter and "pull down the sheets." He would "gaze long" at my remains.[11] The editor of Scribner's magazine described Lincoln in 1865 as "full of contradictions."[12] He wanted to let me go, but could not! Pa is quoted as having said; "That blow (my death) overwhelmed me. It showed me my weakness as I never felt it before."[13]

The day of my funeral the "heavens broke loose." Secretary Bates, a cabinet member, made an entry in his diary on February 24, 1862: "The trees were laid low, roofs were blown off, steeples toppled." A Lincoln biographer commented; "Nature seemed to be in a convulsion of grief."[14]

The funeral services were held Monday at 2:00 p.m., some four days after my passing. In the Green Room of the White House my body lay for several days. There the funeral services were held. Pa preferred it that way. As we know, he called upon his clergy friend, Dr. Phineas Gurley, to conduct the service. He knew the family and the family knew him. He appreciated that Pa was satisfied to think of himself simply as a member of the one great church, invisible and indivisible.

Pa later wrote the pastor for copies of the funeral oration and sent copies to his friends. One flowery sentence in the eulogy stands out: "It is easy to see how a child thus endowed could, in the course of eleven years, entwine himself among the hearts of those who knew him best."[15]

Pa contributed all of $5.50 to the pastor. He had found that amount in my pants pocket. Dr. Gurley persuaded Pa to use the pastor's study for seclusion and meditation. This Pa did, and some Sundays he would sit in the pastor's study with the door ajar. He was able to worship in private.[16] For the record, at least one check was later made out to Reverend Gurley and signed by Pa. The date was January 25, 1863. The amount was $25.00. It was drawn on The Bank of Riggs & Co., Washington, D. C.[17]

During the days I lay in state, the White House was heavily draped in black. Mother was too ill to attend the ceremonies. The press reviews of the ceremony had my hands crossed with a bouquet held in one hand. Mother secured the bouquet later. One reporter wrote of the "beautiful" embalming job.

Secretary of State William Seward sat through the service at, what must have been for him, an ordeal in diplomatic reverence. General McClellan, not always a friend of the family, sat weeping.

Father's continued anguish at the loss of his favorite son led him to extremes. Twice he had my body exhumed from the grave. A third time was not for observation, but for transportation. Several motives have been suggested.

An amusing account gives credit to the embalmer, Dr. Brown, who was employed by the undertaking firm of Alexander & Bryan. Dr. Brown is supposed to have worked "such a seeming miracle" with my body that it was "so life-like." Pa had to have another look, not once but twice![18] Pa had his melancholy moments. "The twists and idiosyncrasies" of his nature were most evident.[19] It was not merely a matter of morbid curiosity, nor was it abnormal, prolonged guilt. It was his genuine attachment out of control.

The funeral of Secretary Stanton's infant son did not help. It took place six months after my death.[20] Instead, it came as a forceful reminder.

In my death the ever increasing war toll was personalized. Over two million boys under 21 were at the front lines. One hundred thousand of these were children "less than fifteen."[21] For Pa, more and more they became 'his boys.' The awesome responsibility of his war-time office, coupled with a sense of war guilt, added to his depth of feeling. Some maintain he was on the verge of suicide.[22]

Outbursts of public indignation at the extensive recognition of my death, while the youth and the cream of the country were being slaughtered, was understandable. My death was unheroic. No patriotic sacrifice was involved. My parents were badly hurt. It would have been better if the entire funeral ceremonies had been omitted.

6

My Psychical Pa

One day, among the military, Pa spoke with less conviction. To Colonel LeGrand B. Cannon on the staff of General Wool, Pa, their commander-in-chief, inquired; "Colonel, did you ever dream of a lost friend and feel that you were holding sweet communion with that friend?" Then Pa dropped his head on a table and sobbed; "Yet you have a sad consciousness, it was not reality.[1] Too often the word superstition has been applied to Pa, when the term sensitive was more suitable. He was spiritually, mystically, and psychically sensitive. Yet Pa was sensible. He had a "genius for common sense."[2] It was his common sense which saved him from going overboard.

A physician who has turned to the study of higher sensory perception refers to Father's moments of precognitive insight. A contemporary of Pa's first coined the word 'sensitive,' meaning psychic. He studied the more reliable sensitives among "the healthy and intelligent members of society."[3]

Some of Pa's precognitive insight, as we shall note, came in the form of premonitions and dreams. The psychic-mystic side of Pa has been either missed or misrepresented. One Lincoln biographer, J. G. Randall, professor of history, University of Illinois observes "a kind of earth-bound quality . . . a ready pragmatism is more to the liking of most Americans than the unballasted flights of the mystics."[4]

No one was more earthbound, yet less earthbound, than Pa. He has been labeled a realist and an analyst by his former law partner, Herndon. Yet Herndon understood that he was spiritual to the point of being mystical.[5] He was a big man, physically and psychically.

"Love is Eternal" was not simply inscribed in Ma's wedding ring, but in Pa's heart throughout his 56 years.[6] The one church creed for Lincoln was "love God and thy neighbor," and, as a second thought came the words "as thy self."

Lincoln's love did not stop the war . . . or did it? A French traveler, attending Lincoln's second inaugual, commented on the use of the term charity in his address: "One discovered an inexhaustible charity, giving to the word its highest meaning . . . that is, perfect love for all mankind."[7]

Some two years before my birth, the Fox sisters, living in Hydesville, New York, had a psychic experience. A third sister, Mrs. Underhill, wrote a book about the experience of the Fox sisters. Soon a religious movement was organized called Spiritualism. It was flourishing before we left Springfield, Illinois. One authority stated that Mrs. Underhill "with many others thought that they had betokened the rise of a new religion. They were unaware that they had only repeated phenomena associated with the early history of Christianity."[8]

This new religious movement, with its emphasis on the spiritual-psychical aspects of all religion, reached my parents. In Springfield they were actively interested in the subject, but never as members of the movement. As the war progressed, so did the movement. The whole idea that Lincoln was interested in any phenomena bordering on the metaphysical was so much "trash" to Herndon.[9]

An early casualty, as you recall, was our friend and former Senator, Col. Edward Baker. Among the official Lincoln papers filed in the Library of Congress is a 'spirit letter' from the Colonel, addressed to Pa. This letter was not discovered until July, 1947. Brother Robert, as we discover, had directed that the official Lincoln papers should remain unopened in the Library of Congress until that date. The Illinois State Historical Society Journal states that the spirit letter from the Colonel "reveals a new facet in Lincoln's character."[10] To those who knew my father, it was anything but a new facet!

During the centennial celebration of Father's birth, *The St. Louis Globe Democrat,* dated May 27, 1909 reported on the Progressive Spiritualist Convention in 1896 at Springfield, Missouri. One delegate announced that Father was "the first Spiritualist of any account in the country." Rev. Thomas Grimshaw, another delegate, arose to offer a correction: "It would hardly be fair to designate Lincoln critically as a Spiritualist, though he was known to have accepted in a general way the truths of our religion."[11] This is a distinction too may Lincoln commentators have either avoided or failed to comprehend.

Father's acceptance of personal survival as a fact of life and of death, led to his own conviction that communication with the departed was logical and real. It was that simple. Father was to find that once this truth became organized or institutionalized, either in the name of religion or science, it was shot! When a Spiritualist said to Pa, "I did not know that you were a Spiritualist," the response was, "well, every religionist is more or less a Spiritualist."[12]

In 1851 Pa was notified by his stepbrother that their own father was gravely ill. Pa responded, "if it be his lot to go now, he will soon have a joyous meeting with many loved ones gone before . . . where the rest of us, through the help of God, hope ere long to join them."[13] This hope was to become a conviction, a reality.

In Springfield, Pa was greatly influenced by the pastor of the First Presbyterian Church. Ma was an active member. The pastor, Dr. James Smith, was well known for his "great ability" on subjects of a metaphysical nature.[14] In our home town of Springfield, Illinois, my parents were initiated into spirit communication.[15] It was there on February 22, 1859, that Pa lectured on "The Art of Writing, the Greatest Invention." In that lecture, he chose some phraseology with a psychical flavor. It strongly suggests an appreciation of spirit communication: "great, very great in enabling us to converse with the dead, the absent, and the unborn at all distances of time and space; and great not only in the direct benefits, but of greatest help to all other inventions."[16]

What other inventions or discoveries did Pa have in mind? The implication behind such language is not surprising to those who knew Pa in Springfield. Back home, among our neighbors, Pa had little or nothing to say about the psychical or metaphysical. Whatever references he made, as in this lecture, would be indirect. The White House was another story. Pa was guarded more than ever. The president, if not his family, belonged to the people. It should be noted that Pa gave the Springfield lecture on Washington's birthday. Father had read the life of our first president. He knew Washington was a slave owner. He also knew that General Washington, during the heat of battle, had a vision. This psychical experience has been related to the Civil War. Could Pa have had this in mind when, on Washington's Birthday, he gave his lecture? Describing his vision, General Washington some 80 years previous concluded, "I found myself once more gaping upon the visitor." "Son of the Republic (repeated the visitor), what you have seen is thus interpreted . . . let every child of the Republic learn to live for his God, his land and Union." The Father of our Country then commented: "I had seen a vision wherein had been shown me the birth progress and destiny of the United States."[17]

Among the diaries and letters of history's great have been found evidences of similar experiences. The great British statesman, William E. Gladstone and Father were contemporaries. They found themselves in accord on the subject of metaphysics. "The work of the Society of Psychical Research," according to Gladstone, "is the most important work that is being done in the world today . . . by far the most important."[18] As for the Confederacy and the Civil War, they were miles apart.[19]

With such support is it not surprising that my father should find some justification for his participation as president in the psychical side of life?

7
Ma's Affliction

I must not neglect Ma. The unfoldment of her inner psychic nature, soon after my death, was no less real than that of Pa's.

Her reaction to my passing was profound. For one reason or another, which will become evident, her psychical life became more dramatic, if not at times unstable.

Too much has been made of Ma's temperamental, emotional side. Between Pa and the Confederacy, she was sorely tried.

Both she and Pa were Southerners by birth. Mother had no fewer than four brothers in the Confederate Army. She had three brothers-in-law who were officers on the Confederate side.[1] She had many southern friends.[2] Her strong southern ties almost tore her asunder. In the midst of her bereavement, one newspaper, *The Liberator,* wrote of Ma as, "a women whose sympathies are with slavery." Another journal spoke of the 'Delilah' in the White House.[3]

Upon my death Mother became withdrawn. She could not bear the sight of the White House lawn, where I had played.[4] Julia Taft, who contributed so much to my childhood, was forbidden to attend my funeral. Her younger brother Bud, my playmate, was treated in similar fashion.[5] The "unhappy division" in the nation was felt in the White House.[6] Pa was not an easy man with whom to live. He had his "abstractions and psychological twists."[7]

Ma's firm acceptance of personal immortality came to the rescue. It was

Mary Todd Lincoln

the increasing acceptance of this truth that set both my parents free.[8] She was sure "her angel boys," Willie and Eddie, were now united. She wrote to our neighbor, a Mrs. Sprigg; "I always found my hopes concentrating on Willie, after the passing of Eddie.[9]

Of those days in Springfield Ma's comment was; "We were having so much bliss."[10] There Ma would go all out for my birthdays. In her beautiful handwriting she would send out 50 or 60 invitations to boys and girls.[11] For Ma, I was the "stay and hope of her old age."[12]

Her sense of loss upon my death was more than she could bear. Never again would she cross the threshhold of the White House guest room in which I died. Nor would she ever enter the Green Room where I was embalmed. She could not face my picture.[13] Ma's grief and guilt, aggravated by her impulsive nature, increased. Pa gently led Ma to a White House window one day, and pointed in the distance to an institution for the mentally disturbed.[14]

The public gossip, stimulated by the news media over the first official White House reception during the Lincoln administration, cut Ma to the very quick. The whole affair was presented as a "heartless exhibition of frivolity in the midst of soldiers dying." In addition, it was declared that my death was "the judgement of God upon the President and Mrs. Lincoln for indulging in world amusements."[15] The cruelest blow came in the form of a widely read poem. It depicted the thoughts of a dying soldier, as he witnessed through a White House window the gayety of the official reception. Written by Eleanor G. Donelly, it carried the brutal title, *The Lady President's Ball.* It was the last straw. Ma cried out against all those who had assisted in plans for the ball. She called them her "evil counsellors."[16] The reception, the war and my death so combined as to consume my parents.

Desperation was not the initial motive in their psychic unfoldment. They had looked 'beyond the beyond' before my death and the war. They were, as indicated, in search of the hereafter during our Springfield days.

8

Ma and the Mediums

Ma turned to mediums. It was out of her great expectation. Ma had her own psychic background. She denied several times any spiritualist connections.[1] She was apprehensive of the professional mediums, and found the private home circles more attractive, if not more reliable.[2] Ma was ten years younger than Pa.[3] She was smarter and discerning in dealing with people.

If she had any doubt about a professional medium, she would call in Noah Brooks or Dr. Joseph Henry. The latter was superintendent of the Smithsonian Institute.[4] Both Brooks and Smith seemed to think most mediums were imposters. They sought to protect Ma.[5] They felt, as others did, that Ma might become "susceptible to the wave of Spiritualism." She might be unable to manage herself.[6] First, they did not know my mother, and second, they were too ready to employ some crude method of exposing any and all mediums.[7] Whatever the faults and the failures of spiritualism, Ma realized it served as a forceful reminder, as stated before, that the very "origin of Christianity was in a marked degree associated with psychic phenomena.[8] There would have been far less speculation as to the role of spiritualism in the lives of my parents if more people had understood this as Ma did. For her, *the goal was spiritual and the means psychical.*[9] What mattered most to my parents was whether a medium or sensitive was a genuinely gifted, sincere, intelligent person . . . one intent upon using his or her gifts of the spirit to the benefit of mankind and its Maker. Such a person they would invariably discover among the non-professionals in a home circle.

This was true at the home of Mrs. Belle Laurie of Georgetown. Here they met the young medium, Nettie Colburn. Sen. Orville Browning entered in his diary that, "to his amazement," Ma had gone to the home of Mrs. Laurie. Then came a statement from Mother: "She (possibly Mrs. Laurie's daughter or Miss Colburn) made a wonderful revelation to her (Mother) about her son Willie."[10] If it was shocking to the Senator, to Mother it was a 'revelation' and a relief.

Ma turned to old Jesse Newton to secure a position for Miss Colburn in the Department of the Interior.[10a] Ma continued to deny that she was a Spiritualist, but not all were convinced. Ma and Pa's reliance on Miss Colburn was unshaken. They would meet her at the Cranston Laurie home. Sometimes they would invite her and Mrs. Laurie to the White House.

At the Laurie home, Mr. Cranston Laurie was a trance medium while his daughter was a physical medium. There was nothing professional about such meetings, but rather more personal and private. The Lauries were honored to have the president and the first lady join a party of friends at their Georgetown home. My parents were glad to get away from the White House. The meetings meant as much, if not more, to them than anybody present. It was a diversion, sometimes productive and profitable.[11]

Professional mediums in those days were held in disrepute by many people, for many reasons. This did not disturb Mother too much. She knew they were human. She allowed for a margin of error, intentional or otherwise. Colchester, a charlatan to some, was a case in point.[12] Brooks, full of prejudice, went after him. Yet among the professional mediums, he was considered a "good test medium."[12a] He was inclined, sometimes justifiably, to "trick or test" the more gullible. As for Brooks and Henry, Colchester, as a medium, was one of "several villains.[13] Colchester was later exhonerated in court, but not until he had been persecuted and prosecuted.[14]

With the acceptance of personal survival, my parents found little difficulty in the acceptance, in principle, of spirit communication. Pa and Ma were given to clairvoyance.[15] This was just as true of clairaudience.[16] By nature they were very different. Their motives in meeting with mediums or sitting with sensitives were different. Pa would go for diversion, when he was not seeking guidance in the affairs of state, or the conduct of the war, or preserving the Union and freeing the slaves. Mother sought primarily to contact her Willie. Sometimes she was too anxious. There are no messages on record which Ma may have received.

My older brother, Robert, probably saw to that. He was reticent about releasing any family data.[17] His attitude on family matters was defensive, if not defenseless. He was supersensitive.[18] He and Mother were too much alike. Robert lacked his father's patience and understanding when it came to Mother. He once wrote, "Mother is one subject not mentally responsible."[19] On December 24, 1866, Robert pleaded with Herndon not to "mention my mother" in his writings.[20] They clashed on many matters, including mediumship. Ma has been accused by more than one biographer of promoting 'spirit practitioners' in the White House.[21] To these accusers Ma is supposed to have influenced Pa. He allowed this 'hocus pocus' in the Executive Mansion just to pacify Ma after my death.[22] The fact is that both parents met with mediums or sensitives in or out of the White House as they pleased. They regarded the White House as their home. Such sessions, private and semi-private, have been attested or verified by numerous independent reliable sources.[23]

The notion that Pa allowed mediums or sittings in the White House to please Ma on some occasions, had, however, an element of truth.[24] The idea that Ma was irresponsible, and that my death "gave impetus to the malady gnawing at her brain," is something else! This sounds like an attempt to explain away Ma's genuine participation in the psychical.[25]

Ma had an inquiring mind, even as Pa did. Once she insisted that Nettie Colburn undergo a test. This was not born of suspicion. One Lincoln biographer, alluding to the mediums, comments that Pa "did not respond to the offer of supernatural aid until after my death."[26] The fact is, neither Ma nor Pa ever used the word 'supernatural.' Nor, please remember. did they wait until my death before consulting mediums. This is among the repeated misconceptions born of bias.

An observation made by a fair-minded historian, underscores the fact that "every Lincoln biography reflects the biographer." The same author adds, "No matter what he (Pa) may have been in Illinois, he became in Washington a figure beyond the comprehension of such men as Lamon and Herndon."[27] This is equally true of Ma. My passing, as we have seen, had much to do with the change which came over my parents. Herndon claims that my father's "forebodings" were due to Mother's "temperament."[28] To understand Pa, one must know Ma. Her hospitality at times was only equaled by her charity."[29]In their devotion, my parents always referred to each other as "Father" and "Mother."[30]

One biographer writes: "certain beliefs (marital or psychical), based upon inaccurate information, . . . become a permanent part of the Lincoln legend."[31]

At first none of our family were welcome in Washington. We were ostracized. We were Republicans![32] Father was not even a church member! As Herndon expressed it, "there were those who could demonstrate that Lincoln was a Catholic, a Congregationalist, a Methodist, a Presbyterian, a Universalist or a Spiritualist."[33] He had been labeled a theist, an atheist, an infidel, an agnostic, a free-thinker, etc.[34]

Mr. John H. Littlefield studied law with Pa. He felt that Pa "arrived at a point in religion without going to church that others strive to attain, but do not reach by going."[35] Yet one of the many critics of our private family life indicated that from November, 1842, the month of my parents' marriage, their life, if not ours, was "one domestic hell."[36] A friend of the family countered by portraying Mother as "a true American woman . . . when we have said that, we have said enough in praise of the best and truest lady in the land."[37]

In recent years efforts have been made to revise the distorted images of both my parents. "Discoloring is corrected, partisan misrepresentation . . . perhaps accepted unawares by the public . . . is exposed; predilections and presumptions are stripped away."[38] At no point has the 'discoloring' been more evident than in the misconceptions of their active participation in the extra-sensory or the higher-sensory. Many Lincoln composers either strike a discord on the psychic note or skip it. *They are out of tune with the entire psychic symphony and play it down.* That members of the Confederacy should aim their guns at my parents' psychic side was to be expected. What is more, they very often had the facts, however biased.[39] This can not always be said of some so-called Lincoln authorities, nor some of Father's associates. One bitter Confederate proclaims the noted Lincoln medium, J. B. Conklin of New York, a "drunkard, a trickster and a cheat." Pa also is listed by the same person as a "sneak and a coward."[40] As for "Mary's marriage to Abraham," it was, to the Confederate officer, Dr. Fayette Hall, a "flat failure."[42] An astute piece of Lincolnia observes, "Nothing so educates men and women as marriage and the rearing of a family."[43] The Lincoln marriage covered a "stormy period" of 23 years, and they remained faithful throughout."[45]

Pa tended to be a loner. Soon after marriage he would spend days alone riding the court circuit on horseback. Judge Davis, his friend and associate implied a bit facetiously, "it was to get away from home."[45] At one of the official Washington receptions, Pa spoke for himself: "My wife was handsome when she was a girl. I, a poor nobody, fell in love with her. What is more, I have never fallen out!"[46]

9

"He Comes to Me."

My death produced for Ma some personal psychic experiences. As might be expected they were at first dramatic, if not traumatic, but finally comforting.

To her sister Emilie she made the announcement: "He (Willie) comes to me every night. He stands at the foot of my bed. He has the same sweet adorable smile he always had. He does not come alone; sometimes little Eddie is with him. Twice he has come with our brother Alex . . . you cannot dream of the comfort this gives me."[1]

Much to Ma's distress Aunt Emilie was unduly concerned. She recalled that upon my death Ma at first seemed locked in a tomb; each day was like a year. Another aunt, Mrs. Helms, was skeptical of the psychic phenomena.

Ma was almost defiant as she tried to assure her sister Emilie that she was alright; it was simply that people did not understand. Ma was more or less immune to the smirks and jeers mixed with the claim that she was losing her senses. Meantime, beyond the agonizing war and its racking torment, she continued to keep in touch with me. However, my Aunt Emilie noted in her diary: "Sister Mary's eyes were wide and shining, and I had a feeling of awe, as if I were in the presence of the supernatural. It was abnormal, unnatural; it frightens me." My aunt was sure that her sister spoke out of "gloom and despair." She added "Mary longed to touch and hold me."[2]

Books written on the personal psychic experiences of my parents, as we shall see, continue to make all psychic phenomena synonymous with spiritualism.[2a] Ma knew better. Her psychic experiences were real. They were a fact of life eternal.

It is easy enough to classify such an experience as an illusion or a delusion, an apparition or an abberation. For Ma it was a revealing, if not a transforming, experience.

From Frankfurt am Main on November 29, 1869, Ma wrote to her cousin, Mrs. Orne. A few quotes from this rare letter, signed M. L. are worth noting; *Whilst we are of the 'earth earthy' with a mind filled with anxiety and fear, how hard it is to direct our thoughts Heavenward . . . I am not either a Spiritualist — but I sincerely believe our loved ones, who have only gone before, are permitted to watch over those who were dearer to them than life. . . . I should have lost my reason ere this — if I had entertained other views on the subject.*[3] There are those who point to this letter in support of the theory that my mother did not deny she was a Spiritualist until late in her life. This is more assumption. At the close of the letter, Ma expresses a feeling toward friends in the Senate, who may or may not have opposed her views. The comes the sentence, "*The last four years should have taught me more discretion.*" Finally, there is the postscript . . . "*Please burn this — when read.*" This is a bit of rare Lincolnia not yet destroyed.[4]

Little is known as to the full range of my parents' personal psychic life after my death. "Belief in survival and a future meeting with their ancestors has always been a source of calm and courage."[5] As death struck my family and the country during the Civil War, this truth became self-evident.

Looking at my parents from this side of life, the concept of annihilation becomes a figure of speech . . . not a fact of life or of death. Continuation and transformation replaces annihilation or obliteration. *Far more important than any 'law of the conservation of matter' is the conservation of energy, power and spirit.* Science and religion came close to confirming each other. "The things which are seen are temporal, the things which are unseen are eternal." The things to which our five senses respond are illusive, if not an illusion. This is primary to all faiths. Physics has confirmed it.[6]

The fact that men speak of rebirth, and that there is such a conception at all, means that a psychic state which is so described exists.

Carl Jung, Psychological Reflections.

CHAPTER II
SURVIVAL AND COMMUNICATION

1
A Changed Person

A contemporary of Pa's commented: "Lincoln buried his son, Willie. Ever after, there was a new quality in his demeanor — something approaching awe. I sat in the fifth pew, behind him, every Sunday, at Dr. Gurley's church. I saw him on many occasions, marking the change in him."[1] This gentleman explained that during that sickly winter in Washington, he also lost two boys. A whole new world opened to Pa. My death released for both of us certain gifts of the spirit. As Pa became aware of his newly won spiritual-psychical gifts, in their noblest form, he became less interested in professional psychics. Miss Colburn, the child psychic, as we shall discover, never received any pay. Paramount in the very nature of Pa was a higher sensory perception.

If my reference in this account appears to include few historians or biographers of prominence, it is because they have avoided the psychic aspect of Pa's life with which my story deals. Spirit communication based on personal survival, in Father's life, is too often treated superficially or suspiciously. One can scan the index of Lincoln books, or Lincoln Library files, and find little or no reference to Pa's psychical life. Yet my death so stimulated Pa's active interest in the subject, as to contribute to his transformation. He was reborn. An old friend of Pa's on the circuit court was Judge Whitney. He thought of the first part of Pa's life as uninspired. The latter part, especially after my passing, was "supernaturally wonderful".[2] The term 'supernatural' has an orthodox religious connotation. This was not a part of Pa's language. A biographer suggests; "It is time to know about Lincoln's supernaturalism. Your favorite historian avoids the subject."[3] Supernaturalism, if not spiritualism, scares too many people, and such words, as applied to Pa, are unnecessary. Survival of the individual and communciation with the spirit world became facts of life for Father.

Soon after my death the White House artist, Francis Carpenter, considered the change which came over Father as a "true religious experience." Father's roommate of Springfield days was to recognize this change. The Washington Post stated that Reverend Gurley, who presided at my funeral, declared "with tears in his eyes, believed Pa's heart was changed." Noah Brooks, who considered himself one of Pa's confidants, saw a change in both heart and mind.[4]

A thoughtful Lincoln observer claims that "far too little of Lincolnia is based upon scholarly scientific research." Then he adds, "There are many, a great many, who must have believed that some supernatural force, some divine guidance, was behind his (Lincoln's) rise."[5] It is this supernatural force which could stand some scholarly scientific research, as it pertains to Pa's acceptance of spirit survival and communication. Some ten years before my death, Pa wrote, as previously indicated, concerning the personal survival of his own father. This faith for Pa was to become a fact.

Harriet Beecher Stowe said of Father; "As he mounted on a higher plane of action, his view became enlarged and elevated."[6] That higher plane of action included both survival and communication. It was the basis of Pa's change and rebirth. With my death, the president's state papers breathed, "more and more a dependence on a higher power, whose existence he may have doubted in his callow years."[7] We have only to consider Pa's second inaugural address, along with that at Gettysburg, to catch the meaning of this statement. Father, you recall, once admitted, "Willie's death showed me my weakness. I know something of my change."[8] No one came to know my father's facial expression better than the Man from Munich, editor Lorant. He was a most prolific commentator and collector of Pa's photographs. He stated: "In Lincoln's face . . . you can see him change."[8a]

When it came to survival and spirit communication, Pa's motivation did not include 'proof.' Nor did he try to contact me; although quite the contrary we know was true of Ma. On occasions, Pa's acceptance of spirit communication was sorely tried.

Senator Browning, in his diary, records that father came across a "female spiritualist," (Browning's term for any psychic or sensitive) "whose talk was intolerable twaddle, incomprehensible nonsense." Father walked out before she was finished.[9] My death, more than that of my younger brother, Eddie, "had a profound effect on Pa's mature religious belief.[10] Lincoln students, noting Pa's spiritual growth at this period, attribute it to personal and public crises.[11]

The increasing war casualties made death seem the order of the day. My death did something more personal to Pa. Yet there were those close to Pa, who never recognized that a change — the new birth — had come to him. In the course of the war, Pa met with people, some of whom questioned his spiritual status. One day he confessed, "I had lived until my boy, Willie, died without realizing these (spiritual truths) things. That blow overwhelmed me."[12] It is true that such folks as Lamson and Herndon did not begin to see the sort of tranformation which came over Pa. This caused one Lincoln commentator to remark: "No matter what he may have been in Illinois; he became in Washington a figure beyond the comprehension of such men as

Lamson and Herndon."[13] Ma was among those disposed to feel that, in the year of my death, her husband's spiritual senses had been most profoundly stirred.[14] Some saw the transformation as a slow change which caused Pa "to believe in his destiny as a great man."[15] This view should be taken with some reservation. Pa thought of himself as one of the 'common' people. *The ordinary man is the most extraordinary man* is an axiom which applies to Pa.

A theologian with some insight wrote about "the acceleration of Father's religious (spiritual) development" which followed my death.[16] This acceleration was accentuated by the war. In one paragraph, which puts a finger on Pa's pulse at the time of my passing, he concluded, "There can be no doubt that this was one of the crises in Abraham Lincoln's inner life. To those who were nearest to him, he seemed different after those days; always a religious man, he had undergone some new initiation into the mysteries of the Spirit."[17] The phrase, "an initiation into the mysteries of the Spirit" would appeal to Pa.

Another interpretation of this change which merits attention declares, "it was not a violent change . . . but merely a better harmonization of the outer and less significant part of him (Father) with the inner and more significant. His religion continued to resist intellectual formulation. He never accepted any definite creed."[18] One is reminded of Pa's familiar quotation: *"When any church will inscribe over its altar a condensed statement of the law and the gospel: 'Thou shalt love the Lord thy God, with all thy soul and mind, and thy neighbor as thyself,' that church I will join, with all my heart."*[19] Pa was saying, if the church must have a creed or a doctrine, let that be it, nothing more nor less!

Let us pinpoint in (earth) time when Pa's transformation or change took place. We know it was soon after my death. We know the change led to a reaffirmation of his belief in personal survival and consequent communication with the spirit world. Upon my death, Ma feared for Father's sanity, even as he was concerned as to Ma's state of mind.

A clergyman was called to the White House. It was an emergency. Ma secured, by chance, a distinguished visiting clergyman from New York City. He was Dr. Francis Vinton of the famous Trinity Church on Broadway, at the foot of Wall Street. He took Pa in hand and he was firm. Mother had briefed him. Dr. Vinton spoke of 'overindulgence in grief.' Such indulgence was unworthy of one who believed in the basic concept of personal survival. The clergyman then struck a responsive chord. "Your son is alive, in Paradise. God is not the God of the dead but the living. All live unto Him." Father, sobbing, repeated over and over "Alive! Alive!" The clergyman was persistent, and Pa was patient. He listened. The clergyman continued: "Seek not your son among the dead. He is not there. He lives today in paradise."[20]

That was it. The tide was turned. Pa followed up this initial conference or conversion by inviting his clergy friend, Dr. Gurley, to meet with him from time to time in private at the White House. Pa was an early riser. Dr. Gurley was seen to leave the Executive Mansion early one morning. A friend asked the nature of his call. Dr. Gurley was frank. "*We (Gurley and Lincoln) have been talking of the state of the soul after death. That is a subject of which Mr. Lincoln never tires. This morning, however, I was a listener. Mr. Lincoln did all the talking.*"[21] Pa was discovering for himself that "beyond death there is the fullness of life."[22] Meantime, Dr. Vinton, at Father's request, had sent a sermon on survival. Pa read it many times. He had a copy made. The change which came over Father was noticeable within our family.[23] He had accepted my death as a challenge "toward a firmer faith in Providence.[24] Pa's constant concern for a better understanding of life after death is considered in a later chapter of my story. It must be remembered that this story comes from the 'other side.'

A psychical researcher, Marcus Bach, reports that a *small percentage* of church goers accept personal survival. "Any post-existence of an incorruptible psychic personality is for them so much wishful thinking.[25] Psychical, yet pragmatic, Pa denied any wishful thinking as applied to personal survival and spirit communication.

A noble and courageous scientist, Sir Oliver Lodge, among the few who accept spirit survival and communication, has this to say: "However much knowledge is attained, there is always room for faith. The frontier of ignorance enlarges, too. Those who know most are most impressed with the immensity of the unknown prospect."[26] Father was never too far from the truth. His mind and spirit were stretched to their limits. "His mind struggled for truths and his soul for substances."[27] A member of the American Medical Academy of Science, writing on Lincoln's *Philosophy of Common Sense*, reminds us that Pa, as a young man, "took particular delight in challenging beliefs that violated natural processes."[28] As a changed person, he was less argumentative. He was quietly receptive to the idea "that man in his divine inheritance . . . hears through his conscience the voice of God, if he will but heed and listen."[29]

The ability to heed and listen was, with my death, most essential to Pa. He tells us that he believed in what he called the *doctrine of necessity*. He explains it thus: "The human mind is impelled to action or held at rest by some power over which the mind has no control."[30] This so-called doctrine may well have contributed to Pa's inner change. John G. Nicolay, the president's private secretary, speaks of Pa as "a Christian without a creed."[31] Pa would want us to think of the doctrine of necessity, not as a religious creed, but as a spiritual concept.

He would admire the scientist who dared to announce; "What I contend is that there is satisfactory evidence for the survival of personal consciousness."[32] He had to be content with his convictions as to spirit survival and communication. This same philosopher proceeds further; "There is no other rational explanation of the facts than the hypothesis of survival. Personally, I regard the fact of survival after death as scientifically proved."[33] Pa was all for a rational explanation though he had neither the time nor the inclination to study it. His personal experience was sufficient!

On the occasion of my death, Franklin Pierce, a former president of the United States, was to bolster Pa's belief in survival. A letter dated March 4, 1862 from Concord, New Hampshire, and signed by the ex-president, reads; "Even in this hour full of danger to our country and trial and anxiety to all good men, your thoughts will be of your cherished boy . . . until you meet him in that new life."[34] Franklin Pierce was to speak from experience. Just before taking office in 1853, he witnessed the fatal accident of his son, Benny, at the age of eleven.[35]

During those days of inner change, Pa had a part of me on display. It was one of my paintings, a "framed picture of Illinois" which hung over the mantel.[36] Far more than this painting, there was for Pa the reality of the unseen. One biographer recalls that Pa was "always sensitive to the unseen."[37] My painting and Pierce's letter were reminders of the reality in the unseen. "There was a window in his mind open toward the unseen."[38] Pa had little trouble in keeping that window open. It was a fact of life eternal. Religionists and scientists could deal with the unseen. They could preach and prove, but as one scientist claims; "No candid student of the evidence, so carefully sifted in recent years, can resist the conclusion that there exists an unseen world."[39] So it followed "as the day the night" that with the reality of the unseen there must be some realistic means of communication with that unseen world. This was the 'new' Lincoln. To quote from an able researcher, Carl Jung: "My conscious mind is like an eye which perceives the innermost spaces; but the psychic non-ego is that which fills space in a sense, beyond space.[39a]

In his transformation, there are those who have contemplated the president's dual personality — "Thus the Lincoln seen and the Lincoln interpreted but rarely correspond to the Lincoln that was." "Call it genius, call it the result of special providence, call it but application of profound common sense, I venture the statement that Abraham Lincoln was the greatest intellect yet produced on the American continent. . . ."[40]

This is one glowing opinion as to the new Lincoln, who emerged upon my death. We ask what made Lincoln 'the man for the ages' or what made Lincoln, Lincoln. In substance, it was the certainty that survival, according to Professor Hyslop, "is the keystone to the arch of history, the pivotal point about which move the intellectual, the ethical, and the political forces of all time.[41] The author of that statement adds: "The certainty of survival of personality will put a stop to all the skeptical discussions which postpone its acceptance. . . ."[42] Pa had reached the point of acceptance of personal survival and the practice of spirit communication.

Senator Browning, that loyal Lincoln supporter, entered with some reluctance in his diary, "I know that Mr. Lincoln was a firm believer . . . in supernatural agencies and events."[43] This is the Senator who continues to use the word 'supernatural' even as he employs 'spiritualism' to cover communication with the spirit world. Father was convinced that the day will come when the "effective existence" of the spiritual can be demonstrated. "*On that day the whole outlook on life will be changed.*" This pronouncement comes from a renowned physicist, for whom the spiritual world is real. He explains; "My thesis is that the spiritual world is the reality. This life is but a temporary episode."[44] This physicist, like Pa, was persecuted for his predilections.

Please do not be too concerned over the fact that many of my quotations are from recent time. Many books and authors, unknown to Pa and me once upon a time, are known to us now! Doubt is overcome as two-way spirit communication becomes a reality. We shall return to this aspect of life eternal. Lewis Mumford is credited with the observation that "death has a mystical effect upon the living." This was true for Father. A part of Pa died with me, yet far more of his mystical nature was reawakened and renewed. A new day dawned.

There came a moment of self-discovery. It showed up in Pa's political life, as well as the spiritual. It was then that he was able to let the members of his cabinet, Seward in particular, know who was president![45] Over death and defeat, Pa was ultimately to triumph. The dilemma of those who would produce a profile of Pa was the pressure to preserve the prestige of the presidency, and yet to portray Pa's psychic life. William Herndon, who felt he knew all there was to know about Lincoln, wrote: "I know nothing about Lincoln's belief or disbelief in spiritualism."[46] In resorting to séances and some forms of spiritualism, it was the soul of Pa seeking out the reality and wisdom to the unseen.

Pa's reading and writing of poetry played up to the spirit-psychic in his life. Lord Byron was one of his favorite poets. Byron, like many great poets, presents the psychical. A student of Byron refers to this aspect of his poetry: "There is too little insight into such matters today. Literary criticism, like the rest of our culture, avoids facing these challenging (psychic) problems."[47] Father would repeat from memory passages from Byron.

> *Sleep hath its own world,*
> *A boundary between the things misnamed death and existence:*
> *Sleep hath its own world,*
> *And a wide realm of wild reality.*[48]

For Pa the words "misnamed death and existence" were underscored. The title of this poem was *Dreams.* Like some of Pa's dreams, most of which were precognitive, it made an indelible impression upon him.

As Pa saw Shakespeare, it was packed with psychic meaning. Who better understood the "sweet mysteries of life and death?"[49] Pa would share Shakespeare with a group of his friends. One of them wrote: "Few men could read with equal expression the plays of the great dramatist."[50] In his chapter on the Growing Proof of Survival, Lodge wrote: "Poets deal in reality, not illusion. Ultimate realities are in the unseen and are things of which our ordinary life may leave us quite unconscious."[51] Yes, Pa was inspired and inspired others by the depth of my death, not to mention the war dead.

In his book, *Lincoln, the World Emancipator,* John Drinkwater has William Shakespeare sitting on a fallen tree, conversing with Father. By way of introduction the author states; "The modern prophets of spiritualistic science, who announce personal continuity with so pure a faith, might take comfort from the poet's occupation."[52] Then follows a soliloquy. First, Father speaks: "That's what a lot of folks about me could never realize — that I, too, was more than half poet at heart . . . That was what I most wanted to do — to bring a poet's understanding to the work-a-day government of a nation."[53] Pa had learned some passages from most of Shakespeare's plays by heart. My death was reminiscent of a passage from *King John,* in which Constance bewails the loss of her boy: "And Father Cardinal, I have heard you say that we shall see and know our friends in heaven; if that be true, I shall see my boy again."[54]

Senator Sumner was deeply moved as Father would read and reread from *Macbeth:*

Duncan is in his grave;
After life's fitful fever, he sleeps well;
Treason has done his worst;
Nor steel nor poison.
Malice domestic, foreign levy,
Nothing can touch him further.[55]

Sumner, a member of that small group to whom Pa presented his poetical leanings, knew well the trials, public and personal, which prompted much of Pa's love of poetry. In support of his premonitions or precognitive dreams, Pa quoted the Bible. His interpretations at times upset Ma. In 1894 the editor, J. B. McClure, gave a "slightly different, but clearer, picture of Lincoln's power of psychic interpretation" when it came to dreams.[55a] (It was Martin Luther King on the steps of the Lincoln Memorial who repeated over and over, "I had a dream!") In one response, Pa sighted Shakespeare: "Somehow the thing has got possession of me. Like Banquo's ghost, it will not down!"[56]

Pa was known to have read or quoted the Bible to the colored help in the White House.[57] In Pa's transformation, a distinction should be made between the spiritual and the religious. Ma maintained that Pa "had no religious faith in the usual acceptance of the word. Religion was a sort of poetry in his nature."[58] An able historian declared "more words have been wasted on the question of his (Pa's) religion than any other part of his life.[59] Mother was of the opinion that between my death and Gettysburg, we see Pa's poetical nature. His words at Gettysburg have been termed an "immortal prose poem."[60] A young Springfield resident recalled that the Bible was Pa's "richest source of pertinent quotations."[61] As time went by, these pertinent quotations from the Bible alluded to the psychical . . . a word that neither appears in the Bible, nor was it used by Pa.[62] It was the "prophetic signs and the revelations of good and bad portent" from the Bible which Pa memorized.[63] A psychic researcher remarked, "From Genesis to Revelations it is a 'spiritistic' book. . . All the psychical texts are the magnificent notes of a prelude to the greatest overture of all, the Resurrection."[64]

In Pa's second inaugural, we see a bit of the biblical poetic cadence; "The Almighty has his own purpose. . . . Woe unto the world because of offences! For it needs be that offences come but woe to that man by whom the offence cometh."[65] Father has been described as a "secular mind, clairvoyant of a spirituality" . . . if he ever found a church "roomy enough of spirit," that would be his church.[66]

As a young man back in Indiana, Pa turned his thoughts on survival to the writing of poetry:

O memory, thou midway world
T'wixt earth and paradise,
Where things decayed and loved ones lost
In dreamy shadow rise.

This is but one stanza of a lengthy poem, largely reminiscent, if not remorseful.[67] There was also the light, poetic Pa. It was from the "wild regions" of Indiana that Pa, at the age of 14, gave us his first doggerel:

Abraham Lincoln, his hand and pen;
He will be good, but God knows when.[68]

Perhaps the deadening effect of war turned him again to doggerels!

Mr. Hay, one of his secretaries, happened to find one on his desk. The doggerel is in Pa's longhand. At the bottom of the page is noted: "Written Sunday morning, July 19, 1863, attest John Hay." Was it written for his own amusement? He did not suspect even his secretary would see it. Nor was it anything of which Pa could be proud. It does, however, like some of Pa's stories, reveal his primitive background. This background plays, as we shall see, a significant role in his psychic development. The doggerel read:

In eighteen sixty-three,
With pomp and mighty swell,
Me and Jeff's confederacy
Went forth to sack Phil'del.

The Yankees, they got arter us,
And gin us partic'lar h--ll,
And then we skedaddled back again
And didn't sack Phil'del.[69]

Pa had a favorite poem. When asked if he wrote it, he expressed a wish that it were so. The probable author is a Scotchman, William Knox. He died in 1825 at the age of 36. The reason for recalling the poem here is that it reflects Pa's thoughts on this 'temporal pilgrimage.' The original poem had 14 stanzas. Pa could recite from memory at least 12. The first staza begins:

O why should the spirit of mortal be proud?
Like a swift fleeting meteor, a fast flying cloud,
A flash of the lightning, a break of the wave,
He passeth from life to his rest in the grave.[70]

On April 18, 1864, Pa sent a copy of the poem to "Friend Johnston." In the accompanying letter, Pa was not so sure the poem expressed his 'feeling.'[71]

Pa had his melancholy moments, the origin of which, with its psychical consequences, we shall consider in another chapter. Pa pensively reacted to the somewhat morose sections of the poem. One historian informs us that the poem was introduced to Pa by Ann Rutledge. That courtship you may recall, ended with her sudden death. We are told that Ann would sing the poem as a hymn. My death restored Pa's interest in the poem.[72] As we have seen, Pa, in his finest hour dwelt upon my death, not as the end, but as the beginning. As one Lincoln biographer refers to the poem and to Pa . . . "unquestionably this wistful pilgrim (Pa) of the spiritual often pined for some tenement of the corporate clay, to ease the austerity of the holy heights which he often climbed."[73]

During much of his spiritual-psychical life, Pa would resort to the verse, *Why Should The Spirit Of Mortal Be Proud?* There was the implication of survival, if not communication, with the spirit world.[74] It came in handy. It gave Pa strength in a predicament. The press media of his day included this quotation: "The highly sensitive, poetic and extremely spiritual nature of the man forces him to turn to some supernatural force for confirmation of his destiny.[75] Such a quotation has some truth. Pa's prophetic, visionary nature is described by ex-president Theodore Roosevelt in these terms: "Lincoln saw into the future with prophetic imagination usually vouchsafed to the poet and the seer. He had in him all the life toward greatness of the visionary without any of the visionary's fanaticism and egotism. . . . The goal was never dim before his vision; he picked his way cautiously without either halt or hurry . . . through morass of difficulty, that no man of less courage would have attempted it. . . . He lived in days that were great and terrible, when brother fought against brother, for which each sincerely deemed to be right . . . to Lincoln was given the *Supreme Vision.*"[76]

Among the poets Pa read were Bryant, Whittier and Holmes. He was "excessively fond" of Thomas Hood. He would take Hood to bed. In the middle of the night he would rise up, with Hood in hand. He would wander into the room of his secretary, and read aloud from *The Haunted House* and, like Banquo's ghost, for Pa "it would not down." One can conjecture as to what drove Pa through the halls of the White House in his nightgown, with *The Haunted House.* One answer is that a strong psychic impulse impelled him. His fascination for the ethereal since my passing was stimulated.[77]

Another factor which entered into Pa's transformation at this time was his affinity for the Society of Friends, the Quakers. Their concept of the Inner Light struck a spark in his soul. For him the appeal was both personal and universal.[78] It is no mere coincidence that the pamphlet entitled *Further Communications From the Spirit World* should bear Pa's signature on the upper right corner of the title page, while on that same page, in print, is an announcement of a section on *The Right of Man* by George Fox. The latter was founder of the Quakers.[79] The Spiritualists claimed him, even as they claimed Father. A book dealing with this psychic soul bears the title, *The Torch Bearer of Spiritualism.* It explains: "By the Inner Light, George Fox meant the voice of the Divine Spirit . . . instead of assuming the Divine Spirit to be a metaphysical mystery, he gave it a literal interpretation . . . The voice of the Inner Light spoke to him as it spoke to Socrates." The book describes Fox as "this deadly earnest shoemaker, from Leicester, England, in his leather suit, equipped for a revolutionary task."[80] Fox lived from 1624 to 1691. Pa's attachment to the Quakers is in part traceable to his Quaker ancestry. This applies also to members of his cabinet. They were called the Quaker Cabinet. Stanton's mother was a Quaker minister. Bates and Chase were "closely connected with the Friends Society." General Halleck was a Quaker.[81] Inner illumination became a cardinal principle in Pa's transformation following my demise. His mysticism was closely related to that of the Quaker community.[82] Fox, in his day, would hold community meetings "packed with psychic power." He was Clairvoyant, he went in trance and was a healer."[83] We shall come to the matter of Pa's Quaker ancestry.

Meantime, Pa had his Quaker followers. In a letter dated March, 1862, soon after my death, Pa addressed himself to Dr. Samuel Boyd Tobey of the Society of Friends. He explained that his delayed reply was due to a "domestic affliction." Then came this sentence: "Engaged as I am in a great War, I fear it will be difficult for the world to understand how fully I appreciate the principle of peace inculcated everywhere by the Quakers."[84] Pa was to experience the peace "that passeth all human understanding." Those around him and within his official and personal family often were not at peace.

Another Quaker friend was Jesse W. Fell. He was a Hicksite Quaker who waited 'in silence' upon the Inner Light. Pa wrote to Mr. Fell from Springfield, Illinois on December 20, 1859, enclosing his autobiography. In Pa's handwriting there appears the notation: "Of course it (the autobiography) must not appear to have been written by myself." The autobiography states; "My paternal grandfather, Abraham Lincoln, was of Quaker ancestry."[85] We know that there were "many intermarriages between the Lincolns and their Quaker neighbors in Berks County, Pennsylvania."[86] A former librarian at the department of commerce, Cassie Moncure Lyne, kept a scrapbook devoted to American Quakers. In longhand there appears this reference: "Abraham Lincoln's family (grandfather) and their relatives, the Boones, were Quakers. The Boones were kinsmen of Daniel Boone." Attached to her scrapbook are two pages (17 and 18) from a biography of Daniel Boone. A significant entry on the Library of Congress card for this book in the rare book section is: "The influence of the Society of Friends on Robert E. Lee."[87] An elderly Quaker lady holding Father's hand used the phraseology and precepts of the Society. "Thee must not think thee stands alone, dear friend Abraham . . . The Lord hath appointed thee. All our hearts are with thee." To this Pa replied: *I know it is not hope I have, but knowledge that He is sustaining me. Otherwise my heart would have broken long ago.*[88]

Yes, the Society of Friends in large measure gave rise to the new Lincoln and sustained him. Groups of Quakers would visit the White House. On September 28, 1862, Pa spoke at the Executive Mansion: "If after endeavoring to do my best in the light that He affords me, I find my efforts fail, I must believe that for some purpose unknown to me, He wills it otherwise."[89] Pa remained steadfast to the end. Years after this meeting with the Society of Friends, Pa addressed a letter to the Quaker, Eliza P. Gurney: "My Esteemed Friend; . . . we must work earnestly in the best lights He gives us . . . Surely he intended some great good to follow this great convulsion . . . In this hard dilemma some have chosen one horn, some another . . . I have done and shall do the best I could and can, in my own conscience, under my oath to the law.[90] Out of this "hard dilemma" and through this "great convulsion," guided by the Inner Light, Pa's personal spiritual-psychical unfoldment was something to behold! Like George Fox, he was "equipped for a revolutionary task." One Lincoln biographer, Nathaniel Stephenson, explains that Pa "was prone to turn away from the outward life and to lose himself in the inner."[91] That is my Quaker Pa. The original name for the Quakers was Friends of Truth. If they were of a guilty conscience, they quaked![92]

Few people knew Father better than his artist friend, Carpenter. Said he: "I believe no man had a more abiding sense of his dependence on God; a faith in the Divine government, and in the power and ultimate triumph of Truth and Right in the world."[93]

2

Discerning the Spirits

The biblical injunction, *discern or distinguish between the spirits,* whether they be true or false, was neither unfamiliar nor inconsistent with Pa's attitude toward communication with the spirits. As this book attempts to show, the day is fast approaching when *matter may not matter* any more. The fundamental nature of matter may prove matter to be anything but matter. The discerning of matter may yet vindicate the discerning of spirits.

The European Center for Nuclear Research in Geneva Switzerland, operating under the nickname of CERN, is a project "for the advanced research into *The Fundamental Nature of Matter.*"[1] Now it is no longer simply a matter of discerning the spirits but of discerning matter.

Since Pa's time, spirit communication has been considered in a much wider context, and in new dimensions. Examination of the other waves, for example, now offer considerable promise to the psychical researcher. "It is through the ether that we ourselves really act upon matter. I suggest it is there, in that connecting, all-permeating medium, that we must look for the permanent basis of life."[1a]

There are those who have presented a strong case for the relation of the radio and telephone, as well as the telegraph and television, as a means of arriving at a clearer concept of communication with the spirit world. But none of these avenues were available in the 1860's! The novelist Upton Sinclair provokes serious thought among psychical researchers in his book, *Mental Radio.* It is a factual account of telepathic powers developed by the author's wife.[2]

A newspaper correspondent provides a scientific theory. He maintains our nerve cells have built-in receiving sets. We are reminded that our nerve cells have their roots in a "world transcending that of the physical world of space and time."[3] His book, *Telephone Between Two Worlds,* has gone through eight or ten printings. Involved in spirit communication are the elements of telepathy and what is loosely called mind-reading.

A great scientist, Sir William Barrett, writing on *The Threshold of the Unseen,* quotes Lord Kelvin, a fellow scientist: "Science is bound by the everlasting law of honour to face fearlessly every problem which can fairly be presented to it."[4] Spirit communication has qualified on this premise over and over again. Pa was never frightened by names nor deterred by ideas out of the ordinary. He had neither the time nor the inclination, however, to study psychic phenomena. In his own way he experimented and explored. Pa's inquiring mind comes in for further study. He was a born explorer. The frontiers of the mind intrigued him. The topic of telepathy, whether confined to the earth plane or beyond, incited his interest. A book, *How To Make*

ESP Work For You, by Harold Sherman, a layman, includes a telepathic experiment between New York City and the North Pole.[5] This is relevant to Pa's communications with the spirit world.

Perhaps the most far reaching or effective method of communication will ultimately come through thought transference and spirit communication. Charles Lindbergh has told us that he found "the mechanics of life less interesting than the mystical qualities they manifest." With these conclusions, he "began studying supersensory phenomena."[6]

A courageous clergyman stepped out when he wrote: "Scientific methods in our time (his time) have been increasingly applied to a number of areas of perennial human experience, which from the dawn of history have pointed to the extension of the functioning of the person beyond the space-time continuum in which he is set."[7] Such testimony would appeal to Pa, if for no other reason than the fact that it indicates the doors of the church will yet be forced open to that which is fundamental to their faith.

The Pentecostal phenomena of speaking with tongues, is but a phase of spirit communication. Another churchman, Morton Kelsey, had dared to submit a scientific study on this subject which has been published.[8] Further mention will be made as to his contribution. Father would be the first to concede that spirit communication, whatever form it takes, loses much in translation. The human factor interferes. *You can be a Delegate to the United Nations Through Thought* is the title of a recent leaflet. Father reserved judgment on many aspects of survival and communication with the spirit world.[9]

Discerning or distinguishing the spirits inevitably presents a problem. Since Pa's death, the claims by those who were in contact with him are too numerous to mention. Pa understood that spirit communication was a two-way street. Even as Pa had received messages from the spirit world, so the day came when he was to send them. In the Library of Congress is a copy of a communication in which reference has been made from our dear friend, Gen. Edward Baker, new in the spirit world. This communication takes the form of 'mirror' or automatic writing. We shall give further consideration to this particular communication. It has been preserved it its original form. There are still those who have their doubts. Pa is ever ready to have us examine this spirit message from General Baker, even as he has no objections if we look at some of the spirit messages attributed to him. He is aware that some of these messages *from* him, have aroused more controversy than did the communications he received from the otherside.

Senator Richmond, for example, a respected citizen from Chicago, was a long time personal friend of my father. He was a leading business executive in the grain and shipping industry. While chairman of the Committee on Banks and Corporations in 1870, he wrote a book entitled *God Dealing with Slavery*. In this book he produces letters which under psychic influence he sent to President Lincoln.[10] It is fair to assume that a man of such business acumen approached all spirit communication with some trepidation. Within a few months after Father's passing, he began to receive spirit messages. The native shrewdness of the Senator must have been taxed when he discovered that the 'guides' or 'controls' were former statesmen – Franklin, Jackson, Webster, Penn, and others! Pa at times controlled the medium. The Senator acknowledged each spirit communication with a certain caution. The initial reaction was a mixture of shock and satisfaction. The Senator was all for discerning the spirits!

One spirit communication, signed by Father, was dated October 24, 1869. It reads in part: "I can now perceive that I was simply an agent or instrument in His hands, to conduct the rebellion in such a manner that slavery might be abolished."[11] What could be more Lincolnesque! Yet the historian eliminates the claims of the Senator, not as to his personal veracity but as to the validity of the messages. To the historian, the fact that this Senator once indicated that it was his intention as a congressman to serve the president as a "battery of brain, mind and thought," becomes a reason for ridicule.[12]

The historian relegates to a footnote the mediumship of Grace Garrett Durand. She too, received the spirit messages from Father. One passage in her statement sounds plausible. "Mr. Lincoln told me, had he followed his mother's advice the day of his assassination, he would not have gone to the theater that fateful night, as his mother had warned him not to go."[13] There were countless such warnings. Pa's step-mother was apprehensive. Had any one of these warnings been heeded, Pa might have been able to carry out his plans for reconciliation and reconstruction. That was not to be. Nor does Pa now have any regrets, as we shall see.

A contemporary of Father's was Bishop Gilbert Haven. In 1872 he received his appointment as Bishop of the Methodist Church at the general conference in Brooklyn, New York. The Bishop's messages, along with related material, are filed in the rare book section of the Library of Congress. Gilbert Haven graduated from Wesleyan College, Middletown, Connecticut, 1842. His first pastorate was Northampton, Massachusetts in 1851. A spirit message in automatic writing came from the Bishop in 1890, through an "excellent" medium in Springfield, Massachusetts. The message is included here because Bishop Haven, who functioned during the Civil War, even as Pa, was not concerned about the spread of Spiritualism as another religion. *"I warn you if you do not want your thinking ones to go out into Spiritualism, to bring Spiritualism in the purest sense into the church. Hundreds are seeking surreptitiously that which every one should be free to seek in the light of day."*[14]

Unlike the Bishop, Carl Schurz was one of Father's trusted generals. No one could have been more amazed to hear from his late commander-in-chief, then deceased, of his forthcoming appointment as Senator![15] This spirit message from the president to his general was fulfilled.

A Washington physician, Dr. Hausman, was "skeptical of all spirit manifestation" until he suddenly discovered his gift of the spirit. This is a familiar testimony. The physician had resided in the Capitol since 1853. One day he received a spirit message signed by Pa. In part it read: "I had Belle Laurie at the White House many times during the stormy rebellion to seek advice . . . how to proceed from the higher realm. I got it, Sir, and followed it. Our emancipation was born in heaven. My order came from that source. I struck the blow as ordered by the *Invisibles*. It was mighty for it was from God."[16] As spirit messages go, Pa would not consider this one far "off the beam."

Among the more significant messages were those received by Judge Edmonds. The Judge, you recall, had corresponded with father, during those days Pa occupied the White House. Judge Edmonds was then assigned to the New York City Court of Appeals. He was a Supreme Court Justice. Soon after Pa's assassination the judge was to receive messages from the other side. The first message concerning father read: "When he awoke to consciousness in the spirit world he was surprised and somewhat confused. He had no idea he was dead! This condition did not last long, as he was familiar enough with spiritualism to understand what death was." The judge then described "how Lincoln awaited the coming of Booth. When they met, the sadly misguided man was treated with kindness and compassion."

Some years later Lincoln came through to Judge Edmonds again. In November 1873 Mr. Lincoln claimed he had a message for the people on Reconstruction. So important did the Judge regard this message, that he "declined to publish it until he had verified the names, places, and statements." A search of the Congressional Records, and various libraries, convinced the Judge as to the accuracy of the message.[16a]

We have a series of spirit messages from such other personages as Phillips Brooks, General Grant, William James, Henry Ward Beecher, and Julia Ward Howe. Pa was included among distinguished company. The messages are dated from October 15, 1910 to January 28, 1911. The record consists of 400 pages of handwritten notes by Charles McArthur. The séance was held in Brooklyn, New York. As one pursues the section devoted to Lincoln, it becomes clear that it lacks Lincoln language.[17] This could well be because of faulty interpolation . . . where the medium gets in the way.

Finally there is the mediumship of an elderly lady. She discovered her gifts of the spirit late in life and then found herself in touch with Pa. She assures us that Pa was a "believer in spirit communication" and, after his death, became a "spirit communicator." The messages she received made it plain that Pa was now a "leader of rescue work, and a powerful Peace Band," the latter "composed of 'great souls' who are doing what they can to bring peace on earth." She adds, after some study, this statement: "No man, without exception, has had his interest in spirit communication so well documented as had Lincoln."[18]

We must remember, as previously mentioned, whether one is involved in spirit communication as the receiver or the sender, "there is overwhelming evidence that messages from the transcendental world are modified by the mind . . . our organic habits give them their shape. The most we can affirm is that they indicate foreign causes, subjectively interpreted."[19]

One typical Lincoln biographer informs us that Pa "even went so far as to dabble in spiritualism." Then, as if to correct any misapprehension, we are told that "Lincoln's mind was an open one. He brought all the experiences of his nature to the test of his own shrewd common sense."[20] Pa, from his Springfield days, was alert to the pitfalls of the psychic. The judgmental historian differs in his opinion as to Father's response to spirit communication. Father would appreciate the distinction made by one scientist, Sir William Barrett; *The psychical order is* NOT *the spiritual order . . . the psychical deals with the external, though it be in the unseen world. Its chief value lies in the fulfillment of its work, whereby it reveals to us the inadequacy of the external, either here or herafter, to satisfy the life of the soul.*[21]

Pa was quite capable of discerning or detecting what one biographer chose to call the "mummery of the mediums."[22] The spirit of Judge Douglas came through at one mediumistic session. Pa's discerning response was: "I believe that (communication), whether it comes from spirit or human."[23]

Another Lincoln observer, Editor Warren — *Lincoln Lore*, admits that after my death, a number of séances were held at he White House, attended by both Pa and Ma. Then comes this sentence; "Just how much they (Pa and Ma) were influenced by these demonstrations is a matter of conjecture."[24] Both parents were discerning when it came to spirit communication. They were not inclined to be 'taken.' However strong Father's acceptance of spirit communcation in principle, it must not be forgotten that he was, upon my passing, "predisposed to a spiritual view of life and conduct."[25] Speaking for himself, Pa once said: "I have felt His hand upon me in great trials and I have submitted to his guidance. I trust as He shall further open the way, I shall be ready to walk therein."[26]

To make Pa's meeting with mediums or his messages from the spirit world a matter of major concern, is to risk loss in the labyrinth of Lincoln lore. As president, and as a person, Pa was pragmatic. One Lincoln historian, Norman Graebner, describes him as a "supreme realist; in one respect he was often ready to abandon realism."[27] Much of the time there was, for Pa, far more realism in the *unseen* than in the *seen*. There was for him no substitute for direct communication with the Supreme Spirit. "In those dark days, he found strength in communing with God."[28] As he would turn to the

Almighty, so he was convinced the Almighty relied upon him. "That the Almighty does make use of human agencies is one of the plainest statements in the Bible."[29] These words, as we learn, were spoken in confidence to Pa's Registrar of the Treasury, L. E. Chittenden.

Spirit communication, beginning in Springfield, Illinois, was never an end in itself, but rather a means. The end was to be mentioned in his Springfield farewell message. "I hope you, my friends, will all pray that I may receive divine assistance, without which I cannot succeed, but with which, success is certain."[30]

A perceptive proponent of the psychical and the spiritual has written on *Lincoln and the Unseen.* He stresses that Pa's acceptance of survival does not make him a spiritualist. At the same time, "this construction of Lincoln's spiritual beliefs in no way denies his psychic sensitivity."[31] In fact, Pa's psychic sensitivity enriched his spiritual beliefs and vice versa. There is little doubt even as his enemies charged, that Pa's participation in spirit communication affected his conduct of the war and the administrative decisions and responsibilities of his high office. Yet he assiduously avoided the various organizations, political or religious, which would lay claim to his mind and spirit. Addressing himself to the providential will, Pa insisted, "If I can learn what it is, I will do it."[32]

In his private diary, one of Pa's political partners made this entry: "I know Lincoln believed . . . that his own destiny was shaped and controlled."[33] In discerning the spirits as to their source and motive, Pa was doing what came naturally. Meantime, the Spiritualists could claim him, but there is no indication that he claimed them. The psychical researcher, William Barrett, concluded: "Reviewing the numerous séances I have attended with different private and professional mediums during the past 15 years, I find that by far the larger part of the results so obtained had absolutely no evidential value in favor of Spiritualism."[34] Here is a discerning spirit!

3

Sensitives and Séances

If sensitives and séances could put Pa on a higher plane, he was all for them. Others could shrug their shoulders, and cry Spiritualism as some cry Socialism, but on Pa's shoulders there was a national situation crying out for some sensible solution now or never. The whole subject of spiritualism in Pa's day and since has been bandied about so as to cast doubt on the sincerity and the integrity of those involved. With all its faults and failures, spiritualism has done more than any science or religion to keep alive much of the truth of personal survival and spirit communication. Pa, with his biblical background and predispositon for the psychical, understood this. We owe much to the long maligned Spiritualists for standing by the sensitives and séances, whatever their obvious imperfections.

One Lincoln historian, Jay Monaghan, writing on spiritualism in relation to my father, tells of "the setback" to the movement in 1863. Then he adds: "All manner of quack séances were held by swindlers and persons mentally deranged."[1] Sensitives and sitters alike are constantly made aware of this aspect of an otherwise honorable, if not challenging, human endeavor. Why must we be suspicious of all sensitives, séances and spiritualists because of some? Why must we assume that what is real and true for one person will, in a similar situation, be so for another? Why should we expect a sensitive or a séance to reproduce, on demand, what is beyond their control? Such questions were on Pa's mind as mediumship gained his attention, and for the most part his respect.

After the first few centuries A.D., psychic phenomena was thought to be the work of the devil. Yet some gifted psychics became saints. One such person was St. Francis of Assisi.[2]

Father's inherent cautiousness was apparent when he was invited by Congressman Soames to attend a séance. At this séance young Miss Nettie Colburn, a medium, was to outline on a map a northern military strategy. Pa remarked: "It is astonishing how every line she has drawn conforms to the

Nettie Colburn Maynard
photographed from miniature, 1863

plan agreed upon."[3] No sensitive so reached Pa as did Miss Nettie. Years later Mrs. Maynard, the former child medium, was to give us a book on her séances with Father. One biographer, who thinks of himself as Pa's soul searcher, sees little but bias in the Maynard book. "She was invited to the White House where, if we are to credit her story, she imparted to Lincoln very nearly all the wisdom which he possessed during the period of the Civil War."[4] This is to concede that the Colburn child did in fact impart some wisdom. One of Miss Colburn's guides responded to the name Wisdom. This same Lincoln biographer is no less pontifical in judging Walt Whitman's writings on Lincoln. He sees Whitman indulging in pretense, if not fabrication.[5] Nettie Colburn (Mrs. Maynard) and her book will come later in my story. Suffice to say here, that in the drama of sensitives and séances as they enter into Pa's life, the two central figures are the author and her book entitled, *Was Abraham Lincoln a Spiritualist.* There are those who declared that about all we know concerning sensitives and séances, in or out of the White House, emanates from the works of Nettie Colburn Maynard. We shall discover this to be one of those derogatory exaggerations. As for the title of the book, it is from Father's viewpoint most ambiguous. It raises the old issue of who or what is a spiritualist?

Mrs. Maynard's book was published by a Philadelphia printer, Rufus Hartranft. From his Last Will and Testament, it appears to be the only book of its kind he published.[6] Mr. Hartranft makes it indelibly clear that he never was a Spiritualist. Nor does he claim that Pa was a Spiritualist. Why then the title, *Was Abraham Lincoln a Spiritualist?* A clue may be found in the publisher's important and elaborate introduction. A copy of the first edition in 1891 must be secured, if one is to catch the full significance of the Hartranft introduction. He quotes from an editorial in a New York daily: "If it can be proven that Abraham Lincoln was in any way connected with spiritualism or did take council from any medium at a time when the Nation's weal or woe hung in the balance, or was in any manner governed by such council, it would be the literary event of the century and the most astonishing statement of modern times."[7] As the publisher wants it understood he is not a Spiritualist, so he makes it no less plain that his purpose in printing the book was not to convince the public that Pa was a Spiritualist.[8] Nevertheless, the book was sure to attract attention by such a worn out, controversial and sensational title. The introduction is full of testimonials. Some of them take the form of affidavits. Most are from highly reputable citizens. All of them merely affirm that the author, whatever her infirmities in later years, was a respected member of a respected family.

Among the Maynard testimonials, there is one from our friend, Francis Carpenter, the White House artist. "I have known Mrs. Maynard for some years. She is a talented woman; I do not believe she would tell an untruth; she is a medium of remarkable ability. I know that Mr. Herndon knew Mr.

Lincoln better than any other man, up to the time of his election in 1861. After his election, Herndon knew but little of him (Lincoln); and absolutely nothing of his mental or spiritual condition before the sickness of his son, Willie, nor after Willie. I must say that Mr. Lincoln's mind underwent a vast change after that event."[9]

It is the vast change, as we have seen, which explains the contents of this book. Carpenter adds that he is not "prepared to state that Mr. Lincoln was a Spiritualist."[10] This testimonial, as well as the others, verifies the fact that after my death, sensitives and séances were a part of Pa's life. Some of them, without identifying themselves with the religious movement, acknowledge that spiritualism has made a contribution and deserves examination.

Before we leave this key witness (Nettie Maynard) to Pa's experience in private séances, we should consider one of the more common criticisms of her book. The story is told by a medium who some thirty years later, and on her sick bed, attempts to recall, perhaps partly in trance, the details of an historical séance in which she was the sensitive.[11] Pa would agree this is a fair criticism. Yet considerable poetry and some prose could be thus discredited. What about much of our sacred and ancient biblical literature? Historian Jay Monaghan has attempted an appraisal of the Maynard book. His article has the title, *Was Lincoln Really a Spiritualist?* As Pa would see it, the spiritualist controversy is only prolonged. The article raises more questions than it begins to answer. Séances and sensitives are all wrapped up in the one word spiritualism. Pa and his Miss Colburn, whom Monaghan calls the "little vixen," would nevertheless find the article coming from a noted historian, a significant contribution. This same historian refers to "detractors" who "for almost eighty years" have insisted that Pa was a spiritualist.[12] In this historian's view the Maynard Book constitutes some of the "best source material."

Then we learn about other source materials which serves as valuable "corroborating evidence" for the authenticity of Nettie Colburn Maynard's ministry. This is an important point, made by recognized historian Jay Monaghan. In brief, this is not a rehash of Maynard material. In this somewhat objective, even knowledgeable study of the subject, he concluded there are at least two other works, along with the Maynard material, to which any Lincoln student can safely "apply the accepted rules of evidence."[13] The two other works, authored by Dr. Fayette Hall and Col. Simon Kase, will be considered later in this account. Suffice to say here, they give validity to the work of Mrs. Maynard. It should also be proclaimed that they provide independent data. This adds up to substantial support for the sensitives and séances related to Pa.

The question of spiritualism remained for Father a moot question. For the news media it was anything but a moot issue. Headlines read, "Spiritualism at the White House." Then followed: "A few evenings since Abraham

Lincoln, President of the United States, was induced to give a spiritual soiree in the Crimson Room of the White House . . . "[14] "Spiritual soiree" set the tone of the report. We should not forget that Spiritualism had hit the Nation's capitol with a capital S.[15] Hartranft did not publish his book until 1891. He was very much aware that Lincoln and Spiritualism was highly controversial and still very much alive! He assures us that his personal interest in the subject is from a "purely historical standpoint."[16] Mr. Hartranft died soon after his publication, at the age of 37.[17]

"The piano jumped so violently and shook us up so roughly that we were thankful to get off it."

Monaghan regards, along with other Lincoln students, the séance of February 5, 1863 as the most authentic."[18] It would appear that the next day, a Friday, saw the famous session of "the waltzing piano." For Pa this was a moment of levity and levitation. The historian, Monaghan, does not doubt the Maynard account. Pa volunteered to hold the instrument down! Two others, including Colonel Kase, mounted the grand piano, but to no avail. Pa then spoke of the "weight of evidence."[19] Pa's reference to "an invisible power" brings from Professor Monaghan the comment; "No one will question that statement."[20]

Remember, there was a lapse of almost thiry years between the Lincoln-Colburn séances and the publication of the Maynard book in 1891. A newspaper article provides insight in the belated writing and printing of the Colburn Maynard book. The editor of the *New York Sun* in 1891 was N. B. Dana. He sent a reporter, Paul Tynar, to the home of Mrs. Maynard who lived in White Plains, New York. It was Friday, April 3, 1891. We are informed that as Nettie Colburn, the child medium, Mrs. Maynard had kept "careful notes on all the important communications." Years before, she had completed a manuscript based on these notes. She had turned the material over to S. B. Brittan for publication. Soon thereafter the gentleman died. The manuscript was subsequently lost! Again we are faced with the mysterious disappearance of original material related to the more important séances which Pa attended. Mr. Tyner found Mrs. Maynard on her sick-bed, attempting to recall and rewrite her experience of some twenty or more years ago. Her condition was such that she dare not rely on her memory or her mediumistic powers. For the past two years she had been obliged to lie in one position. Her hands and feet were twisted after some ten years of suffering from a rheumatic ailment.

Mrs. Nettie Colburn Maynard called upon a physical medium to aid, if possible, in securing or verifying some of the dates and details. It is a desperate effort to achieve some degree of accuracy. *A reliable physical medium is the rarest of souls.* It was a dramatic moment in the life of Mrs. Maynard and Tyner was called upon to report it.[21] Friends and relatives of the family had gathered. Pa, as you remember, had witnessesd the psychic phenomena known as levitation. A physical medium, if successful, can produce a materialization. Pa, to the best of my knowledge, had never witnessed this rare phenomena. Dr. Raynor Johnson, that impeccable scientist, a retired professor of physics, has given us a chapter on "The Materialization Phenomena" in his book on *Psychical Research.* At the beginning of the chapter he names some of the world's leading scientists who have witnessed this rare phenomena. He adds, "These men were fully aware of the possibility of fraud . . . none of them were easy to convince. They had nothing to gain by stating their conviction of the existence of these things."[22] The *New York Sun* reporter provides a comparatively complete account of what happened at the bedside of Mrs. Maynard. He names those attending the séance. He also gives us the names of those who appeared in materialized form. One such person was Congressman Soames of Maine. He was Pa's intimate friend. He had participated with Pa in the Colburn séances. He was able to give "some precise dates."[23] Most of those who materialized were familiar figures to Father, and highly respected. Pa himself put in an appearance in some form. He had little or nothing to say. He was an honored guest.

If we are accepting the New York Sun account as that of an honest observer . . . a reporter who tried to give a fair impression and expression of what occurred . . . that in itself is fair enough. Any story which involves the phenomena of materialization is subject to speculation, suspicion and skepticism. There will be those who will pass it off as pure spiritualistic sensationalism. Pa would undoubtedly reserve judgment had he observed materialization in his day. As for Mrs. Maynard herself, he would have *no* reservations. She was a sincere seeker. Her illness and the loss of the manuscript accounted for the lapse of time. It is to be regretted that the original material, based on the notes taken at the time of the Colburn séances, was no longer available. Under the circumstances Mrs. Maynard did her best to produce a manuscript. The *New York Sun* article, on behalf of Mrs. Maynard and Mr. Lincoln, attempts to make a plausible, if not valuable, contribution to the Colburn case. Further consideration of this aspect of the Maynard story will be found in the section entitled *Epilogue* at the close of this book.

In the various accounts of the séances, the historian is quick to detect a discrepancy in some dates and details. This did not deter Monaghan from making a serious study of the subject. It is, as we know, when anyone thinks of spiritualism as synonymous with psychism that provokes Pa's dismay.

It was Nettie Colburn, not as a spiritualist, but rather as a sensitive, which caused Pa to remark: "My child, you possess a very singular gift. That it is of God I have no doubt. It is more important than anyone present can understand. I thank you for coming here tonight."[24] One does not have to

Mr. Lincoln and young Nettie

accept this quotation, word for word, to catch Pa's thought. Pa took part in the singing of some Scotch songs as a prelude to the séance. He then took the initiative by inquiring, "Well, Miss Nettie, do you think you have something to say to me tonight?"[25] Then came the control, old Dr. Bamford. "His old-fashioned methods of expression and straight-forwardness of utterance made him quite a favorite with the President," so Professor Monaghan informs us.[26] Through Miss Nettie as the sensitive, and Dr. Bamford as the control, there came the instructions which led to the Emancipation Proclamation.

The Lincoln Life Foundation introduces us to Earl S. Haines, the gentleman discovered the Kase material. Haines claims the Kase pamphlet was not actually published until the late 1890's.[27] Haines, however, maintains that Colonel Kase first met Pa on Sunday, December 29, 1861.[28]

One account informs us that the President was attending séances at the home of Mrs. Stewart, in Georgetown. This was during the summer of 1861. Pa would go with "a few gentlemen friends" in a cab. The cab was dismissed some distance from the residence. Then Pa and his companions, along with a few other friends from different quarters, met by appointment for these services."[28] Some of this apparent secrecy may explain the difficulty in dates. As early as 1850, Colonel Kase was in Washington on business.[30]

To resume the main theme of our story, Pa "believed in the open door between two worlds — the mortal and the spiritual realms; that is to say, in the possibility of mortals communicating with departed men and women.[30] Call it what you choose, it was the premise, not necessarily the motive, upon which Pa participated in séances. That Pa was directed by 'spiritual teachers' was clear enough to his artist friend Carpenter, in whom Pa confided.[31] Professional mediums were in some degree a part of Pa's psychic life. It was, however, the non-professional, unpaid child medium, Nettie Colburn, who, as we know, held his respect and attention. Pa would concur on several conclusions reached by the historian Monaghan in his careful study, if he uses the term spiritualism in the context of a religious movement as founded by the Fox sisters. The historian is sure "the stories about Lincoln's belief in spiritualism are contradictory."[32] Such a summation is in keeping with Pa's views. It was simply spirit communication, as derived from an acceptance of personal survival, which struck a responsive chord in Pa. He found people quite ready to believe in personal survival, yet shy away from spirit communication.

A noted sensitive, Arthur Ford, has explained for us what he calls the "communications system." It consists of four individuals; "the discarnate originator of the message, the discarnate control, the medium and the sitter." The control has about the "same energy pattern" as the sensitive. He maintains that "conscious fraud" is not the main problem of mediumship. It is self-deception of the "unconscious kind."[33] The acceptance of the hypothesis, supported by scripture, that man has a physical and spiritual body is essential to spirit communication, as related to personal survival.[34] This current leading sensitive states: "My purpose is to teach and demonstrate survival."[35] He cites the pioneer in astronautical engineering, Professor Wernher Von Braun: "Nature does not know extinction. All it knows is transformation. Everything science has taught me, and continues to teach me, strengthens my belief in the continuity of our existence after death."[36] This expresses, in substance, the principle upon which Pa participated in séances. When Pa first met Nettie Colburn, she may have been, according to Jay Monaghan, around 12 years of age.[37] That was about the age at which my transition and Pa's transformation came. As in my passing, so in the coming of Nettie Colburn, Pa had fresh faith that " a little child shall lead them." A sociologist, Earl Fornell, has outlined the spread of spiritualism during the Civil War. He acknowledges Nettie Colburn as a noted medium.[38]

4
Guilt by Association

Pa was a lawyer. He was familiar with guilt by association. He saw this process applied to sensitives. He understood the claim that the Bible condemns mediumship because of one 'bad' medium.[1] All witches are evil because some witches (the Witch of Endor) are evil. About 100 years before Pa was born, a devout Christian "held firmly to a belief in witchcraft." His name was John Wesley. In spite of the evil superstition which attended witchcraft, he was convinced that it was not all bad. A doctor of medicine contributes to a newspaper column this comment: "Many witch doctors possess psychiatric secrets that have been passed from generation to generation."[1a] There was 'undeniable,' although 'unexplainable' evidence to this effect.[2] A student of mediumship tells us: "The superstitions of today sometimes become the facts of tomorrow and vice versa."[3]

Pa knew his Old Testament. It distinguishes between "the good and evil mediums."[4] Pa would ask, if a person can accept personal survival, why can not such a person believe in communication with the spirit world? As the Bible indicates, the gifts of the spirit may not always include spirit communication. A person may have the gift or talent and fail to exercise it. Many of us are undeveloped sensitives! Pa was such a person.

Had church schools included a course in the biblical concept of spirit communication based on personal survival, then this gift of the Spirit would be better understood, if not practiced. "Some tell us that nature or providence does not intend us to know about the future life. . . . The same type of mind told us that we should not inquire into the processes of nature."[5] A leading scientist and philosopher, James Hyslop, argues that both religion and science have "blocked the way" to a study of survival and communication. Their reasons for doing so are "mutually destructive."[6] This same scientist declares that spirit communication in itself is not sufficient proof of the eternal survival of personality.[7]

Pa was a self-made mathematician. He had conquered Euclid. "The book, *The Elements of Euclid,* went into his saddle-bag as he went on the circuit. At night, with other lawyers, two in a bed, and eight and ten in a hotel room, he read Euclid by the light of a candle, after the others had dropped off to sleep."[7a] It was all part of his logical mind. He was intrigued by geometrical formulas and trigonometrical propositions. His mind went in for syllogisms. "All men are mortal. Socrates is a man, therefore Socrates is mortal.[8] This was sound logic, and Socrates went in for personal immortality and spirit communication, even unto his death. Nicolay and Hay report that in a debate with Stephen A. Douglas, Pa said: "I believe this is a sort of a proposition in proportion, which may be stated thus: As the Negro is to the white man, so is the crocodile to the Negro. As the Negro may treat the crocodile as a beast or a reptile, so the white man may rightfully treat the Negro as a beast or a crocodile." Pa was responding to a figure of speech used by Judge Douglas in which he said: "As between a crocodile and a Negro, I take the side of the Negro. As between the Negro and the white man, I go for the white man every time."[8a] Pa's mathematical, if not his legal mind was at work. Pa was quick to sense illogic. Nothing irritated him as much as the reasoning that séances are silly because something trite or funny or peculiar happened at one séance, such as a waltzing grand piano. In a book by a physician, George Johnson, under the title *Does Man Survive?* we read: "Levitation of inanimate objects are exceedingly common. They have been witnessed by a number of scientists and eminent men, among them Abraham Lincoln and Sir William Barrett."[8b]

Pa knew how easy it was for a false premise to produce a false assumption. Professor of philosophy and logic Hyslop, reminds us, as previously indicated, that "messages from the transcendental world" are sometimes "modified by the mind that receives them."[9] This logician was to become the first President of the American Psychical Research Society. Pa's legal, logical training did not prevent him from becoming a victim of guilt by association. He was a spiritualist in the minds of some, because he attended a séance or sat with a sensitive. The mental institutions (insane asylums as they were called in Pa's day) are full of people who hear 'voices' or see 'visions.' Therefore, argue some, the Lincolns were unstable. They were indulging in unstable activities, in and out of the White House. They associated with people who were 'queer'. For the president, the commander-in-chief, to be thus involved was unthinkable. One psychical researcher concludes, "if a man offers evidence that he has a soul, and may expect life after death, he is called insane. . . ."[10]

Because table rapping or the Ouija board became parlor games for many folks, that is all there was to it. It was child's play or worse. This line of reasoning would amuse and aggravate Pa. It horrified others. One gentleman entitled his book, *The American Heresy.* He made the statement: "A few experiments in table tapping were his (Lincoln's) only traffic with Heaven and Hell."[11] Pa's antagonists considered him crazy — he had something to do with table rappings! One such author discusses the possibility that General McClellan's command was the result of table rapping. Then he adds, "If the spirits rapped him in command at one sitting, they at another may have rapped him out again."[12] This disenchanted author, Quinn, entitles his book *Interior Causes Of The War,* with a subtitle *Nation Demonized and President Spirit Rapper.* This is one Lincoln book few, if any, take seriously. Meantime, more than one noted scientist has given the subjects similiar to table rapping, etc., serious scientific examination. No scientist has accomplished such study without the ridicule of his fellow scientists.[13]

When it comes to psychic phenomena, persecution is no respector of persons. "*The scientist has always insisted that we relax religious obstinacy and prejudice in the consideration of hypotheses that seem to conflict with preestablished ideas. It therefore becomes obligatory upon him to practice his own preaching in the consideration of supernormal phenomena.*"[14] This is the sort of logic which appealed to those like Pa, interested in the supernormal. We are told that in the seventeenth century "table turning" was practiced in Jewish circles. However, in 1614 it was "denounced as magic."[15] Who denounced it in those days? The very people who are convinced by circumstantial evidence that psychic phenomena must be the work of some demented dupes.

There is the scientist who takes the position that the supernormal does not lend itself to scientific investigation. It is too subjective and too far out! As we know, Pa did not require scientific proof. His experience was sufficient. Nor did he expect acceptance, only tolerance. He could not understand, however, why the supernormal was not entitled to an open mind . . . why it did not serve as a challenge to the imagination of science and religion.

Some 40 years ago (by your Christian calendar, earth time), it was said that science, in the narrow sense, tries to exclude "everything that is not metrical and exact and repeatable at will under laws that can be formulated."[16] Pa was simply asking that the psychic and psychic phenomena be considered innocent until proven guilty. This is what Thomas Henry Huxley was pleading for. "Sit down before fact as a little child; be prepared to give up every preconceived notion, follow humbly wherever and to whatever abysses nature leads, or you shall learn nothing." This famous scientist went on to urge "entire surrender to the will of God."[17] Another eminent scientist, investigating the supernormal, writes, as essential, the "loss of self." This is the self-surrender which enables the consciousness of God to enter our life.[18] How sweet such solemn words coming from top men of science would have sounded to Pa. He was surrounded by those who accused the president of treason for allowing mediums to enter his administration. The fact that Father accepted both survival of the personality and communication with the spirit world 'proved' that Pa was *not* a Christian. Yet all Christology support both! One clergyman, Rev. Dr. Savage, has sufficient stamina to state: "If a Christian minister preaching God's word has no right to consider spiritualism and its phenomena, pray who and in what manner does possess the right?[19]

Pa was on trial before a Kangaroo Court. The trial made little sense. Pa was convicted before he was tried. Pa's plea was consequently "non-cul." One psychic researcher takes the position it would be "very odd if spirit communication were to confine itself only to proof and no more."[20] It was the 'more' that to Pa was most important. The desperate demand was for more and more wise guidance, not proof. Pa was invariably faced with the fact that it is "one thing to prove that a statement comes from a Spirit . . . and very different to prove it true and valid."[21] Yet "cold blood evidence is vouched for, and this it is which must be examined without prejudice either way."[22] Pa left to others the examination of the "cold blood evidence" for communication with the spirit world. An able witness, Sir Oliver Lodge, in defense of spirit communication writes, "I take it that the preamble of all religions is the existence of a spiritual world. We who have gone into the matter believe we are in touch with the spiritual world."[23]

'Guilt by association' plagued Pa during much of his career. If it was not politics, it was religion. His universal, transcendental nature caused people to cross sectarian and party lines to claim him as their own. The Spiritualists were understandably "among the most persistent."[24] One such Spiritualist, who saw Pa at more than one séance, declares, "I mention this because many prejudiced people deny that he (Pa) was a Spiritualist. *I know he was!*"[25] There you have the kind of evidence, which overstated, often convicted Pa before the court of public opinion. A Lincoln biographer counters: "There might be a certain element of truth in the Spiritualist conception of Lincoln . . . but not all truth." Then he adds: "Most of these quarrelers are inclined to see in Lincoln beliefs they themselves espoused."[26] The Spiritualist claims have been labeled by Lincoln students as myths and legends. Under such labels we find the statement: "Spiritualists, on the strength of the few séances that Lincoln allowed Mrs. Lincoln to have in the White House, claimed him of their beliefs."[27]

A most ardent 'Lincoln' Spiritualist recently passed over at the age of 80 or more. In 1864 Pa appointed the Spiritualist's paternal parent as a County Attorney in Kansas. This gentleman tells how he constantly "heard a bunch of old Lincoln cronies in his father's Topeka office discuss Lincoln's psychic life." He continues, "They all *knew* Lincoln was a Spiritualist. He made great decisions on the advice of those we wrongly call 'dead.'[28] Our Spiritualist friend then adds: "Even the most devout Catholic admits spirit communication is true if it comes through Catholic sources." Faulty logic, and guilt by association, is admissible when this Spiritualist applied it to Catholicism. The news media, as we shall see, never too accurate and inclined to exaggerate Pa's participation in spirit communication, reported that Ann Todd, (presumably Mary) as a mystic, persuaded her husband to hold séances in the White House "every week."[29]

To suggest that "only a Spiritualist" would attribute the Emancipation Proclamation to "spirit intervention" is one of those assumptions born of bias. This is no less true of the declaration that all historians say 'no' and all Spiritualists say 'yes' in response to the dubious issue of Spiritualism and Pa.[30] Some Lincoln biographers and historians make no distinction between Pa's psychic life and Spiritualism. There are those on the side lines who are not impressed one way or another by the evidence. It is too circumstantial.

Why we lack firsthand information from Pa, as to his affiliation with psychic groups, will be considered, though not answered, as we come to the confiscation of Pa's private papers. Meanwhile, there is ample direct evidence that spiritualism had become 'big business' to the distress of some and delight of others during the Civil War and within the Lincoln Administration.

To venture beyond the accomplishments of this psychically fantastic age, sensory perception must combine with extra sensory. I suspect the two will prove to be different faces of each other.

Charles Lindbergh, Letter to Life Magazine, July 4, 1969

CHAPTER III
HONEST ABE A WITNESS TO TRUTH

1
Watch Your Language

Even among earthlings, something is lost in translation from thought to language or words. Witnessing to eternal truth is not limited to any one sphere or plane of life. In its highest sense, Pa was a medium or sensitive. In conveying the truth, he grasped both the power and the limitation of words.

Honest Abe, the lawyer, sought to become a clear channel for truth. In his book, *Life on the Circuit with Lincoln,* Father's friend, Judge Henry C. Whitney comments: "If a witness told the truth, without evasion, Pa was respectful if not patronizing. He would score a perjured witness unmercifully."[1] Pa was a stickler for the truth. "He loved and idolized the truth for its own sake. It was reason's food."[2] To those who would tamper with the truth, Pa would warn, "Watch your language."[3] There is in all he said a tone of truthfulness. Words fail when we seek to clarify an experience which transcends the human. A research chemist at the General Electric laboratory claims that "the higher power can never be expressed in terms of the lower." "We cannot understand clairvoyance until we become clairvoyant ourselves."[4] Father has been described as a "secular mind, clairvoyant of all spirituality."[5] This made him susceptible to the psychical-spiritual field of endeavor. Quite unexpectedly, he would use their language. Mention has been made of his Washington's birthday lecture in Springfield, Illinois on "The Art of Writing" in 1859, in which he comments; "great, very, very great in enabling us to converse with the dead, the absent and the unborn at all distances of time and space."[6] Someone listening to that lecture and those words must have murmured, "watch your language!" Pa was a political figure. He was soon to become the nation's chief executive. Pa watched his language! He wanted others to watch it too. Washington's birthday, as you recall, may have reminded Father of the General's psychic vision at Valley Forge.[7]

As Nobel Prize physicist, DuBose, has suggested, ". . . the secrets of spirit communication, if not personal survival, may yet come not through the

language of the psychic, but rather that of the physicist."[8] The subtitle of a book by Geoffrey Murray, the British scientist is: *Inquiry into Spiritualism, Faith Healing and Psychic Research.* It is an impartial approach to the subject. Dean Matthews, former dean of St. Paul's Cathedral remarks in the book's introduction that Dr. J. B. Rhine, the parapsychologist (a term which would appall Pa), is concerned because we "know more about the atom than ourselves." Professor Murray also maintains that "the mediums are held to be links in a system of communication analogous to telephones and radio sets."[9] This concept, as we know has also been put in the language of laymen by authors, Upton Sinclair and James Crenshaw.[10] Science for the most part has steered clear of this area. Those who have touched it, have found it a burning issue among their fellow scientists. A satirical attack in a scientific journal calls Sir William Crooks a spiritualist. His reply was that: "nothing that I have ever written can justify such an unfounded assumption."[11] Pa was familiar, as we have seen, with just such an unfounded assumption. Whatever he said to the contrary made little difference. Experimentation by those best qualified in science and religion for psychical work has been defeated by name calling.

The Old Testament book of Leviticus employs the word "medium." It appears in a negative context. For the literalist, this proves that mediumship is sacrilegious. For others, it merely indicates that mediums are people, and not without error.[12] A tyranny of words operates in the name of religion. A medical researcher, Dr. Shafica Karagulla, who has dared to turn her talents to higher sensory perception, recommends as essential to the understanding of the psychical a "more adequate terminology."[13] She adds that "some terms used for the past 150 years are out of date."

On October 26, 1864, Pa resorted to some legalistic observations: "We know all this exists, even better than we could know an isolated fact in the sworn testimony of one or two witnesses; just as we better know there is fire whence we see much smoke rising than we could know it by one or two witnesses swearing to it."[14] Far more convincing than language or words were the smoke and fire. Pa wanted to see the evidence. Yet psychic experiences were real enough. He observed and participated in them.

One biographer, Professor Current, bemoans the fact that much Lincolnia is full of "preconceived notions," and adds that, "a great deal of the Lincoln literature is controversial and controversy begets more controversy."[15] Nothing in all Lincolnia is quite as controversial as Pa's exercises in spiritual communication. As we have seen, sworn testimony and signed affidavits by some people were given to prove that his active interest in the psychical made him, to some, a Spiritualist! Confusion was thus compounded. The meaning of language is lost in the heat of controversy. This in part explains the absence of original material setting forth Pa's personal testimony.

He was in the main a silent witness. Some Lincoln research now in progress is based on Dr. Randall's essay, *Has the Lincoln Theme Been Exhausted?* To the question, "what made my father the man he was," the researchers reply, "in the end we shall find out all of our learning is imperfect. . . . Was it something deep in the heart, something in the soul?"[16] The purport of Pa's phraseology, as in his lecture "The Art of Writing," went far beyond the topic. This was obvious — if not intentional.

A news columnist took it upon himself to lift out of context a series of passages from Father's lectures and letters. He composed what he described as "a mosaic of Lincoln sayings, some of which would highly commend Lincoln to the Communist Party."[17]

In the book, *The Legends That Libel Lincoln,* the author observed: "inaccurate information of the past still lingers in spite of more recent discoveries . . . there are still differences of opinion among authorities. Many points about Lincoln's life are in need of correction and clarification."[18]

A prerequisite for those who would speak or write on Father's behalf is an open-mindedness — a characteristic of those who have reached the heights, whatever their vocation or avocation. (The first chapter of a recent book dealing with higher sensory perception carries the title *Journey of the Open Mind.*[19]) Some people have been blessed with spiritual-psychical insight. But science, no less than religion, has for the most part suffered a 'blind spot' in researching this type of phenomena. There has been a decided lack of open-mindedness, accompanied by the familiar language barrier. Professor Hyslop has written that "from no one has Psychic Research met more opposition than from scientific man. His attitude is explicable, but not always excusable. The conquests of physical science are supposed to have eliminated the supernatural from human belief. Most scientific men think that psychical research threatens to restore that beast to power. But there is no danger that past conceptions will find currency, and no serious consequences can happen from giving the term 'supernatural' as clear a meaning as that of 'natural'."[20]

At times Pa played with the spirit guides. One such meeting, as mentioned previously, took place in the Crimson Room of the White House. A newspaper reporter attending on this occasion was a Mr. Melton, friend of the medium, Charles E. Shockle. The event was recorded in Boston's *Saturday Evening Gazette,* datelined Washington, D.C., April 23, 1863. The message came through in code, in the form of table rapping. Pa was not too convinced. Addressing the guide, Pa exclaimed, "Well, opinions differ among the saints, as well as among the sinners. They don't seem to understand running the machines among the celestials much better than we do. Their talk and advice sounds very much like the talk of my cabinet." Several members of his cabinet were present, among them Secretary Stanton of the Army and Secretary Wells of the Navy. Pa turned to the latter asking; "Don't you think so, Mr. Wells?"[21] During this affair the medium recognized an Indian guide. In the language betraying his frame of mind, Pa addressed the guide; "Well, Sir, I should be happy to hear what his Indian Majesty has to say. We have recently had a visitation from the red brethren, and it was the only delegation — black, white or blue — which did not volunteer some advice on the conduct of the war."

Carl Sandburg was quite upset by the manner in which Father thus conducted himself. His language was not becoming of a president! It was "bordering on horse-play . . . amid the ludicrous, the shallow and the bottomless."[22] This same author questions Pa's motives "in allowing the séance to be held in the White House and in permitting a news reporter to be present."[23] Such writers, however competent, do not understand Pa. He had nothing to hide. Yet he was quite aware that the dignity of his office demanded some reservations. Honest Abe was not pinned on Pa for nothing! A Lincoln writer observes: "His great and general life was honest. He was justly entitled to the appellation, *Honest Abe*. Honesty was his great polar star."[23a]

Back in Springfield during the presidential campaign, he was informed that only three out of twenty-three clergymen intended to vote for him. In language no one could misjudge, Pa reacted; "*I know there is a God, and that he hates injustice and slavery. I see the storm coming. I know that He has a hand in it. If He has a place and a work for me . . . and I think He has . . .*

I believe I am ready. I am nothing, but TRUTH is everything."[24] Be it slavery or a séance, the truth would come out. Pa counted himself for naught.

Father remained a church member at large. He was sure the finite cannot give full expression to the infinite. The more the finite tries (in or out of church), the more the finite fails. One Lincoln commentator concluded, "It is quite probable the Almighty does not think as we do, in terms of human language. It is not likely with Him that the meaning of a law, physical or spiritual, depends on the turn of a word in any language."[25] If there is such a thing as a universal tongue, Pa, in the course of time, developed it. Pa could have been interested in the psychic phenomenon known as "glossolalia." The United States Government at one time awarded a research grant for this project (glossolalia). A graduate of Dr. Carl Jung's Institute in Switzerland, Rev. Morton Kelsey, an Episcopalian cleric, has written a book on this subject, entitled, *Tongue Speaking*. He reminds us that tongue speaking is spiritual-psychical in origin and transcends the limitations of finite speech. Pa may well have been familiar with the subject through his extensive Bible reading.[26] An authority in the field of ESP, Harold Sherman, comments on Marcus Bach's latest book: "*The Inner Ecstasy* speaks in a new way about speaking with tongues. It is a spiritual phenomenon worthy of exploration in search of hidden religious meaning."[26]a Any hidden religious meaning was forever a challenge to Pa!

Author, P. D. Packard, is convinced that "men with Lincoln's mental and moral endowments are not drawn to sectarianism or cults. In his (Lincoln's) case, he would thus be deprived of his inherent right to spiritual kinship with men everywhere."[27] The growth of Father's soul was often reflected in his language. Whether at Gettysburg or in Springfield, his life and his language became as one. In language more dramatic than Pa would prefer, we read, "fiercer white light than ever beat on many a throne makes every day that Lincoln lived as familiar to us as our own yesterdays."[28] It is true that some of Father's deepest feelings ran the gauntlet from slavery to séances. Far more of his words on slavery have been preserved — and with more accuracy. Without fear or favor, he stuck to the truth as he understood the truth.[29]

My death, as we know, made the psychical far more than a passing phenomenon for Pa. The psychical became the pathway to spiritual guidance. His position on spirit communication, which seemed novel, if not untenable in the 1860's, became far less so in the 1960's. Former president of the American Psychical Research Society, James Nyslop, informs us that, "in the course of 30 years' work . . . an immense amount of data collected now leaves the scientist no excuse for ignoring the supernormal element in human experience."[30] In thought, word and deed, Pa had courage *not* to ignore the claims of the spiritual and psychical upon his life. The founder of psychoanalysis, Sigmund Freud, used language which today might startle some members of the American Medical Association. As for Pa, he was delighted when Freud said; "If I had my life to live over again, I should devote myself to psychical research rather than psychoanalysis."[31]

In defining both the psyche and the psychic, Webster makes the mind synonymous with the soul. Yet language used for defining the soul is quite distinct from that of the mind.[32] The words of Alfred North Whitehead, one of the great minds and souls of any age, are always relevant — "Most of what we say with our conscious minds and speech is shallow and superficial. Only at rare moments does that deeper and vaster world come through into conscious thought and expression. These are the memorable moments of our lives when we feel, when we know, we are being used as instruments of a greater force than ourselves for purposes higher and wider than our own."[33] Dr. Jung, in his book, *Modern Man in Search of a Soul*, constantly uses the term psyche, and in his introduction to the German language edition of Stewart Edward White's, *The Unobstructed Universe*, appears the comment; "I do not hesitate to state that I have observed a sufficient number of such psychic phenomena to be completely convinced of their reality."[34] It can be said of Father, . . . what you think and do is what you are. And what you are is what you communicate.

2
Silence of Eternity

Pa's close associates remind us that "No one has a right to say he knew Lincoln intimately. There were areas of his life which he shared with no man."[1] Pa practiced the silence of eternity. The deepest area in his life defied definition. He referred to his silences as a "process of crystalization." Another expression he used was "not to be heard of men." He would say to himself, "I like that phrase!" He mastered the eloquence of silence. "I should be the most presumptuous blockhead upon this footstool if for one day I thought that I could discharge the duties which have come upon me since I came into this place, without the aid and enlightenment of One who is stronger and wiser than all others."[2] Pa had an *impelling impulse.* It made him sensitive to the domain of the spiritual and the psychical. A contemporary recalls that; "Things came about (for Pa) not so much by preconceived method as by impelling impulse."[3] *He was led!* He sought and waited upon guidance. The hour of decision, whether it was the timing of the Emancipation Proclamation or some move at the front, required the silence of eternity.

The last three years of his life on earth, following my death in 1862, caused Pa more than ever to feel that he was "driven by a Power Greater." "I have so many instances when I have been controlled by some other power than my own. I cannot doubt that this power comes from above. I frequently see my way clear to a decision when I am conscious that I have no sufficient facts upon which to found it."[4] This higher sensory perception dominated his life during the last years of the war. It accounts for his quiet acceptance of the psychical. His silence explains in part the absence of first-hand data as to Pa's psychic life. When a communication came through a medium, if Pa believed it to be from a higher plane, it made sense to listen. It was a relief from the conflicting counsel of his cabinet and Congress!

Father's innate ability to remain silent on occasions was reported in the *New York Times.* Pa had received the news of the presidential election while in Springfield. He was smothered with advice. People were making proposals as to his cabinet and what to do with the secessionists; "But the truly Republican President passes it off with a smile, and keeps mum." Then the Times reporter adds a personal note; "I never knew a public man who knew so well how to hold his tongue, and yet not offend his best friends."[4a]

Pa's associates, in the main, did not share his convictions nor his silence. Outstanding public figures, however, both in and out of Congress, were influenced by the new religious movement called Spiritualism.[5] Pa was cautious and he kept his views to himself. James Hyslop has warned that "whoever accepts the belief in spirits, from scientific evidence . . . if he has any respect for the good-will of his neighbors, he will let the subject entirely alone."[6] Pa was far from letting the subject alone. It was enough to keep silent.

Not even father's private secretary was aware of his 'subversive' activities. Nicolay confessed; "I never knew of his attending a séance."[7] A devoted friend was Sen. Orville Browning, whose aversion to psychic phenomena was recorded in his personal diary. He did admit that the phenomena "seemed to indicate the presence of intelligences." Yet the idea that messages came from the "spirits of deceased men" was too much.[8]

Pa knew what it meant "to stand alone." The strongest man on earth is the man who stands alone. He was a lone seeker, hence, "he was fated to enter upon a life of isolation."[9]

In a letter signed A. Lincoln, this confession appears: "I claim not to have controlled events, but confess plainly that events have controlled me."[10] These are the words of one who waited for guidance and Pa's prayer invariable began, "if it be thy will." On July 4, 1864, the Battle of Vicksburg proved to be a turning point in the war. Pa admitted he had previously sought guidance and urged his friends not to reveal this fact "lest people might laugh, you know."[11] One of Father's oft quoted passages from the Bible was, "go and tell no man." He knew its spiritual-psychical background atop Mt. Hermon. Pa was most anxious to secure silent wisdom in the timing of the Emancipation Proclamation. We will touch more on this. His words then were: "I said nothing to any one; I made a promise to myself and (hesitating a little) to my Maker."[12] Pa felt fraternal with the Eternal; it made for the silence of eternity.

Pa's melancholy mood attributed, for some, to his silence. Mention will be made of this later. Herndon expressed the opinion that these moods were born of the occult.[13] That was Herndon! While the psychical runs all through religion and theology, Father "seldom communicated to anyone his views" along these lines.[14] During the first presidential campaign, Pa spent most of his days at home in Springfield. He would receive visitors and write letters. "On political matters, he kept his lips tight," as previously noted. We also learn that "Lincoln made a resolution not to write or speak anything on doctrinal points."[15] This applied to the religionists in general, and for good reason.

For too long the psychical has been considered abnormal. A person with an unusual talent of this sort has been suspect! Psychically gifted children have been punished. This was true of the great Irish medium, Eileen Garrett.[16] Parents continue to scold the child who shows signs of psychical sensitivity.[17] The subject remains taboo. Hence much of the secrecy. Father remained "extremely reticent on the subject."

His critics in the press and in politics had a field day![18] Accuracy was not the hallmark of their profession, yet there "is ample evidence that Mr. Lincoln attended at least four séances, and perhaps several similar conferences, in his (White House) office."[19]

There was in New York City, as noted, "a lawyer of sufficient ability to become appointed Justice of the Supreme Court" in that state. He wrote two volumes "of great interest to so-called parapsychologists." "His first psychic experience came through his own daughter."[20] The judge wrote the president, inviting him to accept copies of his books. Pa signed an office memo, addressed to his friend, Sen. Edwin D. Morgan. The original document has been preserved. Pa asks the Senator to please inform the judge that the "books would be gratefully received."[21] There is no indication that Father read both volumes. There is some indication, in securing the books, that Pa sought to avoid undue publicity.

Father once granted a rare newspaper interview. He was asked if, as "an unknown individual," he had attended a séance. Pa's response was succinct, even sardonic; ". . . the one falsehood in the statement (report) is that half of it has not been told. The article does not begin to tell the wonderful things I witnessed."[21] Confirming a similar event, there is the report that the discovery of the presence of the president incognito almost threw the séance into chaos.[22]

At times Father would break his silence in the company of one in whom he had confidence. One such person in Pa's presence questioned the wisdom of keeping the public ignorant as to the psychic depth of Father's spiritual life. Father could only reply, "I know. I am obliged to appear different. I think more on these subjects than others. I have done so for years. I am willing that you should know."[23] In a note to Judge Whitney, Jesse Dubois wrote that "after having been intimately associated with Lincoln for twenty-five years, I now find that I never knew him."[24] In a recent book, *Beyond Words and Thoughts,* the author warns his readers not to share their deepest spiritual experiences with their immediate family or relatives. Only those who have had a similar unfoldment can understand your experience."[25] From a reputable medium comes this admission: "The inadequacy of words to express emotions, thoughts and feelings has from time to time created a barrier between me and others. It has made it impossible for me to explain myself, and my method of functioning, to most other people."[26]

Pa had a manner of communicating his thoughts without the use of words. His language was spiritual rather than verbal. "The medium is the message," is an expression employed by Marshall McLuhan, a current authority on communication. His "basic concept is that the *way* people communicate with each other is more important than what they say." He contends that "The communications technology compels people to adapt to particular ways of behaving, thinking, and reacting."[27]

3
Burn This

There are those who suspect my brother Robert, or one of Father's private secretaries, along with others, of confiscating considerable Lincolnia. Perhaps I can help to set the record straight. One source, Hans Holzer, quite sympathetic to my father's psychic life, states that "Robert may have burned some important papers of his father's, bearing on these sittings (séances), along with the political plot to assassinate Father. According to the record, he (Robert) most certainly destroyed many documents. . . .[1] Whatever the method employed, it can be assumed that 'reticent Robert' reserved the right to dispose of Father's personal papers in any manner he saw fit. Robert's "almost abnormal shrinking from giving out any personal information about his parents," was increasingly apparent.[2] As if to react against his very nature, Robert once "modestly affirmed that he made his father President!"[3]

No one was more averse to Pa's psychic leanings than Father's private secretary, Nicolay. He had his own blacklist on file in his office. It contained the names of persons and projects he deemed devisive or detrimental to the presidency. One such project listed was Spiritualism. At the bottom of this list appears the quotation, "you can fool all of the people some of the time."[4] Numerous volumes on *The Life and Work of the President* appeared under the authorship of Nicolay and Hay. Robert, we are told on reliable authority, "had the final word as to what went in and what stayed out" of those volumes. Robert's attitude toward the psychical was no less adamant than that of Nicolay. One professor of history tells us that Nicolay and his associate "had to submit to censorship, line by line," and adds that "Lincoln amounted to no more than Robert was willing for the world to know."[5] Herndon is blamed for the "Burnt Book Myth,"[6] but this is not an impartial opinion.

A more important issue, which can only be surmised, relates to material destroyed! Robert insisted, in his Will, that only certain of the Lincoln collection in his possession should be released. This was to be accomplished almost 100 years after our father's death! We are told that Father "left no written words on some other matters of secrecy by which to be accused."[7] Father was never consulted. One can but guess as to the nature of "some other matters". One original piece of Lincolnia preserved for posterity does bear on "some other matters of secrecy." It carries, you will recall, Mother's postscript, "please burn this!"[8] The purport of this Lincoln rarity leaves little doubt as to the reason for the postscript. We have a clearer concept of my clairvoyant Pa.[9]

Ma was given to the burning of some personal psychical correspondence. Is it too much to assume that her alter ego, Robert, was involved in a similar process? We can only speculate as to the degree and nature of Robert's burning desire. By one method or another it was either fulfilled or curtailed Dr. Nicholas Murray Butler of Columbia University gives a detailed account of his intervention.[10] The details of a confrontation with Robert, as reported by Butler, has been doubted, but no one has questioned his efforts. Any psychical material, in particular that which Robert considered might cause embarrassment to his family, could have been eliminated any time before or after Butler's intervention. Butler discounts the claim that Robert's primary concern was some correspondence which implicated Stanton in the conspiracy to assassinate Pa. He has said, "*My own impression is that the letters contain records and evidence of various happenings in Abraham Lincoln's own life and family which it was just as well not to make public, certainly not while his son was living.*"[11] One can draw his own conclusion as to the *various happenings!* One Lincoln scholar dealing with the Butler story concluded; "Robert was Victorian through and through." He was afraid that a biographer would reach the wrong "conclusions."[12] Pa, who was anything but Victorian, would share no such view.

On July 23, 1863 Pa sent a telegram to General John M. Schofield. It contained this non-committal statement; "I care very little for the publication of any letter I have written." However, it provokes the cryptic comment — "It is a great injustice to the memory of Abraham Lincoln to build up a purely hypothetical propositon that only certain papers were burned or suppressed by Robert Lincoln as the guardian angel of his father's reputation."[13] We know that brother Robert became the self-appointed guardian of Pa's reputation. We are aware that he burned or suppressed certain of Pa's papers. The term certain papers really tells us nothing . . . but am I not entitled to draw my own conclusions based on my understanding of father and brother ? Nobody knows unless it is Robert. And if I know my brother Robert he is not about to say, particularly if it relates to the psychical

The distinguished E. Joy Morris was appointed ambassador to Turkey on June 8, 1961.[14] He had graduated from Harvard University in 1836, speaking several languages and twenty years later, from 1856-1861, served in the House of Representatives. Morris is reported to have attempted a recovery of a monograph "in which Father set forth his views on Spiritualism." Nothing is known as to the outcome of his endeavor. An air of mystery surrounds the disappearance of the monograph and the report.[15] On September 19, 1862, soon after my death, the secretary of state informed Morris "of the reoccurence of religious or other domestic disturbances in the Capitol."[16]

Senator Browning tells us in his diary that spiritualism had become a "Washington Fad."[17] This condition of affairs in the Capitol will come up for further consideration. On May 21, 1862 Pa was presented with a volume called *Further Communications from the World of Spirits.* On the title page, in the upper right corner, appears Father's signature of ownership.[18] This is one more item which escaped the hands of the censor. A historian who came upon the volume, now in the Oliver R. Barrett Collection, remarks that "it bears no sign of use."[19] This is one historian's opinion. It did however, affirm some of Lincoln's views.

What bothered Pa was the mixture of the psychical and the spiritual, to form a newly organized religion. In his mind, psychicism and spiritualism were not synonymous. One day Father listened at length to the reading of a paper which emphasized spiritualism. The insistent reader asked for the president's comment. This was Pa's chance. He said, "For those who like this sort of thing, that is the sort of thing they like."[20] One reliable historian refers to a "monograph on Deism," written by Father and burned by a friend.[21]

4
Careful Historians

The Howard Chandler Robbins Professor of Religion at the Episcopal Theological School in Cambridge, Massachusetts, was William J. Wolf. He has given us a searching account of Father's religion. The author refers to the "careful Historians" . . . "who shy away from the religious dimensions" in Pa's life. These dimensions have not been within the purview of the average Lincoln historian or biographer. One can search through many such books and come to the conclusion that Father's spiritual-psychical dimensions were negligible.

In Current's book, *The Lincoln Nobody Knows*, the author recognizes a reluctance to deal with the psychical side of Pa. The constant religious and counter-religious claims could cause many a historian or biographer to shy away.

Father once referred to a profound New Testament psychic event of the spirit in these words: "I doubt the possibility or propriety of settling the religion of Jesus in the models of man-made creeds and dogmas." Father continued, saying; "Probably it is my lot to go on in the twilight, feeling and reasoning my own way through life, as questioning and doubting did. But in my poor, maimed way, I bear with me as I go on seeking a spirit of desire for a faith that was with him of old time, who, in his need, as in mine, exclaimed, 'help Thou my unbelief.' "[1] To what biblical quotation did Pa allude? None other than the reappearance of Jesus in the spiritual body, after his crucifixion, when the Master appeared several times, walking through walls and locked doors.

The American historians tend to be too cautious in their appraisal of Lincoln's religious dimensions. But Ralph Shirley, an astute Lincoln observer from Great Britian remarks, "it is not to be wondered at that a man, who had so deep a realization of the spiritual side of life, should have had his own strange experiences of the psychic forces ever present around us."[2] Another Britisher displays an astute depth of knowledge relative to Pa's struggle with the spiritual-psychical. He speaks of Father's "dim sense of another world surrounding this, the belief in communion between the two. These are the parts of him that are based unchangeably in the forest shadows." Then he adds, ". . . the spiritual passion, the ecstasies, the vague sensing of the terribleness of the creative powers — to them he (Lincoln) always made silent response."[3] The 'careful historian' is careful, not alone because of the nebulous, ethereal aspects of the subject, but for an American historian to couch the prestigious office of the presidency itself in an aura of psychic mystique, would seem to them inherently unpalatable and inconsistent with the national and historical perspective. No such mental block appears to exist among the British however, as can be discerned from the comment, "*Strangely enough, those interested in psychic matters in England — and the number is impressively large — seem to be more familiar with Lincoln's mystic life than we are in his own America. That the English revere him for it, I know, as we shall when we, too, come of age psychically, as well as scientifically.*"[4]

My father was familiar with most philosophers and Kant in particular.[5] Historians and biographers who deal with the life of Kant or Hegel or Shopenhauer tend to disregard the fact that these great minds were "convinced of the existence or reality of psychic phenomena."[6] When Swiss psycho-analyst, Jung was asked what his attitude toward psychic phenomena was, he replied, "I have always taken it very seriously. In matters like that, you cannot always come right out into the open. Even if you merely hint at them, you are at once misunderstood and exposed to bitter attacks by your professional colleagues."[7] How many history books include George Washington's psychic experience at Valley Forge?[8] There is some justification for renowned Spiritualist Sir Arthur Conan Doyle's complaint; "The reader might, I fear, search every history of the great struggle (Civil War) and life of President Lincoln without finding reference to this vital (psychical) episode.[9] The vital episode, to which Doyle refers, is the part played by the child medium, Nettie Colburn, in the issuance of the Emancipation Proclamation but more on this later. Spiritualism is apparently anathema to the careful historian.

Some relevance can be seen in Hyslop's statement that, "there can be no doubt in the mind of the present writer that the phenomena of the Fox sisters never received their deserved investigation; but the spiritualists did not take a course that would invite the interest of intelligent people. They succeeded only in giving to the word spiritualism a meaning that has made it almost impossible to use in a favorable sense among respectable people."[10] Father would not deny that but would none the less add that spiritualism had kept alive one of the primary tenents of all religion. It has afforded psychical research a continued base of operation. A strong statement comes from Sir Wm. Barrett, a leading British scientist; "The humble spiritualists have had to try and do the neglected work of science in this very difficult region of inquiry. Now having done it to the best of their ability, they are scorned and pelted by the educated world and told they are guilty of intellectual whoredom. Their painstaking effort to enlarge the sum-total of human knowledge is stigmatised as the recrudescence of superstition. . . ."[10a] Meanwhile, the attitude of the average Lincoln historian can be detected in such passages as the "rigamarole of séances" or "the mummery of mediums." The same author acknowledges that Father was not gullible and could detect the "hocus-pocus . . . the juvenile passages that came through." He claims father "did not become a Spiritualist, either." Then by definition he states; "The word spiritualist has a more general meaning. It refers to any person who has a sensitivity to the unseen." Only in this general sense does the author conclude Lincoln, was a spiritualist.[11] Another historian, Ruth Randall, after narrating the Georgetown séances attended by my mother and father, admitted to a certain skepticism. This same historian projected her own feelings upon my mother. She is sure that Mother, out of her suspicion of skepticism, demanded a test of young Nettie Colburn. The test applied to Gen. Daniel E. Sickles, who was disguised. Miss Nettie's guide, or control, was to identify the General. The historian concedes the identification was correct! The control described a "crooked knife" or a sickle.[12]

Those who are troubled by the term trance, should consider the Webster definition; "a complete mental absorption or deep musing."[13] Such a definition includes some of the more inspired thought forms in both prose and poetry. Henry Wadsworth Longfellow is credited with this prose; "*The spiritual world lies all about us, and its avenues are open to the unseen feet of phantoms that come and go. We perceive them not, save by their influence, and when at times a mysterious Providence permits them to manifest themselves to mortal eyes.*"[14]

Historians in general are not equipped to make a scholarly and scientific psychical research into the "huge bibliography of Lincolnia." One Lincoln scholar states that "far too little has been made of this approach."[15] But psychical research is making progress. "It's been nearly 90 years since the British Society for Psychical Research was founded at Cambridge. Now, for the first time, is the idea of extra sensory perception — or ESP — acquiring a flavor of scientific respectability."[16] Perhaps this story about my Pa should have been called "ESP in the White House!"

Dr. Nandor Fodor informs us that in the periodical *Spiritual Scientist* appears the notation; "On four succeeding Sundays, Mr. Conklin the test medium, was a guest at the Presidential Mansion. The result of these interviews (visits at the White House) was the president's proposition to his cabinet to issue the Proclamation"[16a]

One historian, Jay Monaghan, confirmed a Laurie 'home circle' séance.[17] The careful employment of an adjective or adverb, gives away his motive. Earl S. Miers, editor-in-chief of *Lincoln Day-by-Day,* tells us that Pa "allegedly" attended White House séances.[18] In Chicago, there is The Lincoln Book Shop. Ralph Newman, the proprietor, has long been a careful student of Pa's history. He writes of Father's *apparent* interest in the psychical.[19] One historian debates the issue with himself! "How did such activities escape the eagle eye of John Hay, who kept a remarkably frank diary about the 'Tycoon' (nickname for Pa) . . . it seems odd that John G. Nicolay could not recall a séance ever being held in the White House."[20] Why is it so odd and strange? These two men were private secretaries. They were trained to protect the president. They had a known aversion to the psychical and the president was not oblivious to their feelings. The *New York Tribune* once described my father as "one of the most reticent men who ever lived in regard to his own spiritual exercises."[21] Father was prudent. It was, in part, a matter of policy.

Lincoln student, J. Snider, with a mind for the extra-sensory has said "Lincoln's biography reveals the inner psychical movement of a biography, his life reveals the essential process of every completed life."[22] This provides an insight far deeper than most Lincoln scholars comprehend! The cautious historian, Professor Current, assures his readers that "it is true," a few séances were held in the White House.[23] Upon personal pressure, he is "no longer sure."[24] What does this reflect? He defends his position by saying: "The historian does not claim to arrive at perfection. He does hope for fresh inquiry to come nearer to past reality."[25] Pa would have appreciated his use of the term reality. By friend and foe, whether past or present, he was considered a realist.[26] Those who have accepted psychic phenomena in my father's life as a reality have, with some justification, referred to "Lincoln's timid biographers who suppressed and ignored the actual documentary evidence right under their very eyes."[27]

Many a careful historian becomes involved, as we have detected, in the ambiguity or anomaly of classifying Pa's participation in psychic phenomena as spiritualism per se. This gives rise to the comment that, "Lincoln's detractors for almost 80 years have maintained that the Emancipator was a Spiritualist"[28] — the key word being detractors!

One notable researcher coined the term "spiritistic hypothesis" as a compromise. He comments that, "the prejudices and ignorance of a century are organized against even the use of this term."[29]

Among Father's numerous biographers, William E. Barton deserves some careful consideration. He expresses disappointment, even disillusionment, with the Lincoln historians and biographers. He feels that Father has "eluded" most of them,[30] and alludes to "the *last* attempt to make out Lincoln a Spiritualist."[31] Barton's book was written in 1920. Many attempts to make Lincoln out a Spiritualist have been made since and will no doubt continue into the future.

Miss Ida M. Tarbell devoted her life to the task of probing into Pa's personal life. She confessed "I am such a slave to facts, dates and things, I fail to see the greater facts."[32] Any real examination of the greater facts would certainly portray Pa's psychic profile.

A specialist in American history at the Library of Congress is critical of one Lincoln historian for "begging the question" as to séances in the White House. This same specialist states that "independent witnesses place the séances either at the Soldier's Home, or in Georgetown." Then he adds that, "only the Spiritualists claim any séances were held at the White House."[33] Few historians, and perhaps even then with some reluctance, are willing to admit that séances were, in fact, held at the White House.

One promising Lincoln historical project makes the assertion that, "It is the purpose of this paper to examine the unexplored areas and the deficiences in the Lincoln theme. . . ."[34] Hopefully, these unexplored areas and deficiences will include the psychical. The dilemma in which Lincoln devotees find themselves is in painting a portrait of Pa which preserves the dignity of his high office and still includes the psychical! Pa would be the first to agree that this is an aspect of his life which needs to be approached with some reserve, and an element of reverence. Lincoln student, Frances Grierson, writes that "it is time to know the truth about Lincoln's supernaturalism. Your favorite historian avoids the subject."[35] Father himself, as we have learned, avoided the word supernatural. What seemed supernatural, became natural.[36] With the use of such terms by historians and others, the fear of the unknown becomes more fearful.

5

Free Press

Carl Schurz was one of the inner circle and one of Father's few trusted military officers. He traces, you will recall, his ultimate appointment as United States Senator from Missouri to a psychic, precognitive experience. This former general in the Union Army gives us a detailed account of several personal experiences with psychic phenomena. They occurred after Father's assassination. Schurz, of German ancestry, was brought into touch with German poet, Friedrich Schiller. The poet, long deceased, succeeded in contacting Pa on the other side. He sums up his psychic life saying, "I give here my own experiences. I do not offer any theory or hypothesis upon which to explain them. The believer in spiritualism may see it in it striking proof of the truthfulness of his belief."[1] This could well have come from Pa. The free press printed the 'proof.' Schurz paid tribute to Father's inherent honesty — "Beyond the circle of those who had long known him, the feeling steadily grew that the man in the White House was still Honest Abe Lincoln."[2]

Pa's insistence for honesty did not influence the power of the press. Schurz stated; "In vain did the journals of the opposition represent him (Pa) as a light-minded trifler . . . it may be said that few men in power have been exposed to more daring attempts to direct their course, to severe censure of their acts and to more cruel misrepresentation of their motives."[3] Schurz was well acquainted with the controversial issues of slavery and séances. He goes back to New Salem and Springfield to underscore Father's determination to get at the truth. "He (Pa) became a successful lawyer less indeed by his learning than by his effectiveness as an advocate . . . it may be truly said that his vivid sense of truth had much to do with his effectiveness . . . he would abandon cases in the midst of a trial . . . he would refuse to act as attorney for a personal friend if he felt the TRUTH was not on his side."[4]

Pa's hold on the truth brought him little but ridicule from the free press. It related to Pa's position in the psychical and political arenas. One Lincoln commentator, Brand Whitlock, wrote that "abuse and criticism he could endure." Father seldom read the newspapers . . . "I know more about it than they do," he would say . . . "the newpapers and the pulpit became full of abuse, because they were not heeded."[5] Pa was receiving his counsel from sources far beyond either the press or the pulpit! This counsel he found more convincing. "The principal newpapers of the large cities became the mouthpiece of the extremists. Their fanaticism spared neither Lincoln nor his Cabinet."[6] Pa adhered to honesty as the best policy, and rode out the storm!

The free press was "full of ads by mediums," yet it continued to attack mediumship. A British correspondent was moved to write; "It is strange to see a journal which professes to represent civilization and intelligence of the most enlightened people on the face of the earth carry advertisements of sorcerers, wizards, etc."[7] The Free Press reported Pa's attendance at a séance in an article datelined New York City, April 20.[8] It appears to be the same as that recorded in the Boston Gazette on April 23, 1863. The reports contained the usual spiritualist slant, and what was not put in print, was featured in cartoons.

In January, 1863, "The kindly ghost of King George III tries to enter into conversation with the stiffly stupid ghost of George Washington." The significant caption of the cartoon is "The Latest From *Spirit* Land." King George is addressing Washington: "Well, Mr. Washington, what do you think of your fine Republic now, eh?"[9] "The London *Punch* which castigated Lincoln during the Civil War, had a change of heart after Pa's assassination. *Punch* published a poem entitled *Abraham Lincoln Foully Assassinated April 14, 1865* composed by Tom Taylor. One verse reads:

The Old World and The New, from sea to sea,
Utter one voice of sympathy and shame!
Sore heart, so stopped when it at last beat high,
Sad Life cut short just as its triumph came.[9]a

There were a barrage of books and pamphlets which had no mercy on the president or the mediums. *Interior Causes of the War . . . A Nation Demonized* has been mentioned. This book has been denounced by one historian as part of an unsigned, whispering campaign.[10] One portion of its tirade against Pa claimed, "Mr. Lincoln is a spiritualist of the abolitionist school . . . In the Cabinet and in Congress are many other men equally reliant on spirit communication, but without the same honesty to declare their secret springs of action."[11] There was just enough truth in this, coming from the enemy, to make it hurt! It substantiates what was too often denied or dismissed by many of Father's friends. Another attack was made in a book by Fayette Hall with the tell-tale title, *The Copperhead or The Secret Political History of Our Civil War Unveiled.* It says, "Let spiritualism be true or false. The President is placed in his position and has taken an oath to abide by the law and the Constitution. His authority emanates from this sphere, and from no other! It was just as much treason to receive and obey orders from that (spirit world) source as from any other foreign power. I also believe that the spirits, believing them to be such, were devilish! No honorable spirits would require the President to violate his oath and obligation, and perjure himself to carry out and obey their orders by employing the army and the sword."[12] Pa was accustomed to most any kind of attack, as were other presidents before and since.

Hall was admitted to the White House in good faith and allowed to interview the president. He was later permitted to meet some of the mediums close to Pa. He witnessed some psychic demonstrations by these same mediums and was favorably impressed! Historian Monaghan, claims the author was soured after, rather than before, his interviews with the president and Nettie Colburn. Hence the exposé! Nevertheless, his book, however biased, is accepted as valuable source material — it comes through with a distinct southern accent![13]

Before my family left Springfield, the printed page "prophesied evil times under the President-Elect."[14] During the 1860's, *The Atlantic Monthly, The Scientific American* and *The Nation* printed serious articles speculating as to the validity of claims made by the Spiritualists.[15] A sensational article appeared in the Cleveland *Plain Dealer* attacking Pa as a Spiritualist.[16] The article was published in March, 1864.[17] In the early days, to avoid being maligned, Pa would address a letter to a news publisher. On August 11, 1846 he sent a letter to Allen N. Ford of the *Illinois Gazette* at Lacon, Illinois. Pa sought to disclaim a charge made by his political opponent that he was an infidel.[18] Pa soon discovered little was accomplished. A Lincoln

Centennial edition, 1909, of the *Chicago Sunday Tribune* couldn't refrain from this headline: "President Lincoln Gets Spirit Advice on War." In observance of Father's one-hundredth birthday, there appears one of those uncomplimentary cartoons. The president is pictured as a ghost. He holds a human skull.[19] The Civil War, was again, "Lincoln's War." In his last public address, on April 11, 1865, Pa repeated that "as a general rule I abstain from reading the reports of attacks upon myself, wishing not to be provoked by that to which I cannot properly offer an answer."[20] One knowledgeable Lincoln biographer commented; "When a Washington correspondent found the White House well dry, he turned naturally to those streams of gossip, complaint, criticism and intrigue, the Congressmen, whose anti-Lincoln pronouncements all too often agreed with the prejudices of his editor."[21] One of the most powerful newpapers of its day was the New York *Herald*. The editor, James Gordon Bennett, was anti-Lincoln from the start. The president "was a joke incarnate . . . his inaugural address was a joke . . . his title 'Honest' is a satirical joke."[22] This would be neither the first nor last time the press was after the office of the president.

6
Religious Crisis

The military and political crisis during the Civil War was not enough. The capitol and the country were plagued by a religious crisis of no mean proportion. Séances were ridiculed whenever they took place. The crisis was aggravated by the press and put Pa on the spot. Addressing Congress on the state of the nation, Father had said "the dogmas of the quiet past are inadequate to the stormy present."[1] This had a familiar ring, both in the halls of Congress and to organized religion. A thorn in the side of orthodox religion was the newly-organized religious movement called Spiritualism.

If I seem to put undue emphasis on Spiritualism it is because it was a dominant factor in father's day. "A wave of Spiritualism was sweeping the country as always, in the wake of war."[2] Church institutions, Catholic and Protestant, considered Spiritualism their common enemy. The Catholic and Protestant denominations at one time or another had laid claim to the president's allegiance. Were the spiritualists not equally justified?

Father Charles Chiniquy was for half a century a Catholic priest. He is largely responsible for the myth concerning Father's Catholicism. As a young lawyer, Pa had defended the priest.[3] Reverend Chiniquy quoted Pa with strong Catholic religious overtones. He related the numerous prophecies of the president's assassination. "The disclosure was far more Chiniquy than Lincoln."[4] The priest's words served to confirm many a Catholic hope. This same priest was to turn Protestant and wage a holy war on the Jesuits.[5]

Pa was amused because his ancestors, as indicated, were Quakers,[6] and Father leaned in that direction. His religious heritage also included a sect known as the Campbellites. Alexander Campbell, a Lincoln contemporary, shared Father's gifts of the spirit, and like Pa, Campbell was born psychic. He was not prepared to admit it yet, but the record speaks for itself.[7]

As a young man in Indiana, Pa came under the spell of the 'hard shelled' Baptists at Pigeon Creek, and from them came Pa's strong belief in predestination.[8] Campbell was associated with the Baptist church in those days. "His talents, learning, boldness as a controversalist, and skill as a writer made his publication 'The Christian Baptist' exceedingly popular. . . ." To what extent this leading Christian gentleman's views on predestination, coupled with his personal psychic experiences influenced Pa, stimulates a provocative line of thought.[8a]

Pa's association with the Campbellites may well have been much closer than the Pigeon Creek Baptist Church. His father and stepmother, Sarah Bush Lincoln, became members of the Church of the Disciples. This was during his Illinois days. The disciples were nicknamed Campbellites. Pa's devotion to his stepmother is well attested. What is not so well attested is that privately Pa was baptized (immersed) "by a minister of the Disciples of Christ Communion."[8b] There can be no doubt, that in a larger sense, Pa was immersed by the Holy Spirit, including the spiritual-psychical aspects of the New Testament experience.

What made the national religious crisis so unnecessary, if not unholy, is the fact that Catholics, Protestants and Quakers have all produced psychically endowed individuals among their numbers. We have already mentioned St. Francis of Assisi, John Wesley, and George Fox.[9]

The rise of the newly-organized religion called Spiritualism, did not disturb Pa, but the traditional religionist saw the Spiritualist as a threat or curse! The Spiritualists insisted upon being institutionalized. They had to be recognized to be accepted.

With the inevitable proselytizing the religious crisis began. The explanation was clear to Pa. While the other sects had long since accepted the basic concepts of Spiritualism, they had not put them into practice. The Spiritualists were now attracting adherents from the old-line churches.

Spiritualism soon followed the pattern of all organized religion. They turned their attention to politics. Through a political power block, the Spiritualists succeeded in securing favorable legislation. Not a few Congressmen were impressed by the new religious movement. No less than 15,000 Spiritualist constituents signed a petition addressed to the Congress. It was presented to Congress by Senator Shields. It urged the appointment of a commission "to make a study of the apparent attempt of beings of the other world to set up an actual liaison with the mortal world. Political agitation by the Spiritualists was to make itself felt some six to seven years before Pa took office. But if it was not Spiritualism, which concerned some Congressmen, it was Catholicism or Protestantism (so it seemed to Pa).

On February 12, 1856, a representative from Pennsylvania denounced the Roman Catholic lobby on the floor of the House, claiming satirically; "To vigilantly protect free inquiry into spiritual as well as secular matters, has in itself become political heresy."[19] Prominent senators under pressure "read into" the Congressional Record, "petitions and memorials" in the interest of Spiritualism. "The Spiritualist Lobby was reported in the New York *Tribune* of March 28, 1859,"[11] thus, by the time Pa reached Washington, there was "widespread interest" in Spiritualism "among some leading Americans."[12] Pa found himself in the middle of the growing religious crisis. He was neither for nor against Spiritualism, Protestantism, or Catholicism. Pa felt it was *organized* religion that killed the truth. That was the one and only evil. James Russell Lowell describes Pa's predicament in his poem, *The Present Crisis:*

Truth forever on the scaffold,
Wrong forever on the throne,
Yet that scaffold sways the future,
And behind the dim unknown
Standeth God within the shadow,
Keeping watch above his own.[13]

In the capitol, Spiritualism, as a religion, became a craze. Publicity was given to visitations and séances in homes, in hotels, and on steamboats. For a time, even men like Horace Greeley became interested in the phenomena. Spiritualism flourished in the North, rather than the South. This was due to the fact "that it became part of the radical transcendentalism of the period" which was associated with the crusade against slavery.[14]

One Spiritualist writer informs us that abolitionist leader, William Lloyd Garrison, and my father "gave some sort of testimony to the movement during that period."[15] The tenor of messages which came through mediums at a séance were against slavery. "Father listened, believed, and supposedly was relieved."[16] Along with the war, the flames of a religious crisis were being fanned by organized Spiritualism.

Another Lincoln biographer noticed something in the "make-up" of Pa, which made him sympathize with some aspects of Spiritualism, although there is nothing in records "to prove" that either Pa or Ma "ever had any connection with the organization."[17] But Pa's antagonists continued to maintain that "spiritualism was one of the chief factors in the management of national affairs under Lincoln," and that, "Lincoln's nomination took place at a séance."[18] If a religious crisis had not been in the works, such sensational claims would have started one.

The court trial of the medium, Charles Colchester, accused of being a fraud, aroused considerable acrimony. It became a public scandal, and contributed to the crisis. Colchester, as we know, had more than a passing acquaintance with Pa. He was held in esteem by those in his profession. At the trial, the presiding judge pronounced the defendant guilty "because he refused to demean his God-given communicability in the degrading and compulsory circumstances."[19] As Pa realized, the judge thereby convicted himself in the name of justice. Not even a medium can be expected to become a clear channel for any communication in the midst of muddy waters. The bare essential for a psychic demonstration is a climate conducive to its fulfillment.

There followed the Colchester case, a long drawn-out public debate by two distinguished gentlemen, James Gordon Bennett and Justice Edmunds. It was hardly comparable to the Lincoln-Douglas debate, but it did add more fuel to the fire. "In hundreds of thousands of families, at countless firesides, where imposture would be sacrilege, and in circles of mutually cherished relatives and friends, between whom the ideas of deception would be even stranger than facts, we were asked to believe Spiritualism is undergoing the test of daily experiments . . ." So wrote the angry editor of a New York daily.[20] This was written months after the crisis and the fires were still burning.

It was whispered that Pa's psychical spirit had "rubbed off on General Grant." The latter was seen at a séance conducted by a "celebrated medium of the day."[21] All of which adds substance to this story of Pa's psychic life.

There was an eternal crisis being promoted by the opposing religious customs, creeds, dogmas and denominations. Within organized Spiritualism, there was increasing evidence of some internal troubles. "By the summer of 1863, with many frauds exposed, Spiritualism was having a setback."[22] Fraud, fakery, chicanery or hypocracy are not confined to any one human institution! Spiritualism however, in the minds of some, had more than its share. In the unholy tug-of-war between organized religions, Spiritualism had a rough time.

There is this rather revealing interpretation: "He (Lincoln) was rather interested in Spiritualism, but as the occult art of communication with the denizens of the unseen world had not attained such a degree of perfection in his day as in ours, his opportunity for investigation was limited to a few séances, given by peripatetic mediums, which, however, instead of increasing his faith in intercommunication with the names of the departed, only excited his disgust for the fakers who laid claim to the power of summoning spirits to mortal presence."[23] These lines were published some 40 years after Pa's passing. They reflect the condition of affairs in and out of the White House, and a state of mind during the crisis. Pa could assent to the report, but with reservations.

The East Ohio Conference of the Methodist Episcopal Church produced another report on "Abraham Lincoln's Religious Views." The preface to the report reveals the religious undercurrent. "Much could be said of the claims made by the Spiritualists, insisting that Lincoln looked with favor upon their peculiar doctrine. Likewise the Universalists have come in to announce that Mr. Lincoln threw out friendly glances at them." The account then adds that "the author has sufficient material upon the religious glimpses of Lincoln to fill a five-hundred page volume."[24] Father would be the last to deny it. However, he would emphasize that his religious views were not confined to the Methodist Episcopal or any other church.

Spiritualism as a religion had its first boom and bust period during Pa's administration. It was not the last, but it did contribute to the religious crisis of the 1860's. The increasing war casualties as noted made for an abundant demand that personal survival be real and inter-communication between two worlds could provide relief.

The poet, John Ruskin, at one time had lost his belief in personal immortality, only to regain it. "The unanswerable evidence of spiritualism" was Ruskin's explanation of his renewed conviction in personal immortality. Then the poet adds, "I know there is much vulgar fraud and stupidity connected with it, but underneath I'm sure there is enough to convince us that there is personal life, independent of the body. *But with this once proved, I have no further interest in Spiritualism!*"[25] This sounds like Pa. He could understand and accept such a confession.

While Pa was concerned about truth, when churchism professed to promote it, that was another matter. Dr. Nando Fordor, a graduate of the Royal University of Science, received his doctorate in 1917. He was to become director for the International Institute for Psychical Research. In his book, *Between Two Worlds,* he comments on Spiritualism during Pa's tenure as president. He concludes that Lincoln was a firm believer in life after death. "That did not make him a Spiritualist! And it was a misnomer to label him as such!"[26] More than one Lincoln historian concurs.[27] *In every crisis, religious, political, or domestic, Pa was sustained by the psychical-spiritual around which Spiritualism and all religions are built.* Although neglected, these concepts remain constant in more than one religious faith.

An impartial study of Spiritualistic practices provides some historical insight into Pa's attitude and the crisis which the Spiritualists generated. "One effect of my inquiry," said Dr. Fodor, "has been to increase considerably my respect for the Spiritualists. They are not the cranks I had imagined them to be. Nor in Isaiah's phrase, 'Wizards that peep and that mutter'."[28]

It did not take a religious crisis or a Civil War or the president's participation in séances to provoke concern over mediumship. The late Arthur Ford, one of the most outstanding mediums of modern times, and a minister in the Disciples of Christ Church, suggested that the "academicians" who have persisted in their investigation of mediums should themselves submit to a "brief investigation."[29] In the same vein, a British scientist complains of "the scientific psychic investigator who plays the part of an amateur detective."[30] The same scientist gives a "distinct warning," apart from a religious crisis, "against making a religion of Spiritualism." This, he states, is "an argument for the study of the phenomena as a branch of the psychical or psychological science."[32] For Pa, as we have seen, the real victim of organized religion was the truth it sought to uphold.

Herndon, not always complimentary in his appraisal of his former law partner, argues that Pa survived the religious crisis as a 'realist' and not as a 'Spiritualist.'[32]

The color of the ground was in him (Lincoln); the red earth; the smack and tang of elemental things. Into the shape she (Mother Earth) breathed a flame of light, that tender, tragic, everchanging face; And laid on him a sense of mystic powers.

Edwin Markham, *LINCOLN THE MAN OF THE PEOPLE*

CHAPTER IV
MY PRIMITIVE PIONEER PA

1
Uninhibited-Untutored

"The greatest hope in the study of spirit manifestation is among unspoiled. so-called primitive peoples."[1] Any interpretation of the spiritual-psychical Lincoln must include his primitive pioneer background. Civilization has inhibited the instinctive and the intuitive. These human aspects reach beyond the five senses. Psychic phenomena began in pre-history. The great psychics and mystics came out of the East.[2] Primitive tribes, whether in Peru, Haiti or Ethiopia, display genuine extra-sensory perception. Pa's native qualities can be seen in the sentence: "The highly civilized individual must be a highly inhibited individual."[3] It was the "backwoods drama" of his whole life which strengthened his spiritual-psychical posture.[4] It is the clue to his greatness and his genius.

Edgar Cayce, among other sensitives, was a living testimony to the fact that no amount of intellectual or theological training is prerequisite to the development of the psychical or mystical. Quite the contrary is the case. Formal education "might destroy and impair native aptitude . . . to break through spirit barrier and pierce the impenetrable veil."[5] The primitive and the pioneer in Pa made him more psychically receptive. Primitive tribes have their psychic midwives who observe the severance of the spiritual umbilical cord. "Death is a form of rebirth."[6] Former President James A. Garfield spoke of Pa as "gifted with an insight and a foresight which the ancients would call divination. He sat in the midst of darkness and obscurity, the logic of events, and forecast the results."[7]

In most people there is a paradox which Pa shared. Man lives by a faith that Providence did not "intend us to know about the future life."[8] The pioneer primitive in Pa merely sought to penetrate the unknown. As one Lincoln authority explains: "His concern about dreams and some inquiries into spiritualism were survivals of the primitive biblicalism and backwoods superstition that characterized frontier religion."[9] We have pursued this viewpoint to some extent. Pa's Pigeon Creek Baptist predestination, coupled with his premonitions, preserved and enriched Pa's firm acceptance of spirit survival and communication.

There was far more to life than his five senses could detect. Carl Jung tells us that "whether primitive or not, mankind always stands upon the verge of those actions that it performs iteself, but does not control."[10] The influence of Pigeon Creek Church stayed with Pa. Nathaniel Stephenson, one of his biographers, writes us that "even at nineteen, for anyone attuned to spiritual meaning, he would have been struck by the note of mystery, faintly perhaps, but certainly."[11] What began as mystery took on more meaning through the years. Pa tried to detect and to determine his direction. Life for him was one great schooling of the soul. Prediction of events, and events themselves, however terrible, came under that category. Pa, as we know, wanted only to become an instrument in the hands of the Almighty, the ruler of the Universe. War and peace could come and go but life went on forever!

Pa's predominant acceptance of personal survival placed him on a plane from which he could carry on amid extreme adversity. Sen. George Sewall, who was a delegate to the convention which nominated Pa for the presidency made this observation: "The schools create nothing; they only bring out what is; but as long as the mass of mankind think otherwise, an untrained person like Lincoln has an immense advantage over the scholar in the contest for immortality. In this particular, the instincts of man have a large share of wisdom in them. When we speak of human greatness, we mean natural, innate faculty and power."[12] This is a personal appraisal of Pa which fits my present theme.

Pa called his kind of "plain people" the "children of nature." He had "profound respect . . . for their collective wisdom . . . touching matters belonging to the domain of the psychical mysteries."[13] As a child of nature himself, he could read the mind of the common man. His friend, Senator Cole, spoke of Father's "uncanny prescience taking us quite off our feet." The Senator quotes Pa: "Let me discourse on a theme I understand. I know all about trees by right of being a backwoodsman."[14]

Many who were to consider Pa as merely uncultured and uncouth were to see him clothed in robes of a high order. Higher sensory perception has been discovered or recovered among folk like my father. Many of these people are ignorant of the scientific training which would have hindered their achievements, a discovery which has recently been confirmed by a medical scientist.[15] While Jefferson Davis and Robert E. Lee went to West Point, "Abe Lincoln went right on educating himself."[16] It was this self-education which allowed for the development of his gifts of the spirit.

It is true that Pa was not one to "grace fashionable society." He "hated clothing of all kinds." He would invariably remove his boots "to allow his feet to breathe."[17] Many, including Ma, were distressed. Ma had had a

Mrs. Mary Lincoln
from a photograph presented by Mrs. Lincoln
to Mrs. N.C. Maynard

formal education. She was "well-versed in literature," foreign and domestic. She was an "attractive girl, with great charm," but she could also be caustic.[18] My mother was often tardy for social occasions. Pa would explain "she'd be ready as soon as she gets all her trotting harness on."[19] Ma's "trotting harness" was elaborate and plentiful. Mother once wrote; "It must be remembered that (she) had the . . . most undomestic and unpalatable figure of a husband to carry with (her)." She is supposed to have indicated that this "would have been a terrible handicap to any woman."[20]

Lincoln historian, Philip Stern had the insight to see that, "underneath his uncouthness, she (Ma) saw possibilities of growth that she was clever enough to recognize."[21] It was the inner thrust of the spiritual-psychical forces to which much of that growth can be traced. Carl Jung, a psychic observer of note, said, "the great decisions of human life have as a rule far more to do with the instinct and to other mysterious unconscious factors than with conscious will and well-meaning reasonableness."[22] Pa, at the same time, could be very unreasonable if not stubborn! Pa's close associate, Judge Whitney, respected Pa greatly, yet he remarked; "Lincoln had no regard for manner, politeness, etiquette, official formalities, fine clothes, routine or red-tape."[23]

My primitive pioneer Pa was a problem. After one of my parent's visits to an army camp, a cavalryman wrote: "His Lady is charming enough to make up for all his deficiencies."[24] Pa's looks, as well as his outlooks, became a factor in his future. He was a frontiersman at heart.

Pa's countenance was a measured contrast to his conduct. The comptroller of the currency under the Lincoln administration was Honorable High McCulloch. He remarked, "I thought when I first saw him, he was the ugliest of men. Now that I know him well, he seems to me perfectly charming."[25] The comptroller concedes that much of Pa's charm emanated from an inner light. Noah Brooks, who thought of himself as a friend of the family, describes Pa's native dignity as . . . "a certain simple yet influential grandeur" . . . "one soon forgot in his immediate presence the native ungainliness of his figure," and felt he was "in the personal atmosphere of one of this world's great men."[26] Such a testimonial, is sufficient to substantiate Pa's sources of strength. Pa was younger in spirit than either his appearance or attitude would imply.

Pa took office at the age of 52. He died at 57. Those five years took their toll. We know how personal and bitter was the opposition. One New York newspaper constantly referred to Pa as "that hideous baboon at the other end of the avenue . . . Barnum should buy and exhibit him as a zoological curiosity."[27] Pa reached the breaking point when such talk came from his official family . . . Stanton and others. Pa was then overheard to say: "I would rather be dead than, as president, be thus abused in the house of my friends."[28] It should not be forgotten that it was soon after becoming chief executive Pa was hit by the Civil War and my death as a 'favorite' child. One historian would remind us that "none of Lincoln's greatness is lost when one points out that his uncouthness has been exaggerated."[29] "The most typical American figures in my view," wrote syndicated newspaper columnist Sidney Harris, "are Abe Lincoln and P. T. Barnum and one would be hard put to say which looms larger in our national character as our particular Dr. Jekyll and Mr. Hyde."

Irrespective of his appearance, Pa could transform an audience. The "rail splitter" cracked through any resistance when he rose to the occasion. His former law partner, Stephen T. Logan, commented; "He was tall, gawky and a rough-looking fellow. His pantaloons did not reach his shoes by six inches." The Judge adds that once Lincoln "began speaking, he held his audience.[30] It was Pa's spirit, more than his mind, which came through. His appearance at times worked in his favor. Writers agree as to "the remarkable effect produced by Lincoln's personal appearance . . . by the originality of his manner, his angular features, his long limbs hanging loosely in his ill-fitting clothes, the strange ungainliness of his figure."[31]

The sculptor, Leonard Volk, made a mold of Pa's right hand. It was scarred. Pa once explained it happened during his rail-splitting days . . .

"The ax glanced and nearly took my thumb off."[32]

In speaking out for Pa, my intention is simply to affirm his hidden gifts of the spirit. Now, closer than ever to my father, it is possible to better understand him. His rebirth followed my death. Indeed, so did my own rebirth come with death. An able psychologist describes rebirth as "an assertion which belongs to the primordial assertions of mankind."[33] It is this primordial assertion which provides some real insight into my primitive Pa.

In him, as I have stressed, the mystic came before the psychic . . . the spiritual before the psychical. Stimulated by the spiritual-psychical combination, Pa suffered the consequences of being ahead of his time. Also, as we have seen, he was a non-conformist, a maverick; but never for its own sake.

If man is a 'political animal,' Pa was no exception. Some people felt he pushed himself into politics. His friend, Judge David Davis, describes a political session at which Pa was present. The discussion which ensued was directed at a potential presidential candidate from the west. Pa promptly offered himself.[34] No one could deny that he was not head and shoulders above every other person present. He dominated most every situation physically, if not spiritually and psychically. He was big and tall in body, mind and spirit.

On December 20, 1859, Pa wrote to his friend, Jesse W. Fell from Springfield, Illinois. The letter was accompanied by a brief autobiography. Pa called it a "little sketch." It did not do him justice. As if to prove it, there appeared this sentence in conclusion: "There is not much of it, for the reason, I suppose, there is not much of me."[35] That was two years before Pa became president. That high office, coupled with the Civil War and my death, tapped Pa's inner resources as nothing had before.

One Lincoln orator was sure Pa "bore a commission from God on High!"[36] Few people were more aware of a sense of mission or destiny. This may account for this sort of estimate — "They sneered at him for his lack of education. Yet he might have been said to be the most perfectly educated."[37] He was perfectly educated in so far as he allowed life to draw out of him those deepest gifts of the spirit.

Seward was one of the more cultured members of Pa's cabinet. He almost defeated Pa for the presidential nomination. "He (Seward) never quite forgave his being put aside for an uncultured, inexperienced Westerner."[38] In the course of time even Seward was to recognize the unfoldment of Pa's power.

John W. Hill, wrote that Pa "acquired his education in such an unusual way that he might be able to speak for his time, and to his time, with perfect simplicity and sincerity." The author added; "We shall err if we look for the sources of Mr. Lincoln's power . . . in the mode of his educaton. It is his spiritual inheritance . . . there is something more in him than the quality called genius."[39]

Pa's spiritual inheritance was sustained by his childhood reading of the Scriptures. "The only school I ever had was in a log schoolhouse. Reading books and grammar were unknown. All my reading was done from Scriptures."[40] In later years he was to find in the Scriptures considerable support for his psychical-mystical experiences.

The two biographers, J. C. Randall and Richard N. Current, deal with Lincoln's primitive ancestory. They make the trenchant analysis . . . "They (his ancestors) were in touch with those original experiences, out of which the higher evolution of civilization slowly rises."[41] The slow rise is often imperceptable, if not impaired, by civilization itself.

In our present day the Spiritual Frontiers Fellowship organization is bent upon recovering or recapturing this evolutionary rise. Any such promising ecclesiastical innovation would have Pa's blessing. What is more, it has the support of the more courageous lay leaders and clergymen among many churches of all denominations. It deals with personal survival, spirit healing and communication as recorded in Scriptures. The work of the Fellowship within the churches will come in for further consideration in this chapter, and reflects much of my father's feeling throughout his life.

In his poem, *The Praise of Lincoln,* the poet Edwin Markham senses so well Pa's primitive intuition:

So hidden in the West, God shaped his man.
There in the unspoiled solitudes he grew,
Unwarped by culture and uncramped by creed;
Keeping his course courageous and alone,
As goes the Mississippi to the sea.
His daring spirit burst narrow bounds.
Rose resolute; and like the sea-called stream
He tore no channels where he found no way.[42]

Quaker founder and leader, George Fox also had psychic-mystic leanings which contributed to his higher evolution. He was also a primitive pioneer. In *The Varieties of Religious Experience* written in 1902 by William James, there is written this sentence concerning Fox: "So far as our Christian sects today are evolving into liberality, they are simply reverting in essence to the position which Fox and the early Quakers long ago assumed."[43] William James has left us a rich heritage of psychical research upon which we can draw.

One of Pa's bodyguards sounded an apologetic note as to the president's peculiar views concerning those interesting mysteries," and said, "the more intense light which is thrown upon what may be regarded as Mr. Lincoln's weakest points, the greater and grander will his character appear."[44] Pa did not think of his primitive, pioneer, psychic heritage as among his weakest points. He would concur with Hyslop that, "all important movements of the kind (spiritual and psychical) have originated among the common people."[45] Pa was proud to be considered as one of the common people.

Father would have appreciated the anonymous tribute, "Had Abraham Lincoln been living today, the Rotary Club would have supplied him with a good set of books, the Lion's Club with a reading lamp, the Cosmopolitan Club with writing equipment, the Kiwanis Club with a wooden floor for his cabin. He would have the protection of the Child Labor Law and Government Old Age Insurance. A kindly philanthropist would send him to college with a scholarship. Incidentally, a case worker would see that his father received a monthly check from the county. The O.P.A. would reduce his rent by thirty per cent. He would receive a subsidy for railsplitting, another for resisting some crops he was going to raise anyway, and still another subsidy for crop he had no intention of raising! *Result: There would have been no Abraham Lincoln.*"[46]

CULTURALLY - DEPRIVED AREA ABOUT FEB 12th 1809

Whether in the 1960's or the 1860's, Pa would have continued to resist much that came under the heading of progress. One Lincoln scholar observed: "He smiled at the anxieties of narrow minds over material possessions. He knew the ephemeral character of such things compared with the permanency of possessions of mind and soul."[47] The immediate family and close friends were at a loss to accept Pa as the primitive pioneer. Pa had a mind of his own. It was not bound by the establishment!

Pa relied on his intuition and seemed to take it for granted. "*Educated reasoning power often stifles intuition, repudiates extra-sensory power, strikes faith with a blunt word, stones hope with a derisive laugh, whitewashes sin or fear with a shrug, and in the end edits meaning out of life, thereby rendering man's reasoning power itself inane . . . As surely as extrasensory perception gives rise to delusion upon occasion, upon occasion unbridled reasoning power elaborates fact until it fabricates a fantasy that is again all reason.*"[48] Others could investigate and try to prove, but Pa was already so constructed and developed, that such an approach was unnecessary. One author wrote, "For hundreds of thousands of years man has acquired an "inner feeling" . . . of the eternal continuity of the living process . . . the educated part of humanity finds it difficult to find their way. They ask for scientific proof. But educated people who can *think*, know that proof of this kind is out of the question."[49]

Pa learned through perseverance, patience and persecution. As one biographer concluded, he became an "educated man . . . in the larger sense."

If Pa had an "alma mater," it was Joshua Speed's store in New Salem, Illinois. It was in New Salem that Pa struggled as a young man and the New

Portrait by Danny Fleckles
February 1957

Salem store where he would meet with Speed, Hurst and Herndon to make up the "nucleus of a literary society."[51] Pa's potential then was unrecognized, and some would think "Abraham Lincoln was a man uncouth, uncultivated and unfitted for the higher walks of life."[52] Yet, if anything was to distinguish Pa from his fellowmen, it was precisely "those higher walks of life," so prominently seen in his mystic-psychic personality.

2
A Mystic-Agnostic

For Pa the mystic always came before the psychic. The spiritual remained fundamental. "For all his common sense, his fine poise and reason, and his wise humor," at bottom Lincoln was a mystic — that is, "one who felt that the Unseen has secrets which are known only by minds fine enough to see and hear them."[1] This opinion was advanced by a leading theologian, John Fort Newton who wrote at length on Pa's life. His reference bears a strange and significant application to my father.

In his book, *The Soul Growth of Abraham Lincoln,* McElroy pleads to "let the theologians wrangle as they will over the dogmas as to the Holy Ghost. Plain people of all faiths will persist in understanding Him as the agency by which the Deity makes His purposes effective."[2] Pa was one of those plain people. There were, as we have seen too often, those who would mix Pa's mysticism with spiritualism. One writer tells of "the President's conversion to mysticism and the psycho-analytical reasons that turned him to spiritualism."[3] This diagnosis would amuse Pa. In his logical, realistic way he was able to make a distinction between all the 'isms.'

Pa was "in the habit of spending an early hour each day in prayer."[4] His prayers, more often than not, were mystical accompanied by deep meditation. Pa has been compared to the Russian novelist and mystic, Leo Tolstoy. They represent "the paradox of a mystic who refuses to profess adherence to any church."[5] This Russian philosopher saw my father as a "real giant in depth of feeling . . . a Christ in miniature."[5a] The frontiers of the spirit are void of denominationalism or sectarianism. This made Pa in the eyes of some, an agnostic. One Lincoln scholar makes the comparison that "what Shakespeare did in poetic expression, Abraham Lincoln essentially did in his personal and official life," and that "the invisible foundations and vertebrae of his character were mystical."[6] This was difficult for the public, the church oriented public in particular, to accept, yet such a profile places Pa in proper perspective.

The imaginative biographer, Gamaliel Bradford, pretends in one writing that Pa is interviewed by the evangelist, Dwight L. Moody. Pa begins: "The Bible is an excellent book. I often read it and recommend it." Moody retorts

"I'm surprised it has not made you a Christian long ago." To this Pa laconically responded: "It is just possible it has." The evangelist persists: "I should like to make you a Christian." But Pa is consistent: "That's awfully good of you. But really I haven't the time; you know I have this blessed Union to patch up."[7] Perhaps both men were exploring the frontiers of the spirit, but from opposite angles.

As former Episcopalian Bishop James Pike saw it, there are "areas of perennial human experience which from the dawn of history have pointed to the extension of the functioning of the person beyond the space-time continuum in which he is set."[8] The Bishop asserts that from the standpoint of many a scientist, this constitutes a new frontier. As Pa saw it, *such a frontier or horizon was new because it was ever-changing and widening.*

It has been said of Pa that "his avocation as a spirit overshadowed his vocation as a mere man."[9] His high office restrained, yet trained him in the divine fulfillment of his destiny as mystic and psychic.

Herndon, although never one to compliment my father, once gave this assessment: "Sometimes it appeared as if Lincoln's soul was fresh from the Creator."[10] Before the presidency, no one entered Pa's personal life quite as did this former law partner. Pa's "superstition of other days merged in later years with the mysticism of his poetic nature."[11] With the prolongation of the war and my passing, this became markedly true. The Emancipation Proclamation artist, Frances B. Carpenter, learned "through the family" that Pa's attitude toward his gifts of the spirit "were from the hour of my death transformed."[12] My story shows that my father's emancipation, not to mention mine, took place upon my passing. This same artist further claimed Pa ". . . lived and breathed and acted from his reason — the throne of logic and the home of principle . . . the realm of Deity in man."[13] Carpenter became almost a resident of the White House for some six months.

Another of Father's friends, a member of Congress and a concerned churchman once inquired about the president's reluctance to become a church member. Pa said it was "because I have found difficulty without mental reservation in giving my assent to their long and complicated confessions of faith."[14] This prompt response reveals that to his death, Pa remained essentially a 'Christian Agnostic.' As if to reassure those who thought an agnostic was unchristian, Pa remarked that "when he found a church that practiced the teachings of Jesus, he would join it."[15] In the judgment of one Lincoln author, if the "best of the authentic stories told of and by Lincoln" were taken out of context, it "would be enough to put him in the category of the irreligious, the sacrilegious and in some quarters the damned."[16]

At the risk of repetition it was the ravages of war, the responsibility of his high office and the loss of me, his little Willie, that induced Pa to search the very depths of his being. There he was to rediscover the gifts of the spirit. As for the church, Pa conceived of it as a community of the spirit, a fellowship of the committed . . . nothing more, nor less. The fragmentation of the Church reflected the division in society.

If the statement that the "greatest achievement of mysticism" is the development of the attitude, "let me know the worst about the Universe — I am not afraid,"[17] then Pa was well on the way. To examine but one aspect of Pa's life is hazardous. It is either over-simplified or overdone.

A magazine article attributes Pa's inclination toward mysticism as part of his "immeasurable femininity."[18] Any evaluation of such a claim, must appreciate the role of the feminine and the masculine valence as they enter into the development of every human. A Lincoln authority discusses at some length the feminine valence in Pa. We are informed that as a boy in the wilderness, "he astounded his father by refusing to own a gun." "He earned terrible whippings by releasing animals in traps." "In him," the author declared, "had come to a head the deepest things in the forest life; the darkly feminine things, its silence, its mysticism, its secretiveness, its tragic patience."[19]

That Pa was a man of some stature, whether physical or spiritual, few would deny. The *Boston Transcript,* some 70 years ago, estimated that "Lincoln, the man, was far greater than Lincoln, the statesman, even as the heart of humanity is greater than any form of human polity." Then follows the observation: "Just now the world of men and of nations stands more in need of the leadings and the adoption of the spirit which rules Lincoln's soul than it is in need of any particular adjustment or beneficence, great as is its need for such measures."[20] Anyone can conjecture the extent to which a feminine valence may have contributed to Pa's empathy toward men of every race, creed or color.

The term mystic continues to earn more respect in our culture than the term psychic. Unless the latter is combined, as in Pa's life, with the spiritual, it becomes shallow and suspect. The mystic for Pa became more fruitful with his practical, logical nature. It was difficult to distinguish the mystic from the psychic-spiritual in Pa's life. The noted psychic, Arthur Ford, reminds us: "The great mystics have warned us against seeking simply psychic experiences. These great souls have again and again stressed the Spiritual Life. . . ."[21] If Pa seldom employed either the term spiritualism or psychicism in any form, (although he did once apply to himself the word mysticism[22]) one can speculate that these terms were eliminated from Pa's vocabulary by someone other than himself. Agnostic is another term which appears to have been avoided in Lincolnia literature. Dr. Leslie Weatherhead, for many years Pastor of the London Temple, defines a Christian Agnostic in these terms: "*Unless we can break out of the prison of old-fashioned expressions, creeds and formularies, we shall never be free to find far more glorious truths which are inherent in the Christian*

Religion."[23] Along with a group of Anglican Bishops and the former Dean of St. Matthews Cathedral in London, Dr. Weatherhead is among the sponsors of the Church's Fellowship for Psychical and Spiritual Studies. The Spiritual Frontiers Fellowship is an American version of the British Fellowship. The mystic, the agnostic and the psychic have much in common!

The late Dr. Bennett, professor of philosophy at Yale University, and authority on mysticism, also speaks for Pa when he writes: "*The soul has never been separated from God, so one cannot talk of it being reunited. There is an illusion of separation. That illusion can be overcome. The mystic refuses to admit that the church can monopolize the channels of revelation. He will not believe that the accumulated wisdom of the priesthood contains all that the human soul needs to know.*"[24]

Columnist Sidney Harris, underscores an idea Pa would likewise profess — "What has been promulgated in the name of Christianity would tempt the man with the greatest idea of all to say: 'I am not a Christian.' "[25]

A book by Joseph W. Barrett, on *The Life of Lincoln* published in 1865 reveals something of Pa's boyhood days at school. "In Kentucky, Lincoln attended two schools . . . one was kept by Zachariah Riney, a Roman Catholic . . . no proselyting efforts were made . . . during religious ceremonies all Prostestant children were accustomed to retire."[26] This respect for all religious faiths marked Pa's attitude toward the church in general.

"Lincoln at heart was both a mystic and a scientist, a combination not conducive to a smooth-flowing, ambiversive personality."[27] The mystic-scientist is essentially agnostic. Pa's agnosticism, as expected, provoked some antagonism. He became the rebel and the heretic. "*No man can undertake, as the mystic undertakes, the task of discovering what his deepest purpose is and of making over his life in the light of that discovery without becoming the most difficult radical of all to deal with, the radical who confronts the existing order not with the intent of pure destruction but with a new standard of what human nature really needs.*"[28] Such a description fits Pa, the mystic-agnostic.

Francis Grierson, author of *Abraham Lincoln; The Practical Mystic,* studied Pa for some 30 years. He concluded that Pa's "whole existence was controlled by influences beyond the ken of the most astute politician of his time."[29] This becomes apparent if we see in the 'practical mystic' the psychical motivated by the spiritual. It has been said, remember, that Pa was "one of the most reticent men who ever lived in regard to his own spiritual exercises."[30]

Pa soon found that the deeper the spiritual experience, the less it lends itself to description. He was surprised at times by the depth of his own spiritual exercises. He was aware that many people were psychic who did not know it and did not want to know it. This applied to the mystic-agnostic. Still others liked to think of themselves as psychical or mystical or both. This condition became increasingly clear to Pa, the President, as he mingled among the masses. More than 50 years ago this became the subject matter of a book in which we read: "The renaissance of practical mysticism is becoming apparent both in and outside the churches."[31]

We have mentioned the Church's Fellowship for Psychical and Spiritual Studies in England. The current literature of the Fellowship informs us that "Christian mysticism is an important feature of the Fellowship. Here the gifts of the Holy Spirit appear as the contemplative Christian develops his sensitivity to the Holy Spirit and to God's higher agents, messengers or angels." There follows a pertinent psychic query: "Is communion with the higher states of life co-extensive with the communication between the 'living and dead' as taught by some?"[32] If Pa's life denotes anything, it is a decisive confirmation of such an inquiry. Psychic sensitivity came to Pa, not through church membership or formal education but out of his personal experience. Pa would also relish the description of the Church's Fellowship in England that "it is a pioneering movement *within the Church.* It is not concerned with denomination. It seeks no dogma. It may well throw light on old dogma!"[33] Dogma and doctrine divided the church. Anglican Church clergy are obliged to accept the credo: "Christ did truly rise again from death, and took again his body with flesh and bones."[34] Pa was well acquainted with Scripture. He could read in Paul's first letter to the Corinthians 15:50 "Flesh and blood shall not inherit the Kingdom of God." So Pa became a Christian Agnostic. The Church's Fellowship for Psychical and Spiritual Studies claim "psychical studies suggest that we have an intermediate body, called etheric or astral, through which activities of a psychical or supernormal order take place. What roles has it to play in spiritual life?"[35] As Pa saw it, *the church has too often miscalculated the mind of man by insisting that he believe what cannot be adequately explained or accept the consequences as a disbeliever.* One result is that the Resurrection, as one of many church dogmas, "remains a total mystery in church teaching — an enigma to many."[36] Pa was one of the many!

Lamon is sure that "Lincoln was no dabbler in divination, astrology, horoscopy, prophecy, ghostly lore, or witcheries of any sort."[37] This could be more Lamon than Lincoln. The fact that Pa was born under the sign of Aquarius, may not 'prove' anything. If in truth astrology has something to say, then it may be relevant to my story. A reputable British physician, Dr. Arthur Guirdham, explains: "Man is at the present moment in the process of changing his nature. He is passing through a phase of evolution which will enable him to live on a more psychic plane . . . He is preparing himself to live in a new and psychic dimension."[38] This evolutionary process takes time. It may not be consummated until the year 2000.

The sign of Aquarius has been described many ways, many times. It is "characteristic of a persistent effort to stabilize the values of living by an adequate realization of life's meaning."[39] A noted psychic offered this definition and the comment concerning the year 2000. He adds; "It doesn't take an astrologer (which I am not) to see that such a program would make a good deal of sense."[40] There are some characteristics of the zodiacal sign of Aquarius which seem to spell out Pa. People born under this sign are "especially intuitive." Their "perceptive powers are extremely acute. . . ." They may be "suddenly confronted with an opinion or a flash of inspiration foreign to their belief. . . ." Such a person "often feels that he is impelled by an unknown force toward concepts or actions . . . he acclaims universal brotherhood . . . he can be delighted one moment, indifferent and moody the next . . . he is sometimes eccentric and unconventional, yet progressive."[41]

Charles Lindbergh among others was born an Aquarian. No one has shown more potential for the psychic and mystic, than this pioneer in aviation. It is said of the Aquarians that "they advocate the higher love . . . preferring to live and let live." The sign is humanitarian and altruistic. It seeks social progress through change ". . . unless they happen to perpetuate change through violence, but not necessarily bloody revolution."[42]

In another section of this chapter we deal with Pa, the bearded soul, in search of a new day — *The Rebel-Heretic,* who always had more than a little in common with the bearded youth in every generation beginning in the first century. His mystic-agnostic characteristic was the source of much of his revolutionary, radical tendency. However, Pa was convinced that unless these influences are brought under the guidance and control of a higher love, everything is lost. The use of drugs to induce and sustain a psychic-mystic state or even a higher love strikes Pa as self-destructive. Yet he understands the bearded youth. A reader of Lorant's Lincoln pictorial biography writes: "This is important — reaching young people with the story of a ten foot-tall hero-figure *who can still hold meaning for today's youth.*"[42a] Pa is sympathetic to the radical revolutionary motivated by the higher love. An eminent physicist, Dr. Raynor Johnson, Master at Queens College, Melbourne University, Australia, in discussing the drug induced mystical experience,[43] reminds us that what started as a therapeutic treatment for the few, has become a national disgrace. Most of the addicts or victims are among the nation's more promising youth. The mystical and the psychical for Pa came naturally, and spiritually, void of drug inducement. One psychical scholar maintains, "*we need above all to revive the spiritual meaning of existence.*"[44]

"It is apparent now that Lincoln alone, of all the great men engaged in the gigantic struggle of saving the nation, rose to a height where he could look down upon that awful tangle of passion and prejudice and behold with God-like compassion its conflicting elements."[45] This compassion showed through the struggle going on within Pa. Carl Sandburg reports of an elderly lady who quizzed Pa asking, "How can you speak kindly of your enemies when you should rather destroy them?"[46] The agnostic cannot be anti-agnostic. In Pa, the Aquarian addressed the agnostic, the psychic and the mystic. "He espoused no system of philosophy. Attempts to describe his beliefs became barren. Lincoln's thoughts found strength in his emotions."[47] Wrapped up in his emotions, was his intuition.

"Although he left Kentucky when a child he was an *old* child,"[48] Pa's spiritual and psychical unfoldment received a head start. "Men of his mental and moral endowment are not drawn to sectarianism. It might have deprived him of his inherent right to spiritual kinship with men of beliefs everywhere."[49] Pa was to shed much of his Pigeon Creek religion.

Rev. Dr. Alexander Campbell of the Disciples of Christ was a born psychic. He describes my Father as "a man of the old prophetic type, as one who sees into the nature of the eternal principles, and draws near to reality. Holding high council with the Infinite, his moral intuitions have immense assurance of a revelation our God."[50]

Pa has been compared to his British contemporary, William E. Gladstone. Both were statesmen; both were inclined toward the metaphysical; both were born in the same year. One writer asks, astutely, "what conspiracy was there in that 'unremembered country' from which every traveller comes — that the two greatest men of the American and British branches of the English race should agree to get themselves born together?"[51] These words were uttered by a British cleric born in 1864.

From an American author, McElroy, we have a relevant query asked and answered. This book deals with the soul of Lincoln. "Must we believe that the age of miracles has passed — that the Holy Spirit long since ceased to manifest itself to man? Did not the same medium (The Holy Spirit) make the equally obscured Illinois boy (Lincoln) the greatest moral power since the Man of Sorrows?"[52] Whether such a comparison would be acceptable to Pa is dubious. It does in some degree speak to Pa's condition during much of his life. He too, was a 'man of sorrows.'

My attempt to narrate the more profound parts of Pa's life has its problems. My vocabulary, or the lack of it, does not do him justice. I am supposed to have inherited much of my father's gift for words. One is invariably hampered in any endeavor to express another person's soul so profound as that of my father.

He was nevertheless, human. He was an ambitious politician. One of the more familiar Lincoln biographers, Dr. William Barton, prided himself on exposing the soul of Pa. He accuses the poet, Walt Whitman, of sharing "the general inaccuracies" of most Lincoln writers.[53] Yet no biographer, including Barton, can claim immunity from "general inaccuracies."

A more sophisticated Lincoln researcher who writes of "delving into the souls of men" comments that, "persons who never met in life and might have scorned to meet come together in this wide, vague world of biographers' imagination."[54] Pa might find it difficult to recognize himself as portrayed by many a writer, whether friend or foe. A noted mystic writes: "Life that is behind appearance, behind what we see, hear, taste, touch and smell . . . remains a mystery."[55] My aim, if nothing more, has been to explore that life in my father.

Lincoln Inauguration 1861

One of Pa's more noted black brothers was Frederick Douglass, who was present at his second presidential inauguration, states ". . . I got a peep into Lincoln's soul" during the inaugural address. If my efforts have provided a "peep" into Pa's soul, then they have not been in vain.

3

A Rebel-Heretic

It is not a far cry, as suggested, from Pa the Mystic-Agnostic to Pa the Rebel-Heretic. Pa's beard had little or nothing to do with either characteristic. Those familiar with this "bewhiskered tale' will understand. Union meant unity, not uniformity. Pa was a rebel on the side of the Union. He became the target of the establishment. He would not be bound by the establishment and "had little interest or belief in administration."[1] Bureaucracy was a curse! He remained a pioneer throughout his life. He was 'too far out' for most of his associates, spiritually and politically. Pa looked with "suspicion" upon organizations and institutions of any kind.[2]

A graduate of Yale University School of Engineering has explored communication from outer space. He declares that at present our institutionalized, technological society "cannot be trusted with more knowledge."[3] Organizations designed and dedicated to the spread of truth become, as Pa saw it, self-destructive in the course of time.

Biographer Ralph Shirley writes: "It is not to be wondered at that a man who had so deep a realization of the spiritual side of life should have had his own strange experiences of the psychic forces ever present around us."[4] As my account attempts to show, the psychic forces in Pa's life became part of the spiritual. Thus, Pa understood the Holy Scriptures and would ask in this context, was not the Master thought of as a rebel and heretic?

"Fortunately in the intimate association of the prairie wilderness, sectarianism and denominationalism lost their stronghold. Tolerance was practiced from necessity as well as inclination."[5] This estimate of father comes from one who holds degrees as a Doctor of Divinity and a Doctor of Laws. It was the primitive pioneer that made Pa appear both a rebel and heretic. His disregard for regulations made Pa anethema to such West Point graduates as Gen. George B. McClellan.[6] This was no less true of Stanton.

It has been said that Pa's "strategical thinking" proved to be "far above that of his generals,"[7] although Pa was far from being a trained military strategist. In addition to his logical, mathematical mind, there existed the intuitive-instinctive psychic talent that sensed strategy. That he did not hesitate to order a change in military strategy as "he saw it," can be seen in the telegraph office incident.

We must not overlook the guidance which Pa believed came from the other side. Attending many of the Lincoln séances, were members of the military and the cabinet.[8] Pa was often accused of having a taint of superstition. Such terms as "superstition" and "spiritualism" have had a way, to be sure, of sneaking into Pa's spiritual-psychical life. This upset HSP researcher Karagulla, who asked; "How can we disentangle the real of psychic-phenomena and superstition?"[9]

Between Pa's psychic sensitivity and his inherent non-conformity, it is not surprising that many military men and members of the White House staff could "never overcome a certain dislike" or doubt concerning Pa.[10] One of Pa's more outspoken private secretaries, Mr. Hay, wrote that "Lincoln was extremely unmethodical; it was a four-year struggle on Nicolay's part and mine." Pa was a free-man . . . free of formality.

He never cared to be called "Mr. President" or even "Mr. Lincoln" —

just plain "Lincoln"[11] This may have been in part his 'rebel' Quaker heritage.

Pa had much in common with the rebels of every age, as he continued to defy the status quo. It mattered not whether it was the church or the state, both "twisted the words around so as to sustain their doctrine," resulting in blasphemy or self-deception. Pa was overheard to say: "*The more man knew of theology, the further he got away from the true spirit of Christ.*"[12] What Pa was saying then, as now, is that there is far more to life than most people can begin to comprehend or imagine; that it will take a lot of tearing down before we can begin to build up. Pa was an iconoclast.

An outstanding psychic and clergyman maintains that "*a minority* of beatniks represent something that is really good. They are revolting against some of the things we have perpetuated. They are refusing to accept some of the things which have not worked for us."[13]

Pa's own words that "the change you seek can be achieved without violence," should serve as a reminder to all would be rebels. What is more, the 'lift' to a higher place comes through "drugless meditation" and "spiritual vitamins."[14] This is confirmed by the genuine sensitives; always rebels in their own right. The genuine rebel or heretic is after a real spiritual transformation around and within. Pa understood this.

Lincoln with Secretaries Nicolay and Hay

Charles Sumner, Senator from Massachusetts, and one of Pa's supporters, once commented: "When Lincoln spoke, the recent west seemed to vie with the ancient east."[15] It is this struggle between the "recent west" and the "ancient east" . . . between the occident and the orient . . . which constituted much of the heretic in Pa and others of like mind. It is speculated in Randall's, *Lincoln, The Liberal Statesman* that "there is perhaps a kind of earthbound quality in the philosophy of most Americans. Ready pragmatism is more to their liking than the unballasted flights of the mystics. America is of the West, not of the East." He added that "Lincoln's head and heart were in balance. His emotions might glow, but his well considered judgment would take command."[16] We have seen the "ancient east" revealed in the life of young Charles Lindbergh. Pa saw the shame and sham which continues to infect western civilized society. Marcus Bach, a highly respected rebel, admitted in his latest book: "I never expected to tell in such detail my early experiences with the 'Baptism of The Holy Spirit.' Nor did I think I would confess my deepest feelings about transcendental meditation and the use of hallucinogenic drugs. But the times demanded it. A situation inspired it."[17] His book carries the significant title, *Inner Ecstasy* . . . not the manufactured kind!

Remember this story comes to you from the other side. If personal survival has any meaning then my Pa and me, his Willie, are reunited.

On April 23, 1954 then President, Dwight D. Eisenhower, said of my father: "He knew that there were devisive influences at work. He knew also they were transitory in character. They were flaming with heat. They were made of stuff that would soon burn itself out."[18] This is eternal revolution or evolution for the mind and soul of man. The combination of the spiritual and psychical for Pa alone held the most promise. One who emphasizes this approach has said "every church in Christendom started as *heresy.* Every man who has ever been of any value to the Kingdom of God has been a heretic. He refused to be bound by the chains of tradition, insisted upon finding truth through an actual and vivid experience, so that he knew."[19]

My father has been called many things. More recently it was a secular saint. "We reserve our final honor for those who discharged their finite duties in the amplitude of the Infinite. Such a saint — a secular saint — was Abraham Lincoln."[19a] Pa's reaction to such labels would be lugubrious. In his book entitled *The Heretics,* Walter Nigg claims that "the religious outsiders, which is what the heretics were, represents a different conception of Christianity. It is essential to understand this . . . Heresy has nothing whatsoever to do with the hostile assault upon Christian religion. *Rather heresy is Christianity,* Christianity felt to its fullest intensity. To be sure, the heretic advocates a view of Christianity different from that of the victorious churches . . . he attempts to bring to the fore the *other side* of the *Gospel.*"[19b]

In his book, *You Will Survive Death*, the late Sherwood Eddy has set forth his personal experiences and acceptance of psychic phenomena in no uncertain terms. In his discourse on survival he comments: "Of all the Presidents of the United States, Lincoln was one of the least orthodox yet the most religious."[20] One might better substitute spiritual for religious. What was fundamental to Pa in Holy Writ was often sacrilegious to others. Throughout the Old and the New Testaments it can be seen that it is the psychical combined with the spiritual which gives substance to the Scriptures. For the President of the United States to participate in séances was considered as a form of heresy and irrational. It was the orthodoxy of his earlier days which possibly lead to Pa's unorthodox attitude in later years. In his rebellion, he was to become, in the best sense, a free-thinker.[21]

Whatever courage Pa had, was strengthened and stimulated as he became more active on the spiritual-psychical level. One psychic researcher observed, "if men are convinced that death brings no cessation of their development, then they will be good soldiers in war and in peace."[22] That was Pa — he seldom counted the cost. Whether in politics or psychics, he was prepared to take the consequences. "His catholicity of spirit . . . made him a churchman-at-large for the United States during the Civil War."[23] Pa would cross party lines if for him the cause was right. Robert Ingersoll, who was also considered a heretic, thought of Pa "as one of his own."[24] But unfortunately, when the free-thinking spiritualists became organized, Pa, as was his custom, stopped short of joining their organizations.

The editor of *Scribner's Magazine* wrote in 1865 that he had ". . . conversed with multitudes of men who claimed to know Mr. Lincoln intimately. There are not two of the whole number who agree in their estimates of him. The fact is that he rarely showed more than one aspect of himself to one man. He opened himself to men in different directions."[25] Even as the name of Lincoln represents most every shade of human thought, so also it is used to sell a variety of products.[26]

There is a universality consistant in Pa's heresy. It could be that he was "all things to all men"! The *Springfield, Illinois State Register* was disturbed at what amounted to an exploitation of the name Lincoln. One of the newspaper's editorials whimsically ended "We are prepared to prove by indisputable evidence that he was a Mormon, and the boon companion of Joe Smith."[27] To label Lincoln was to limit Lincoln although Pa was essentially unlimited by his own estimation. One writer argues, "it would be a falsehood to fix the name of Lincoln to any denomination — a still greater folly to associate him with any formulated creed," however, "much could be said for the claim made by Spiritualists that Lincoln looked with favor on them. Likewise, the Universalists have come to announce that Mr. Lincoln threw friendly glances at them."[28]

The French author of *Les Miserables*, Victor Hugo, (1802-1885) is alleged to have pleaded for an open, receptive mind to all issues of the spirit — that "to abandon the spiritual phenomena to incredibility is to commit a treason against human reason." He testified to the "veracity of a friend's premonition of death."[28a]

William Barton has described Pa's life "as an evolution whose successive stages can be measured with reasonable certainty."[29] After presenting Pa's psychic life with some caustic comments in *The Lincoln Nobody Knows*, "the Spiritualists kept after him almost from the beginning of his Presidency."[30] This assertion is not entirely accurate, since it is apparent Pa's psychic life did not begin in Washington.

Herndon and others tell us that Pa turned "to the spirits of the dead" before becoming president.[31] It did not take much to arouse Pa's psychic personality. My death was a major factor.

When Pa was 37, and in the midst of a political campaign, a rumor spread that he was "an open scoffer" at religion.[32] On July 31, 1846, Pa responded to the charge saying "the habit of arguing thus I have entirely left off for more than five years."[33] Pa lost the election but "he stood square and bolt upright to his convictions."[34]

More than one scientist, either fearing charges of heresy or rebukes from their peers, has remained aloof from taking a stand on psychic phenomena. "In the course of many years the American Society of Psychical Research collected an immense amount of data. It leaves the scientist no excuse for ignoring the immemorial claims of a supernormal element in human nature."[35] A rebel among the scientific hierarchy was Sir Oliver Lodge, the great British physicist who once declared, "the least justifiable attitude is that which holds that there are certain departments of truth in the universe which it is not lawful to investigate."[36] For Lodge, as for Lincoln, one of these departments of truth was the psychical. Lodge spoke out but, it soon became evident his fellow scientists felt he had spoken out of turn. He was censored, and like many a rebel-heretic, he was to be vilified in life and defied in death. As if to dignify the psychical . . . to make it less controversial and more palatable to science and religion . . . the term parapsychology has been coined to define a phenomena for which there is seemingly no *scientific* explanation. Pa would have found the term superfluous!

In the opinion of Edward P. Lindamen, executive for the American space program, "man's desire to go beyond set limits is part of his very nature. To deny this is to relegate him to an animal-like position."[37] In one scientific study of HSP the researcher asserts, "we are exploring the vaster Cosmos of space," and asks; "Are we destined to find in man himself the measure of all things, the vast and the minute? Is he the bridgeway between the microcosm and the macrocosm with abilities not yet identified for exploring and perceiving both? Does he have within himself latent instrumentation for this?"[38] We can almost surmise Pa's sublime answer to such questions. He saw himself ridiculed and misrepresented. Sir Wm. Barrett, a scientist who risked his reputation in the study of the psychic, poignantly commented: "I have failed to find a single person who ridicules Spiritualism who has given the subject any patient and serious consideration."[39] Pa might have said that Spiritualism had jumped in where angels feared to tread!

In his *Philosophy of Common Sense* Dr. Kempt is sure that Pa "maintained consistently . . . that man in his divine inheritance today as in the Bible past, hears through his conscience the voice of God, if he will but heed and listen."[40] In the minds of many this open door policy made Pa a heretic.

"Much has been made of Lincoln's belief in destiny as if it were the sign of an occult faculty or of unusual extra-sensory perception."[41] Such were the naive comments aimed at my father. "Like the prophets of old," Pa continued to believe "that portent signs and dreams gave hints of predestined events"[42] Yet people who respected the ancient prophets laughed at Pa.

There were some exceptions. One was Daniel E. Soames, Congressman from the state of Maine, who had attended some séances with the president. Soames confided to his wife "the remarkable incidents" at the White House séances. Many of the incidents proved to be prophetic.[43] Once the séances became public knowledge, Pa was on the spot. Another exception was to be

White House 1861
Jefferson Statue in foreground

Simon P. Kase whose hometown *Business Directory of Danville, Pennsylvania,* contained the statement: "Such men as Col. Simon P. Kase do not travel in the beaten path. Ever and anon they strike out into new and startling projects that seem to the multitude visionary and impracticable, and beyond reach of human effort."[44] This was written before this business tycoon found himself in the company of the president at the Georgetown séances. The Danville directory could not have been more prophetic of the rebel in the Colonel! Still another exception was Massachusetts Senator John B. Alley. The Senator remarked that Pa was "nearly what people call a free-thinker . . . and by many people he was thought to be a Spiritualist. This was very far from being true."[45] When Pa learned of Alley's comments he exclaimed, "How just and true such sentiments," and pondered, "if the press of the country could be made to inhale something of the spirit of fairness. . . ."[46] While others betrayed Pa, the senator portrayed him as he was, a spiritual-psychic.

Pa would have been amused at the reaction surrounding the claims that in recent years Lincoln's presence has been experienced at the White House! Dr. Nandor Fodor, a psychic scientist, has responded to the skeptics with the retort, "there is no reason why the presence of Lincoln should not be felt at the White House."[47]

Norman Vincent Peal reports that a well-known actor was an overnight guest at the White House. The guest was awakened by the voice of Lincoln calling in distress. The guest found "the lanky form of Lincoln prostrate on the floor in prayer, arms outstretched with fingers digging into the carpet."[47a]

Even in romance Pa was a born rebel. He imagined himself eloping. . . . "That night I put her on my horse. We started off across the prairie."[48] Pa had several romances before meeting Ma. On April Fool's Day, 1838, Pa wrote to the wife of his friend, Senator Browning, describing an unorthodox courtship.[49] Herndon, however, concedes that Pa performed with propriety during his several courtships. Pa has summed up one romance by saying, "I made a fool of myself."[50] Whether in romance or séance, Pa was ready to play the fool if he felt the cause was worth it!

Pa was 28 with just 28 more years to go on the earth plane when he lost Ann Rutledge by death in new Salem. He felt he never really lost her. Then there were the two Marys — Mary Owens and Mary Todd — neither one entirely void of a rebellious spirit. Both Marys were from Springfield, Illinois. Mary Owens, so different from Ma, provided a "strange courtship." Pa wrote her that to marry him she "would have to be poor without the means of hiding her poverty."[51] That ended the romance! With Mary Todd, "there was some serious disagreement between the lovers on January 1, 1841. The engagement was broken,"[52] but in little more than a year they were married. Pa noted later in a letter to a friend, "nothing new here except my marrying, which to me is a matter of profound wondering."[53] Marriage continued to be "a matter of profound wondering," and the rebel in Pa was tempered by his higher love in marriage, as in life.

When Ma allowed her jealous pride to gain control then marriage for her became a mockery. The inscription in his wedding ring 'Love Is Eternal' never-the-less retained its meaning for my father.

A romance seldom mentioned was one with Susan Talbott, which was to remain a family secret.[54] Another family secret which in the minds of some contributed to the rebel-heretic, was the legitimacy or the illegitimacy of Pa's parentage. It did not phase Pa. He contended, and with some justification, that "illegitimate children were ofttimes sturdier and brighter."[55] He might have added spunkier! A present day statesman, Chancellor Willie Brandt of the Republic of West Germany, makes no bones about his illegitimate birth. In one of Herndon's more gossipy communications, dated February 24, 1869, the term "lechery" is applied to Pa's parentage.[56]

Wild charges of weird séances in the White House soon became the order of the day during Pa's administration, yet since his assassination, the subject has become almost *verboten.* Those who have felt obliged to defend Pa, have for the most part only succeeded in revealing their own defensive or offensive attitudes toward the Lincoln heresy. Sensitive Arthur Ford, was told in recent days he was doing the work of the devil. Ford laconically responded, "the devil must be a pretty good guy." This same psychic proceeded to remind us that among the spiritual gifts outlined by the Apostle Paul was that of speaking with tongues. He described this gift "as a legitimate part of psychic phenomena," especially when "inspired by the Holy Spirit." For this he was severely criticized by a Pentecostal group who themselves practice speaking with tongues.[57] It is this kind of shortsightedness with which Pa was most familiar and which he most disliked.

Uncomplimentary letters are not uncommon to those active in the study of psychic phenomena. One such letter caused Dr. James Hyslop to suggest "she (the correspondent) belongs to the class of people who regard such things as psychical research as unholy and wrong, though in other matters she is a woman of education and standing in society."[58] Held in comparison to Pa's background, her attitude may well have been due to "her education and standing in society."

Pa shared the bigness of attitude displayed by Sir William Gladstone when he stated, "I shall not adopt a language of disbelief in all manifestations, real or supposed, from the other world."[59]

With the coming of space communication we are already encountering a psychological barrier on the part of earth people.[60] As Pa sees it, the discoveries in outer space will inevitably cause men to search their own souls. The first man on the moon, Neil Armstrong, put it this way: "We hope and think this is the beginning of a new era; the beginning of an era when man understands the universe around him and the beginning of an era when man understands himself."[61]

One for whom psychology means primarily a study of the soul, has commented: "I stand in deepest awe and admiration before the depths and heights of the soul whose world beyond space hides an immeasurable richness of images, which millions of years have stored up and condensed into organic material."[62] This is the same sort of feeling my Pa might have voiced in a vocabulary of his own.

4
The Inquirer-Explorer

Marcus Bach once posed the question; "Can psychic happenings recorded in the Bible be repeated in our time?[1] Pa must have asked as well, whether man since the beginning of time has been interested in personal survival, and why then does he balk at the possibility of communication beyond earthly existence? An inquiring, reflective mind may draw affirmative conclusions. however "unseen" the nature of man's spirit, though experimentation and demonstration, in themselves, appear insufficient to prove the existence of inner sight. The transcendent quality of psychic phenomena defies man's measure of logic. Perhaps the truth must rest in the nature of the man . . . "in the seer-like quality of his soul," as mused one thoughtful observer referring to Lincoln, "with the window of his mind open toward the Unseen . . . through which came influences, intimations, insights not justified by his relentless logic."[2]

Pa's relentless logic counterbalanced his meditative mind, mixed with apparent superstitions.[3] We have touched on the loose manner in which superstitious inferences have been applied to Pa, but his was a meditative, sensitive, intuitive turn of mind. It is easy to overstress the part played by the precognitive in Pa. Chapters have been written on his presentiments and premonitions; many of which occurred through his dreams. Analyst Carl Jung claims that "in dreams we enter the deeper and more universal truth and the more eternal man."[4] "From his early youth he (Pa) seemed conscious of a high mission."[5] This seemed to him more intuitive than precognitive or anything else — even the intimation, "his life would end with the war."[6]

Pa's intuitive, precognitive characteristics were an obvious stimulant to his tendency to inquire and explore the unknown. A current medical researcher described a member of the space program who has made practical use of precognition in his program of exploration: "He often has dreams about the result of missile firing." He is thus "able to set up photographic equipment in precisely the right way."[7]

In the days before Washington, D. C., Pa was much impressed by a sermon delivered in Springfield. "Gentlemen, you may be surprised and think it strange. When the Doctor (minister) was describing the Civil War, I distinctly saw myself in second sight bearing an important part in that strife."[8] The words came straight from my psychic Pa.

General Schurz, himself a psychic and a friend of Pa wrote, "Lincoln brought to the task aside from other uncommon qualities the first requisite — an intuitive comprehension of its nature."[9] The general indicated that if Pa deserved any credit, it was for the use he made of his psychic talent. One scientist defined premonitions as the "the filtering down from some higher region of knowledge or intelligence into the receptive faculties of qualified people; even though such people are not yet in sufficient state of development to preceive than by their own powers."[10] Most of the time Pa seemed to be in a sufficient state of development to interpret his premonitions.

"For Lincoln," observed one contemporary, "things come about not so much by preconceived methods as by an impelling impulse . . . many people today sense a certain new mystical quality in Lincoln . . . new discoveries into the field of Lincoln lore give us cause to increase research. . . ."[11] More research might reveal fresh insight into both the mystical and psychical nature of Pa. Much has been written of his religion, but little of its mystical-psychical aspects. His meditative, intuitive mind was marked by complete confidence in divine direction.

At the age of 53, on the fourteenth of July, 1862, Pa wrote to Joshua Speed. He assured his friend that his (Speed's) marriage was preordained, adding; "Whatever he designs, he will do for me yet."[12] Pa once commented at some length about his reliance on an overruling Providence, but ended with a bit of wit and wisdom saying; "To be sure, He has not conformed to my desires, else we should have been out of our troubles long ago."[13] There are those who persisted in calling Pa's highly perceptive powers supernatural. Pa, as we know, would shy away from the word but what would appeal to him is the inquiry into progress, into higher sensory perception.[14]

Pa in his meditative, inquisitive moments was a loner, much like "Lone Eagle," Charles Lindbergh, who would achieve the heights on his own. Lone Eagle perceived that "through man's evolving awareness, and his awareness of that awareness, he can merge with the miraculous to which we can attach what better name than GOD. In this merging, as long sensed by intuition but still only vaguely perceived by rationality, experience may travel without need of accompanying life."[15] Such a mind is more open to the highway of inquiry and exploration.

Pa's life testified, to the fact that one can get 'high' without getting 'hipped.' One can be psychic without the aid of psychedelics. In the quaintness of Pa's days rumors were rampant that the president was another starry-eyed explorer into the unknown, losing his balance.

Millard Fillmore was a candidate in the presidential campaign of 1856. Fillmore would enter Pa's office and exalt himself. If, at times, Pa appeared to be losing his head, here was a man, as Pa saw him, in the process of having his head swell. That year the presidential election came on November sixth. On one of Fillmore's visits Pa let go at the next president — "I advise you to go to the polls next Tuesday and vote for ALMIGHTY GOD. He is unquestionably the best Being who exists."[16] Ma was enthusiastic over Fillmore. She "told Pa about the goodness of Fillmore before he heard of it from the young man whom he advised to vote for Almighty God."[16a] Self-adulation inevitably ran contrary to Pa's ingrained concept of man as an instrument of the Almighty. During his administration Pa, the inquirer and meditator of God's purpose, often became the *mediator.* "Biographers put stress on the man Lincoln . . . mediating the World Spirit with the Nation of his time."[17]

Pa's inquiring mind was at its best when, as we say, let go and let God. In one of his more familiar statements Pa explained, "I frequently see my way clear to a decision when I am conscious I have not sufficient facts upon which to found it," and then concluded that, "a man who can put two ideas together knows that such a machine requires a powerful Maker and Governor. Man's nature is such that he cannot take the machine and keep out the Maker."[18]

"Though little of a theologian, he (Lincoln) appreciated intuitively some metaphysical ideas."[19] It was metaphysical ideas which provoked much of Pa's inquiry and exploration. It was in this mood that he approached mediumship. His "imaginative powers made of things Unseen true realities to his sensibility."[20]

Medical students have made a study of precognitive, imaginative powers. The case of a certain outstanding industrialist came to their attention. "He could sit in his own office at his headquarters and focus his mind on one of the offices in other cities and tune in to what was happening."[21] Pa, as we have seen, could sit in his executive offices and see what was happening at the battlefront. Clairvoyance was one of the president's characteristics. Nobody will know how often Pa's psychic intuition saved the nation. "*It was intuition, not learning nor experience, that guided his pen in shaping Mr. Seward's first instructions to Mr. Adams, our Minister to England, and saved the nation from an untenable attitude toward the rebel states, upon which hostile Europe was making haste to seize.*"[22]

On one occasion Pa explained to his clergy friend, Dr. Robert Browne, "With my mind directed to the necessity, I catch the fire of it, the spirit of inspiration. I see it reflected in the open face and the throbbing hearts before me. The impulse comes and goes and again returns and seems to take possession of me. The influence, whatever it is, has taken effect. It is contagious; the people fall into the stream and follow me in the inspiration of what is beyond my understanding."[23] Pa was examining and exploring his extra-sensory gifts and could put his finger on the national pulse. He was sensitive to the trouble spots, but more than that, Pa believed he was possessed by forces fundamental to the future of his country. Though his prognosis of a sick society was not perfect, it was close.

As an interpreter of events, Pa had few equals. His response to sensitives and séances, as we have seen, took on a variey of forms. Those who think of Pa as a genius (a term he would disown), point to his gifts of the spirit. It is reminiscent of a question propounded by one psychic researcher; "Is genius simply a designation of certain types of higher sensory perception?"[24]

Those unwilling to probe the depth of Pa's precognitive personality, resort to convenient and superficial descriptions of supernatural or superstition. In 1842 Pa referred to himself as superstitious.[25] At that time, he was as yet unequipped to comprehend his mystical-psychical nature. He could not then see his premonitions in the context of a sixth sense. Even professional research into Higher Sensory Perception is faced with the problem of how to "disentangle psychic phenomena and superstition from authentic gifts or human talents".[25a]

The Indiana community from which Pa came has been described as having "settlers who believed that witches and lizards were sent to cure the cattle . . . the moon exerted fearful influence for good or evil."[26] Pa would not care to be judged upon so precarious a premise, but Herndon, in particular, has done just that.

It has been speculated Herndon's prejudice may be rooted in one visit to Washington from which he returned soured toward Lincoln. It seems Herndon had anticipated a presidential appointment. Pa must have changed his mind,[27] so Herndon played up Pa's visit to New Orleans. That trip included a session with a Negress fortune teller. Herndon also enlarged upon Pa's "belief in the virtues of a mad-stone."[28] In retrospect it is possible to confuse such episodes as a part of Pa's psychical predisposition. A certain Dr. Johnson comments that "Lincoln grew in an atmosphere saturated with all kinds of superstitious beliefs."[29] How much of this saturated, superstitious atmosphere Pa inhaled in his youth, only to exhale in later years, would be an interesting line of inquiry! Such an inquiry would be too subjective for Pa himself, nor is there any indication he was inclined to make such an investigation.

"Through listening to the goodness of this semi-clairvoyant, subconscious voice in times of doubt, he usually obtained the answer he could best believe and best carry out."[30] It was the subconscious voice which gave strength to Pa's capacity for inquiry beyond the normal. Pa had some mystifying visions which have been mentioned in nearly all of his biographies. The visions have provided ample ground for speculation. To some they were "evidence of clairvoyance; to others they were mere hallucinations."[31]

According to Canon J. B. Pearce Higgins, the Holy spirit "covers a vast range of phenomena from humble ESP and clairvoyance to the highest mystical vision."[32] Certainly not all Pa's visions could be so classified. Yet it falls short of reality to relate my visionary father's temperament merely to his belief in "supernatural portents."[33] Such identification is shallow and superficial. Pa became too able an inquirer and explorer of the unseen and the unknown. He rapidly reached the point, after my passing, when such names meant little or nothing to him, yet he had been called most everything.

Pa's inquiring mind went into operation whether applied to superstition or predestination. John H. Littlefield studied law with Pa. In a conversation with Littlefield, Pa thus described his attitude toward predestination: "Now you take the subject of predestination. You state it one way. You cannot make much out of it. You state it another and it seems reasonable."[34] Sir Oliver Lodge has stated in exploring the subject, "It may be that the course of events of a mental and spiritual kind could be foreknown without being predestinated . . . foreknowledge and predestination are by no means the same thing."[35] In his soul-searching experiences Pa became aware of this distinction. A paragraph in Pa's historical second inaugural address touches on the depth of his exploration into predestination. *"Fondly do we hope, feverently do we pray, that this mighty scourge of war may speedily pass away. Yet if God wills that it continue until all the wealth piled up by bondsmen's two hundred and fifty years of unrequited toil shall be sunk, and every drop of blood drawn with the lash shall be paid by another drawn with the sword, as was said three thousand years ago, so it must be said, The judgments of the Lord are true and righteous altogether."*[35a] As one historian reviews the second inaugural, he finds Pa making Divine retribution a factor in predestination.[36]

Pa had begun his preparation of the Emancipation Proclamation in September, 1862, and again evoked the mystery of unknown forces controlling man's destiny. "We must believe that He (the Creator) permits it (the war) for some wise purpose of his own, mysterious and unknown to us. With our limited understanding, we are not able to comprehend it. We cannot but believe that He who made the world still governs it."[37]

General Schurz, so near to his commander-in-chief, has said of Pa: "His charm is of a different kind; it flows from the rare depth and genuineness of his convictions."[38] Predestination was one of those convictions.

It could be argued that Pa's predestinarianism interfered with his inquisitive, intuitive thought. In a dogmatic fashion Herndon declared that Lincoln's "only philosophy was what is to be will be, and no prayer of ours can reverse the decree."[39] This would make predestination synonymous with fatalism. Pa fully realized how deadly fatalism can be. It hit Pa during his moments of depression — a melancholy Lincoln. This may be to what one historian alluded to and prompts us to examine when he told us Pa's "fatalism grew and developed while he was in the White House."[40]

In Washington Pa felt the weight of the whole world on his back. At such times he would quote Hamlet: "There is a divinity that shapes our ends. Rough hew them how we will." But most of the time Pa carried on as a free-agent, inquiring after the Divine plan, which purpose Pa sought to fulfill. He acknowledged the wisdom of the Almighty and the error of man. He once gave us a bit of his Quaker philosophy saying "meanwhile we must work earnestly in the best Light He gave us, trusting that so working still conduces to the great ends He ordains."[41] "In common with The Friends," one historian explained, "he felt . . . a sense of direct communion with the Unseen."[42] What made Pa a trail blazer was "this sense of direct communion with the Unseen." It was an open road, not without detours which required a sense of direction.

Kempf, states that Pa "believed consistently in free-will to work as he chose for self-preservation — for greater mental and spiritual self-realization." He further comments that Pa "maintained that Bible prophets were not alone in receiving Divine revelations of moral law."[43] In this spirit Pa continued his inquiry and exploration along new horizons.

Pa's spiritual, psychical approach to the Scriptures is one illustration. "No man had a more abiding sense of dependence upon God and in Divine Government,"[44] was the conclusion of one who knew Pa better than most people. Nevertheless few presidents have been plagued in their public relations by the problems of predestination and the psychical.

In the imaginary conversation between Pa and Shakespeare, the biographer has the latter saying, "Curious, isn't it? We are both such great men and so different!" To which Pa responded, "Perhaps you exaggerate as far as I am concerned. Circumstances just took me up and tossed me about and planted me on top. I have always felt that that was all."[45] If "that was all," Pa gave little evidence of it in the sum-total of his unfolding, inquiring mind and spirit.

Jesse William Weik, who wrote with and for William H. Herndon, explains that Pa's fatalism was "not of the extreme order . . . Lincoln believed firmly in the power of human effort to modify the environment which surrounds us."[46] The constant target of Pa's inquiry was to "modify and improve man's environment."

In June, 1862, Pa was conversing with James F. Wilson. "I believe Providence will compel us to do right in order that He may do these things not so much because we desire them as that they accord with His plans of dealing with this nation, in the midst of which he means to establish justice."[47] In so far as the psychical provided insight into the plans of Providence, Pa was ready to participate. Senator Browning made this entry in his Lincoln diary: "I know he was a firm believer in a superintending and overruling Providence."[48]

What made Pa's life exciting during the darkest days of the Civil War was his continued search for the 'light that never failed.' Many ministerial delegations made their appearance at the White House. To one such group, during the year 1862, Pa explained, "I am conscious every moment that I am and all I have is subject to the control of a higher power."[49]

The prose of Carl Sandburg, in spite of his negative attitude regarding the psychical, provides a glimpse into the inquiring soul of Lincoln: "Every movement of his long, muscular frame denoted earnestness. Something issued forth elemental and mystical that told what the man had been, and what he was, and what he would do."[50] In an exploratory frame of mind Pa remarked; "If we could first know where we are and whither we are tending, we could better judge what to do and how to do it."[51] This was Pa, the pragmatic seeker.

Pa's line of communication between God and man continued to function even when melancholia overtook him. We must not be mislead by those who refer to the depressions which overshadowed Pa. There were days of gloom and doom when his life processes appeared to be short-circuited. Faith and hope would be cancelled out and the path of inquiry was momentarily blocked. An abundance of studies have been made of the melancholia in Pa's life. One physician flatly states that "to think of Lincoln in terms of true melancholia is *unrealistic.*"[52] But when the condition hit Pa, it would lay him low in spirit.

Pa's extraordinary stepmother "drew him away from too constant introspection and melancholy. She directed his mind toward the acquirement of knowledge."[53] To this dear lady, Sarah Bush Lincoln, Pa gave all the credit for his urge to acquire more and more knowledge.

That far away look which came over Pa on occasion may well have been more mystical than morose. Thomas Hicks, an artist who knew Pa first hand, has said, "it was a puzzled melancholy sort of shadow. It settled on his rugged features. His eyes had a faraway look as if searching for something they had seen long, long years ago. Then, as quickly as the expression came, it vanished."[54] He was soon back on the track. Pa was often sidetracked when he was "searching for something." There were times when Pa was trapped in deep despondency. It occurred when his courtship with Ma was severed. He was broken-hearted and was advised to see a doctor. The doctor recommended a change of scenery. During one bout of despondency Pa wrote to James Stuart, his law partner at that time. "If what I feel was equally distributed to the whole human family, there would not be one cheerful face on the earth." Pa did not stop there. His letter became threatening: "Whether I shall ever be better I cannot tell. I awfully forebode I shall not. To remain as I am is impossible. I must die or be better, it appears to me."[55] From the highest peaks Pa could descend to the depths of despair. He was a sensitive soul. It should be noted this was Springfield, not Washington! It was in Springfield that a member of the Illinois legislature claims that Pa once admitted "he never dared carry a pocket-knife."

General Schurz has said that in later years Pa's melancholia took the form of brooding.[56] As we shall see, this brooding could become creative.

Pa's birth took place at Sinking Spring Farm some three miles south of Hodgen's Mill in Hardin (now La Rue) County, Kentucky.[57] Even the name proved to be prophetic. Pa's spring of new thought became on occasions a 'sinking spring.' Joshua Speed, his young pal back in Springfield, once commented; "I looked up at him. I never saw so gloomy and melancholy a face in my life."[58] Pa was then searching for a way out of a financial predicament, and feeling a "terrible despondency"[59] over the death of his first love, Ann Rutledge. Much of this may be attributable to his youth, but this depth of despair in later life deterred Pa from doing what he wanted most to do; i. e., discover the ways of ending the war, abolishing slavery and saving the Union. When the abolitionists were determined "to sacrifice the American Union if that were necessary,"[60] Pa was driven to despair.

A recognized Lincoln historian, Philip Van Doren Stern, accounts for two of the factors contributing to Pa's melancholy profile, and which may well have a connection with his mystic-psychic development. There is the fact that his life was so full of "harsh and disappointing circumstances," going back to his primitive pioneer days. Another factor was a head injury. "It may have been more serious than suspected." According to Stern, as a boy, Pa had been driving a horse attached to a pole which turned a grain mill. The horse rebelled, and as Pa urged him on, the horse's hoof struck Pa in the head. "He was knocked senseless."[61] There are other accounts which vary slightly in detail. Meantime, doctors have debated the diagnosis and the prognosis of this almost fatal accident. We shall not prolong the debate. In an article dated April, 1952 called, *Lincoln's Organic and Emotional Neurosis,* the author refers to a "fracture of the skull." Pa "was unconscious for many hours," and he was "thought to be dead."[62] Some disfigurement to the left side of Pa's face always remained. There is also some evidence of a change in Pa's personality. Pa was ten years old when the accident took place. It was at a similar age my death had occurred.

Another physician has advanced the theory that Pa's personality pattern was due to a syndrome. His scientific study mentions the high degree of intelligence and "special talents" associated with the syndrome. In the course of the syndrome study, the author sighted the case of another child in which the syndrome produced a "sensitivity." The author appears to correlate spiritualism with superstition. He feels that Lincoln had a "normal degree" of interest in the subject.[63] The prime thesis of the study was to account, not for Pa's personal, but for his physical traits. A Lincoln biographer, writing on *The Real Lincoln,* made reference to another medical analysis which described Lincoln as "the linear type of man, tall and thin . . . such types run to introspections."[64] These studies synchronize, in general, those personality traits we most associated with Pa.

More specifically, it is the mystical-psychical which, it is claimed, grew out of my moody, melancholy paternal parent that we shall now explore. Herndon was among the first to comment on the psychic implications of Pa's near fatal injury. In typical Herndon fashion, he began with a negative note. "As to Lincoln's morbid condition, my idea has always been that it was occult . . . it was ingrained."[65] One learns not to take Pa's former law partner too seriously in his estimate of Pa. It should be noted, however, that the medical article quoted on Pa's emotional life gives some credence to Herndon's observation.[66] The attempt to relate Lincoln's accident as a child to his psychic predisposition is not confined to Herdon.

Lincoln was not the first to display a psychic symptom induced by physical injury. One of the most outstanding psychic's of any generation is the Dutch house painter, Peter Hurkos, who like my Pa, stands well over six feet and is self-educated. He too had an almost fatal injury to his head. When at work, he fell some 43 feet from the top of a ladder. He was hospitalized for some six months. Until that time, Hurkos had not experienced extra-sensory perception,[66a] but has been called upon since to use his psychic powers in assisting the police and others unable to locate the missing link in some mysterious cases. "Many distinguished people are showing keen interest in the psychic ability of Peter Hurkos."[67] If there is anything to the Hurkos or Herndon stories, then Pa's brooding and head injury could be far more relevant to his psychic condition than heretofore assumed.

We have mentioned the case of Mrs. Upton Sinclair whose novelist husband tells of her "special depression" which appeared during a physical ailment. "It might even be that the condition heightened her *telepathic faculty*.[68] Mrs. Sinclair explained that the telepathic faculty seemed to grow out of her depression. She then proceeded to experiment with various psychic phenomena, including clairvoyance and telepathy. She suggested *we may really be fountains or outlets of one vast mind*.[69] This sort of data does not necessarily prove anything concerning Pa but does cause us to ask, as others have, to what degree his physical-emotional condition stimulated his psychical-mystical unfoldment.

Herndon was inclined to put a pathological slant on Pa's emotional life. He has stated that Lincoln had "frequent apparitions and hallucinations . . . he was twice in his life deranged."[70] This is Bill Herndon at his worst, and it was the Herndon who turned against Pa!

A psychological report compiled by a Lincoln student stated "an attempt is now being made to represent graphically his emotional fluctuations. Yet even here there appears to be no evidence of any emotional instability."[71] Pa's emotional fluctuations rose and fell with the war, with the burden of his high office, and with the blow of my death.

Those who were able to detect the depth of the Lincoln mind, realized he was seeking Divine guidance through séances, rather than indulging his emotional fluctuations. One psychiatrist looked at Pa and then criticized those who would "split into segments for exclusive contemplation" the parts of Pa's personality. This, he asserted, is "historically unreal."[72] It is no less unreal to imply that Pa's moody, meditative periods lacked spiritual-psychical significance.

One biographer, dwelling on the introspective, meditative Lincoln, concluded, ". . . Lincoln's intimates are unanimous, and so are later historians, in demolishing ideas that he was a spiritualist,"[73] inferring that the spiritualist Lincoln is none other than a straw man.

Nothing could demolish Pa, the real person — "You can kill the body but not the soul." He searched his own soul in and and away from séances, and sought to overcome insurmountable obstacles. What is more, he was exploring the broad arena of psychic phenomena wherever he found it. One of Pa's more pious kin confirms Pa was "predisposed to depression," and "found solid comfort and permanent peace through a correspondence fixed with heaven."[74] In many of his meditative moods Pa, no longer earthbound, transcended time and space. Pa's pondering's were full of promise. But to the dismay of many, Pa was consistently exploring the frontiers of the spirit. Judge Henry C. Whitney comes to mind again. He was perplexed by Pa's participation in the occult.[75] Those who knew of Pa's admiration for his stepmother felt that her influence kept Pa in line.[76] Pa's creative brooding, inevitably, "made him careless of form in all departments."[77] He could not be otherwise and still be himself. Even Seward soon "learned Lincoln was master . . . that he was able to rise above all personal feeling —" "Surely he dwelt at high altitudes."[78] It was from these same heights Pa functioned best as the explorer and inquirer.

William O. Stoddard, one of Pa's private secretaries, wrote the essay entitled *Lincoln's Vigil*,[79] dealing with Pa's night watches. The watches were interspersed with listening prayers. For one such vigil Pa copied a meditation from Richard Baxter, a Puritan theologian which ended with the words: "You may believe immediately (by God's help) but getting assurance of it may be the work of a great part of your life."[80] Some of Pa's assurance came through private mediums at séances. Some of it came as Pa conferred with the clergy. "My hope of success in this struggle rests on the immutable foundation . . . the justice and goodness of God."[81] For Pa this was not mere talk. Meeting with his cabinet, the military or with mediums, it was the "ground of his being."

One of Pa's meditations began: "O Thou God who heard Solomon in the night, when he prayed for wisdom, hear me . . . I am poor and weak and sinful. Oh, God, who did'st hear Solomon when he cried for wisdom, hear me and save this nation!"[82] At one time, Pa opened his Bible and exclaimed: "Everywhere my eyes fell upon passages recording matters strangely in keeping with my thoughts . . . visitations, dreams, visions and so forth."[83] Pa would explore other worldly manifestations which were for him natural phenomena, however unexplainable.

Our neighbor girl, Julie, who cared for me and Tad, recorded a very provocative experience. Pa had taken Julie's hand allowing it to rest on his knee. Pa then went into deep meditation and Julie became tired. She complained that her arm ached, but hesitated to withdraw her hand. When Pa came out of his trance-like state, he commented, "Why, Julie, have I been holding you here all this time?" In her account, Julie is moved by Pa's ability to absent himself from the world around him, only to enter another world. In childish fashion, she wanted to ask Pa "what he saw out there," and added, "I think he would have told me." But Pa realized that Julie might not have understood and simply left Julie to go in search of us boys.[84] His search for things unseen was abandoned.

One of Pa's more familiar sayings was; "Whatever appears to be God's Will I will do!"[85] He was forever trying to discover the Divine purpose. In one exploration, Major General Daniel V. Sickles was to accomqany Pa to a séance. The general had "left a leg" at Gettysburg. Pa shared one of his meditative moments with the general and his conclusion was "that he had no misgivings as to the result."[86] This is part of Pa's healing ministry to be mentioned further.

Pa did have misgivings, in his meetings with mediums. One Lincoln writer reported, "he was possessed of a curious inquiring nature! According to some, he indulged in sportive comments about spirits."[87] Pa could be sportive and inquisitive. What troubled him as it has anyone who has sought God's will, was making sure it was God's will. One test was mediumship and it was one reason why Pa participated in séances.

In a passage from Stephen Vincent Benet's, *John Brown's Body*, is a fitting commentary:

They come to me and talk about God's will,
In righteous deputations and platoons,
Day after day laymen and ministers.
They write me prayers from Twenty Million Souls,
Defining me God's will and Horace Greeley's.
God's will is this and senator that,
God's will is those poor colored fellows' will.
It is this man's and his worst enemy's,
But all of them are sure they know God's will.
I am the only man who does not know it![88]

Pa's sensitive, inquisitive nature was productive of positive results. When unsatisfide, he would seek to affirm what he sensed to be inner light. He would check with confidants, some of whom did accept spirit communication. This became evident as the zero hour for the Emancipation Proclamation approached. In this connection through all of his seeking and searching, Pa was convinced that "the Will of God prevails" and is in accord with man's ability to perceive His directions. Pa, the lawyer, analyzing the case, saw it this way: "In great contests each party claims to act in accordance with the Will of God. Both may be and one must be wrong."[89]

It was in 1862, not long after my death, that Mr. Lincoln's capacity for spiritual research took on ever larger proportions. "I have been controlled by some other power than my own will. I cannot doubt that this power comes from above."[90] This passage bears repetition.

Pa's contemporaries and sometimes his critics were caught in the Divine dilemma as to God's will. Among them were Horace Greeley and Henry Ward Beecher. They were known to have been engulfed to some degree in spirit communication, and like Pa, they sought Divine direction. A student of the psychical, Dr. Gardner Murphy, has stated; "The reader, who knows . . . Abraham Lincoln well, will find that his experiences must be interpreted in the lifetime of psychological attributes, which he has been known to have possessed. . . . This, as a matter of fact, has already been suggested by investigations now going on, seeking a relation between creativity and the capacity of ESP. . . ."[91] One of Pa's psychological attributes was, as we have discovered, his free ranging thought as it pertained to spiritual-psychical attitudes toward life. For this the 'badge of infidelity,' was fastened on Pa, as on other leaders in free-thought.[92] It is true that on some occasions Pa "would lose his faith in prayer — if certain things did not occur."[93]

A member of the Abraham Lincoln Association and the Illinois State Historical Society urges "increased research into the religious attitudes" of my father. [94] Such an inquiry, if it included an authentic approach to the mystical-psychical aspects of Pa's "religious attitudes," might lend support to the theme of this Lincoln narrative. If my story attests to anything concerning my father, it is that he reached out for God's Will beyond the customary religious attitudes. As one historian, Benjamin Thomas, has stated, he had "a profound religious sense . . . approaching mysticism."[95] The story of his life and thought is ever in danger of over-simplification. It loses much in translation, nevertherless, Pa himself was most adept at tapping and exposing his profound psychic-mystic self.

Often the test for Pa as to whether he was in tune with the Infinite were questions as to; Who were the beneficiaries? What were their motives? Now and then his ego would get in the way and Pa soon found human nature took over. When that happened, self-will had its way.

Pa had innumerable and variable shortcomings. A lack of raw courage in the frontiersman, however, was not one of them. His wrestling encounter with Jack Armstrong has been overdone to the delight of some. As the tale has been told, a saloon keeper placed a ten-dollar bet that young Lincoln could throw the young bully, Jack Armstrong, known as Clary's Grove Champion, where upon Pa threw him for a loop.[96] As Pa grew up, we find that his courage was expanded; he "wrestled not against flesh and blood but against principalities and powers, against spiritual wickedness in high places."

Pa was aware that few men through the ages have shown much courage in exploring the frontiers of the spirit. Pa's courage ran deep and he was fearless in the face of those who deliberately shunned the frontiers.

It took Edwin Stanton to speak of Pa on his death bed, as a man "for the ages." Meantime Pa saw through Stanton, in life, as in death. In recent years one who trod the frontiers of the spirit wrote that, "of all our Presidents, no one has left such a legacy of spiritual eminence . . . about him there was something of a mystery, a pervasive appeal to the latent greatness in us all."[97] Such terminology as "latent greatness in us all" is most appropriate. It was along the frontiers of the spirit that Pa made his pitch to "the latent greatness" in all people. Throughout his short life, Pa "thought for himself and investigated for himself."[98] He would try to encourage others in the process. "A breakthrough in human consciousness is gradually producing greater numbers of people with high sensory perception, who can reshape our world."[99] It was this qualitative perceptability that drove Pa on to other shores of the spirit.

The ship of state was at Pa's command, but much of the time he was under a higher command. As Pa once wrote, he "never adopted a course of proceeding without the approbation of the Almighty."[100] "Hardly ever" may be more correct. Rudyard Kipling described Pa's desire not to prove, but to discover something hidden. *"One everlasting whisper day and night repeated so, Something hidden, go and find it; Go and look beyond the ranges, Something lost beyond the ranges, Lost and waiting for you."*[101]

K. C. Wheare, a British biographer, points to "three important facts" concerning Kentucky, Pa's home state. It was a slave state, but it did not secede from the Union and it was known as a frontier state.[102] Pa's Kentucky ancestry was to color his later life and produce a considerable amount of acrimonious comment.

Pa remained in a 'frontier state' and relished it. A former engineer and his wife find themselves in such a state even now and are convinced that communication with life on other planets is possible. "As we see it, outer space or 'conscious unlimited' can contain anything man can conceive."[103] What a challenging concept to my father. A professor of religion, Marcus Bach, who delves the psychic world, confessed: "I always knew that some day I would relate the spiritual experiences of 'inner space' with man's incredible exploits in outer space. The far-reaching implications of this surprised even me."[104]

When Pa explored, he expanded. He was "reaching toward a new level of being, material and non-material, physical and psychical through which, from which, our too materialistic lives must be restored to balance."[105] Pa kept his balance between the sensory and the extra-sensory precisely because his sensitivity was coupled with his sensibility. Hence, with serenity and nobility he could lay bare his spiritual psychic life. Pa maintained like many a student of the psychic that "the unconscious self of the medium cannot explain all the facts. An external and invisible agency is unmistakably indicated."[106] The "invisible agency" intrigued Pa. It was a Russian savant, Hon. A. Aksakof who, among others, arrived at the conclusion.

An American psychic researcher of long standing, Dr. Hyslop, suggests, "the spirit of openmindedness and impartiality is to the intellectual world what brotherhood is to the ethical."[107] Pa's frontier religion was in some respects retarded,[108] yet it had a sensitivity to the unseen forces of brotherhood.

Pa would find it gratifying to discover the clergy of our day out on the frontiers. Reverend Kelsey has said "psychicism belongs where it began — in man's will to believe. If clairvoyance, clairaudience, spirit communication or any other aspect of spiritual demonstration happened once anywhere, it can happen again anywhere."[109] On this premise, Pa participated in séances as he felt inclined.

Also among the ranks of those thus motivated, is the distinguished physician Dr. Alexis Carrel, who has noted; "The psychological frontiers of the individual in space and time are obviously suppositions. But suppositions, when very strange, are convenient. They help to group together facts that are temporarily unexplainable. Their purpose is to inspire new experiments."[110] This same explorer "realizes clearly that his conjectures will be considered naive or heretical by the layman, as well as the scientist; that they will equally displease materialists and spiritualists. However, one cannot neglect facts because they are strange. On the contrary, one must investigate them."

Metaphysics may bring us more important information on the nature of man than psychology does. The societies of psychical research, and especially the British society, have brought clairvoyance and telepathy to public notice. "*The time has come to study these phenomena as one studies physiological phenomena.*"[111] Pa is quite aware of the progress, not always perceptible to others, that has been made since his day.

Herndon, in one of his more enlightened moments, spoke of Pa as one who "craved light from all intelligences to flash his way to the unknown future of his life."[112] Pa's curiosity drove him on toward the summit. The last book to bear Arthur Ford's name contains the comment; "*What great fear inhibits us from accepting the truths that would liberate man into a new and higher level of consciousness? What stops one from moving bravely and candidly into the meditative dimension?*" This author-medium later referred to "the intense evolutionary effort of man to expand his consciousness into a dimension, by comparison with which the reaches of space exploration shrink to a baseball size."[113]

Pa soon found himself in a field more of exploiters than explorers. Psychics are people and people are psychics. Susceptibility to self-deception is not confined to the sensitive or the sitter. When life and death are involved, both are vulnerable, thus the sitter hears what he wants to hear, and the sensitive gives what the sitter wants. Self-deception, as Pa well understood, can inhabit the subconscious or unconscious recesses of the mind.

The nature of death, as it applied to my father or to myself, does not appear to have been a motivating factor in Pa's psychic exploration. We know that he thought of death as a prelude to rebirth. Dr. Hyslop, is sure that continued exploration of death as the last frontier will verify death to be a fact of life eternal.[114]

Reference has been made to Edward Baker's letter, which came through in mirror script sometime after the Colonel's death. In part the letter read: "I

Lincoln at the front lines

experienced a happy reality — a glorious change, by the process termed death."[115] Was Pa deceived or was he deceiving himself by accepting this message? It is now a part of the Lincoln collection in the Library of Congress. We are told that when Pa first received the news of the Colonel's death, he almost fell in blinding tears as he left the headquarters' tent. Pa had been visiting General McClellan at the front. A telegram handed to him indicated the Colonel had been killed in the battle of Ball's Bluff. This emotional reaction should not be equated with Pa's inclination to explore the last frontier . . . the great divide. Pa respected those dimensions of life "which transcend death." From this base, he "could examine the issues involved at the time of death in such a way that in death, life is affirmed."[116]

Just as you try to explore more effective means of communicating with us on this side, so also we endeavor to discover how best to reach you. Spirit communication through a medium is our most effective method. As your psychic nature develops, you will become receptive to spirit communication. You do not have to wait upon death. "The problem of spiritism," as one investigator explained, "is the collection of evidence to show that consciousness continues after death," but "one difficulty lies wholly in the hypothesis that consciousness is a function of the brain — and requires some such structure for its existence."[117] Pa had no access to such reading, nor would he have had the time to pursue it. He came to similar conclusions instinctively. He was not impressed by well-meaning people who "tell us that Providence does not intend us to know about the future life."[118] Pa was prepared to live by faith, that did not deter him from examining all the evidence in support of his faith. The case for the continuity of life was strong, and not *all* the evidence was in. There was, however, enough evidence to challenge Pa.

Carl Sandburg has Father saying to himself: "Lincoln, you can never make a lawyer of yourself until you understand what demonstrate means."[119] It was then that Pa secured books on logic and mathematics. This legal-logical background was a foundation for his spiritual-psychical inquiry. That his preparation for the proclamation was to be a demonstration becomes more evident.

Pa finally was able to look upon my death as a "visitation from Providence," although it was inexplicable. While his grief was excruciating, his faith was on trial.[120] He had the case, as it were, before the Highest Court, presided over by the Chief Justice, Ruler of the Universe. Pa once commented on the New Testament. "It was a spirit in life that He laid stress on and taught, if I read aright."[121] A Lincoln writer tells us that Pa went to Washington with an aching heart. He lived every day as if it were his last on earth.[122]

Back in 1841 on the twenty-seventh of September, Pa addressed a letter to Mary Speed, the sister of his friend, Joshua. "How true it is that 'God tempers the wind to the shorn lamb.' In other words, he renders the worst of human conditions tolerable while he permits the best to be nothing better than tolerable."[123] Pa was then a young pioneer of 32. Twenty years later he was to become president, and undergo a painful but growing period. The explorer of the last frontier was to become the explorer of new frontiers.

In the opinion of our friend and explorer Professor Hyslop, "emphasis on the importance of death is proportionate to our interest in present living — if we do not value this life, we are not liable to place any high value *on life after death.*[124] This philosophy allowed Pa the patience and incentive to inquire into the great unknown. He came into rapport with the transcendental.

Arthur Ford has made the pertinent statement that "everyone, whether good or bad, low or exalted, smart or stupid, will continue after biological death to live as a personal entity capable of independent thought and action . . . endowed with memory . . . that is a psychic fact."[125] Pa held a similar line of thought; that if life eternal applied to one man, it was applicable to all The Resurrection was a universal experience. Pa would thus interpret the first letter to the people of Corinth (Chap. 15:35) by that intrepid explorer and former professor of philosophy at the University of Tarsus, St. Paul.[126]

"I felt it might be of service for me to come; I did not know wherefore."

The idea of total annihilation was obsolete. Death as an end in itelf was a mockery and a myth. Creation and recreation continued throughout eternity. Pa pursued a spiritual-psychical course of inquiry which he believed from his own experience would set men free. As one recognized psychic researcher has explained: "Our normal isolation from the transcendental world is only the inability to be stimulated by it. A psychic is simply a preson who can overcome the isolation."[127] Pa, in large measure through exploration, had overcome the isolation.

During a séance at the home of Mrs. Laurie in February, 1863, a control came through Nettie Colburn who identified himself as Dr. Bamford. The control described the critical conditions on the Union Side at the front line. Exchanging conversation with the control, Pa responded by saying, "You seem to understand the situation. Can you point out the remedy?" Bamford replied, "yes, if you have the courage to use it!" When Pa shot back, "try me," the control proceeded to suggest "the remedy lies in yourself." According to the guide, Pa was to make an informal visit to the battle front, with Ma to accompany him. Pa was to mix with the men and hear their grievances. He accepted the advise and said, "if it will do any good, it is easily done." Then the answer came . . . "It will do all the good that is required. It will unite the soldiers as one man. It will unite them to you by bands of steel." The next issue of the local press carried the banner headline: THE PRESIDENT ABOUT TO VISIT THE ARMY OF THE POTOMAC. "Subsequent events" proved a "grand fulfillment" of the plan.[128] One can pass over the prophetic outcomes of this psychic council, yet, it is difficult to deny the courage Ma and Pa showed in the face of death.

A psychical research foundation published a bulletin with the subtitle, "For Research on The Problem of Survival after Bodily Death." Dr. Ian Stevenson, professor of psychiatry at the University of Virginia, is on the Board of Directors. Symposiums related to séances are held under the auspices of the foundation.[129]

The more Pa persisted in his exploration, the more he was open to public attack as president. Senator Cameron claimed that Pa's "career was so extraordinary and he was such an extraordinary man that they (his critics) could not destroy him. But they did carry their venom so far as to destroy the social position of his wife"[130]

Pa was rough hewn however, and on April 4, 1864, the day after Jefferson Davis and his Confederate government disappeared, Pa walked through the streets of the Confederate capitol "almost unattended."[131] Few men in public office walked dangerous streets unattended — only those brave spirits, out to explore the unseen.

Lord Charnwood reminds us; "Hardly an action of his Presidency was exempt from controversy."[132] His fellow-countrymen in England proved the point. A piece of British sheet music bore the title, *The Dark Séance Polka.*

The front cover had a photograph, with the inscription *Abraham Lincoln and the Spiritualists,* in which Pa is seen holding a candle in a darkened room. Spectators surround the sensitives. The antics are 'out of this world.'[133] Pa indeed held a candle in a darkened room as he continued his inquiry into the hereafter.

Pa addressed a letter to the Shakespearian actor, James K. Hackett. It was marked 'private' and dated November 2, 1863. The letter ended with Pa saying, "I have endured a great deal of ridicule without much malice. I have received a great deal of kindness not free of ridicule. I am used to it."[134] Persecution is ever a part of the price of the presidency. Pa provoked much more during his psychic expeditions.

As the Civil War came to a close, tolerance and charity were assassinated with Pa. The Confederate leaders were obliged to reckon with Stanton and Buchanan. Vice President Stephens of the Confederacy conferred with Pa during the last days of the war. The issue of a military trial for the rebel leaders was discussed when Stephens remarked to Pa, "we never had much fear of being hanged while you were President."[135] It was this combination of charity and tolerance which marked Pa's life, whether in politics or among psychics.

The Postmaster General in Pa's cabinet was Honorable Thomas L. James, who declared, "Lincoln had extraordinary courage. It was not the courage of brute obstinacy or insensibility."[136] It was on the spiritual-psychical front, Pa's tolerance, born of courage, was sorely tried.

The observation; "The spiritual suffer at the hands of the religious," appears in the book, *The Spiritual Life of Lincoln.*[137] No one better than my father realized how an entrenched religion led to the Crucifixion. God's church someday would come alive with emphasis on spirit survival, communication, and healing. Meantime, Pa was not inclined to 'play church.' Until the church applied the teachings of the master as they related to the spiritual and the psychical, it had little to offer. The Church was the Holy Spirit in action, or it was nothing!

Without first the spiritual, the religious loses its meaning and the psychical becomes pathological! Such conclusions Pa verified by his own experience. His intuitive-inquisitive approach was both constant and courageous. He "remained unmoved and undaunted as he continued on his way."[138] Much of his courage was sustained by the spirit world.

The sort of stamina Pa displayed can be seen in one incident when he was attending a military session accompanied by his old friend Edward Baker. The session almost turned into a riot as the speaker was heckled. The Senator and Pa escorted the speaker to his hotel. Pa later explained to the speaker: "Baker and I were apprehensive that you might be attacked by some of those ruffians who insulted you from the galleries."[139] Pa knew what it meant to be insulted and to have his life threatened.

Early one morning a shot rang out. It was an attempted assassination which left a hole in Pa's top hat. He took the incident in stride, but asked that it remain a secret. "It was probably an accident and might worry my family."[140] Pa was headed for the Soldier's Home that morning on horseback. There he found time for quiet solitude.

Meanwhile the Capitol was packed with dissidents out to impeach the president.[141] They would divide Pa's already divided Cabinet. Such tactics are not unfamiliar to presidents. What saved Pa from this dissention was his determination to follow and study the inner light.

A student convinced of the psychical realities, has contended that many a "would-be coward in the struggle for the right," finds stability in personal survival after death.[142] Thus Pa, in one sense, was sustained in the struggle.

There is also an instance when my fearless father was challenged to a duel back in his Springfield days. It is reminiscent of the Jack Armstrong affair. In both instances Pa's pioneer courage was at stake — as was his firm conviction in Divine destiny and the continuity of all life. The Senator from Minnesota, an Irishman named, James Shields, was ultimately to become reconciled to Pa. But just now his Irish pride had been impugned by a piece of Pa's anonymous satire. The Irishman wanted to shoot it out as both men stood face to face, pistols in hand. Before any blood was shed, however, friends interceded.[143] Pa was heroic, although he never sought to become a hero. The heroic was a byproduct of a life devoted to the discovery of hidden spiritual power in his own life and that of others. It came in the course of reaching and conquering the frontiers of the spirit, all of which led to Pa's personal emancipation and the Emancipation Proclamation. Even Herndon had to admit all this took some rare courage.[144]

Secretary of State Seward spoke for himself and Pa when he asked, "what are we men made for but to encounter and overcome oppositon?"[145] If it was not Pa's psychical activities, it was his political policies that stirred up the opposition. He was portrayed as the devil holding a candle to the Russian Bear.[146] Pa was forever holding a lighted candle; always symbolic of his approach to all matters. He held it up as previously pictured in séances. He held it up to the face of the Russian Bear. He also held it before the American Eagle! That was part of his equipment as an explorer.

A renowned spirit healer and explorer, Edgar Cayce, "experienced a most stormy and difficult life" the moment he employed his gifts of the spirit.[147] As suggested, we might know more as to Pa's inquiries and explorations concerning these gifts had there been less feeling that it might defile or detract from the historical Lincoln profile.

A development within our present day traditional churches has attracted wide attention! The Spiritual Frontiers Fellowship was founded in 1955, in Chicago, Illinois, when some 75 church leaders gathered from all parts of the United States. The Fellowship was formed "to encourage and interpret to the churches the rising tide of interest in the mystical, psychical and paranormal experience." Thousands of church members across the country, irrespective of creed or denomination, today hold study groups "to explore matters beyond the usual range of church worship and activity." The Fellowship relates the non-physical to God in an attitude of scientific inquiry. "All human experiences, including extra-sensory perception, clairvoyance, precognition and other related phenomena, are studied without prejudice for a better understanding of the Invisible World, the nature of man and the universe."[148] What is of special interest to Pa is the fact that the Fellowship functions *within the churches!* He knows that if a change is to come, it must come from *within!* This sort of common sense makes sense to Pa. "In his own heart, Lincoln was ever building the one great church . . . he was a member of the church invisible and indivisible."[149]

What continues to distress Pa is the continued church related divisiveness concerning the frontiers of the spirit. Like most plain folks, he is for one church. Church originally meant fellowship. The early church, without creeds or elaborate organization, without any buildings or finances, neither social, educational or political backing, went out to change and to conquer to world. Its first members were His friends who cherished fellowship with Him.

One church-minded observer warns us that "the effect of public performances accompanied by organized effort to substitute psychic demonstration for worship service" could be courting disaster in many a church.[150]

In the midst of the Civil War, Secretary of War Stanton "requisitioned" one of the old traditional churches in Washington to be used as an Army hospital. Pa happened to be among the congregation as the confiscation was announced from the pulpit. He stood up and said: "I countermand the order. We are too much in need of the church these days. We cannot let it be closed!"[151]

Today the Spiritual Frontiers study groups within the traditional churches "means far more than a fellowship of believers on earth. How much more? To sift and weigh the evidence of the survival of the soul after death as it is presented through psychical research remains a most serious concern." The Fellowship Statement of Purpose reads: "With open minds and seeking to develop spiritual sensitivity, we believe in the reality of the future life and that spiritual guidance and personal communion with our beloved dead are possible."[152] As Pa sees it, a return to the first century fellowship has begun! Miracles today are something to be studied and mastered. As facts are added to faith, so our faith is raised to higher levels. Pa's interpretation of the Pentecost Festival was that it was for the many, not the few. What happened then, and there, can happen again! It remains a challenge, an event, as Pa understands it, for the committed, not for the curious! What occurred on the road to Emmaus can happen on any road. Saul was on the road to more violence when it happened to him. Pa was for exploration, not exploitation the Holy Spirit.

Pa felt a determined need for study in our church schools and colleges with exercises and expression of what has come to be known as higher sensory perception. "More than forty colleges now conduct psychic-research courses under the title of parapsychology. One of the finest examples is St. Joseph's (Catholic) College in Philadelphia."[152a] Pa found the Bible full of such instruction.

This higher sensitivity can be lost if not used. The more civilized we become the less sensitized we are. Pa's life-story illustrates, the more primitive, the more sensitive! Self-protection mixed with skepticism sometimes haunts the traditionalists who find themselves out on the frontiers of the spirit. Their status or standing may be at stake!

More recently, the outstanding Bible scholar and lecturer, Dr. Edward Bauman, took up the work of the Spiritual Frontiers Fellowship. Of special interest to my father is the fact that Dr. Bauman presides over one of the largest and oldest churches in our Nation's capitol. At Foundry Methodist Church, Pa would discover few empty seats at the Sunday services, or throughout the week. Such men, like Pa, have shown faith without fear of the consequences.

Sherwood Eddy, a charter member of the Spiritual Frontiers Fellowship, completed his fourtieth book in 1950. It contains the confession that, "a devout Quaker friend in 1937 felt a concern to lay on my conscience the investigation of psychic phenomena, which might throw light on the survival of personality after death."[153]

In reaching his important decision (The Emancipation Proclamation) there is ample reason to believe that Lincoln had not only endured anxious hours, but had undergone a significant inner experience from which he emerged with quiet serenity.

Prof. James G. Randall, *LINCOLN THE PRESIDENT*

CHAPTER V
THE EMANCIPATON OF THE EMANCIPATOR

1
Mission Impossible

According to my Aunt Mary Father has said, "if to be the head of Hell is as hard as what I have to undergo here, I would find it in my heart to pity Satan himself."

Pa was to face his three final and most impossible years after my death. They were to be the emancipation of the emancipator.[1] Pa was to find his

personal emancipation during a period which proved to be the most destructive years of American life and American property in our history. The Northern states, when they became engaged in the conflict, never dreamed of the gravity of the task that lay before them. Many believed the war would be over in three short months.[2] But it was to become a civil war within a Civil War. What battles did not take place on the front lines, took place on the home front.

It became not only "Lincoln's War," — it was an undeclared war and Pa's "period in office was described by some as a "Presidential Dictatorship."[3] But there were his supporters too, such as those reflected in a letter dated Sept. 6, 1864 to John T. Meir. Meir explained that his son was too young to serve his country but had "saved his pennies to help the sick and wounded among our brave boys fighting for the glorious cause of truth and freedom." The sum of five dollars was enclosed.[4]

The greatest minds in Britain, including John Bright and John Stuart Mills, referred to the war as "fratricidal." They acknowledged that it was a "phase of the eternal struggle for human freedom and liberty. If it was Lincoln's War, it was their war, also." Pa was in constant communication with John Bright, a member of Parliament. There was the ever present possibility that England and other nations might recognize the Confederacy.

Painting by Danny Fleckles
February 1957

Pa had a resolution drawn up, leaving no doubt as to his stand against slavery. It was forwarded to John Bright by Senator Sumner.[4a]

In Springfield Pa had said "if destruction be our lot, we must ourselves be its author and its finisher. As a nation of free men, we must live through all time or die by suicide."[4b] In the meantime, draft riots became more intense. A clause in the draft law, which permitted the payment of $300 to the United States Treasury if one chose to avoid the draft, did not help. Cartoons pictured Father standing by while blacks and whites slaughtered each other in streets of the North. Race riots were the order of the day. The purpose of the Emancipation Proclamation tended to turn the blacks against the whites! For some people, that was the intent! On January 24, 1863, the British weekly satirical, *The Punch*, showed Father attired as Uncle Sam. The latter responds; "You beat enough, Massa! Berry well, I'll beat him, too." The black man is pointing to a white Southern soldier.[5] The cartoons in this country were equally cutting. Pa presided over violence provoked by posters calling for *Civil Rights* and *Student's Rights*. In another cartoon, Pa looks down upon placards labeled *hate, riot, and violence.* Pa was relieved to see himself holding his own placard saying, "our defense is in the preservation of the spirit which prizes liberty as the heritage of all men in all lands everywhere.[6] Finally, another cartoon, which Pa appreciated, depicted him

'With Malice Toward None'

with his back turned strolling toward the great beyond. The cartoon is captioned, "From his council and inspiration comes the grace of immortality."[7] This sense of immortality held Pa in balance.

Before Pa was yet 30, and some 23 years before his presidency, he spoke to the Young Men's Lyceum Club of Springfield, Illinois. He saw then a suicidal threat to democracy, with the "increasing disregard for law which pervades our country."[8] In the same speech he declared, "there is no grievance that is a fit object of redress for mob law."

My reference to cartoons, people and events indicate my awareness of what is happening, irrespective of time and place. This is a fact of life eternal. One Lincoln scholar comments on Father's "deep realization of the spiritual side of life."[9] He was aware of the psychic forces ever present around us.

The discord within the president's cabinet was over the timing of the Emancipation Proclamation. Stanton and Seward, in particular, saw Pa deliberately prolonging the war by postponing the proclamation. As commander-in-chief and president, Pa was concerned that the border states might any day swing to the Confederacy.[10] In spite of the Proclamation issued, on July 13, 1863 in New York City, mob rule continued for another four days. An orphan asylum for black children was "sacked and burned."

From His Counsel And Inspiration Comes The Grace Of Immortality

The governor asked the president for a "postponement of draft," but Father declined. Ultimately the people turned against the mob.[11] Pa remained steadfast.

Riots were not confined to the draft. Some 3000 longshoremen went on strike in New York City. With police protection, Negroes proceeded to replace the whites. This was 1863 and under the Proclamation, Negroes were permitted to enlist in the Union Army. The enlistment was a notable success.[12] Innocent victims of mob violence tested more than ever Pa's continued reliance of a 'Power Creator.'

'There is no grievance that is a fit object of redress by mob law' – Lincoln

Anarchy was not a threat, but a fact. As the Civil War spread, it became less civil in local communities, on campuses and on street corners. As a young man in 1838, Pa pleaded at a youth rally to "let reverence for laws be breathed by every American Mother to the lisping babe that prattles in her lap . . . let it be taught in schools in seminaries and in colleges . . . let it be written in primers spelling books and almanacs . . . let it be preached from the pulpit, proclaimed in the legislative halls, and enforced in courts of justice."[12a]

Political conventions compounded the confusion. As early as the convention of 1860, which was to nominate Pa for the presidency, some "40,000 strangers" arrived in Chicago, shouting for "Old Abe — The Rail

Candidate." "They swarmed around the ramshackle convention hall as though they would lift it, carry it half a block, and drop it in the Chicago River."[13] People were saying to themselves, "what a way to choose the head of a nation in crisis."

Pa did not approve, though he made no move to disrupt the antics of his supporters. His opponent was William H. Seward of New York. The Lincoln forces were led by Ward Hill Lamon who later became a White House bodyguard. He understood Pa's politics, but not his psychics. At the convention, Lamon stopped at nothing. He had a large supply of extra tickets printed and gave them to "certain young men" who signed the names of the "officers of the convention" on each ticket.[14]

What saved Pa from political oblivion, was not his politician friends but the depth of this spiritual-psychical nature. His close, psychic friend, Gen. Carl Schurz, who was to learn psychically of his appointment as the senator from Missouri, would say when Father's "moral spiritual nature was aroused, his brain developed an untiring activity until it had mastered all the

Secretary of State — William H. Seward

knowledge within reach."[15] A similar appraisal comes, surprisingly, from Nicolay and Hay. They did not know all they should about my psychic Pa, yet in their Lincoln biography they comment that "the pressure of the tremendous problems by which he was surrounded; the awful significance of the conflict of which he was the chief combatant; the overwhelming sense of personal responsibility which never left him for an hour — all contributed to produce in him a temperament naturally serious and predisposed to a spiritual view of life and conduct, a sense of reverent acceptance of the divine guidance of a superior Power."[16] These two secretaries would never comprehend that Pa's spiritual predisposition included the psychical!

In times of political stress, Pa would consult a clairvoyant.[17] Indeed, Pa's own clairvoyance came to the rescue on various occasions. The noted psychical researcher, Gardner Murphy, has written of Pa's "capacity for ESP and related psychical predisposition."[18]

On file in the War Department is "the story of a terrible night" during the conflict. Pa had visited the telegraph office in the War Department to get the latest news. One night he rushed in shouting, "get a line through." *He had graphically seen the front line where the Confederate Army was about to cut through the Union line.* The telegraph operator inquired as to where Pa had secured his advance information. He promptly replied, *My God, man, I saw it!*[19] For Pa, this was real, and one less military disaster for the Union Army was avoided. Pa did not always turn to mediums in a time of crisis. He became conscious of his own mediumship, his own powers of intuition or premonition.

In June of 1864, the $300 payment provision, as a substitute for military service, was dropped from the draft law. The politicians were after Pa to restore the clause, but he refused. The politicos feared for Pa's chance for re-election in his forthcoming campaign. "With sad, mysterious light in his melancholy eyes, as if they were familiar with things hidden from mortals," Pa told the politicians, "My re-election is not necessary; I must put down the rebellion; I must have 500,000 more men."[20] Once again the mysterious light, the intuitive mind of Pa manifested — and he spoke as a statesman.

A recent President of the United States observed that "we live in a time Lincoln would well have understood. He heard charges the war was long and wrong. He saw Americans die — 600,000 of them — and he brooded. He saw dissent, riot and rebellion."[21] It was from this climate of conflict the Emancipator and the Emancipation was to emerge.

On July 14, 1862 a White House memorandum was forwarded to the president. It came from a lady . . . an unofficial presidential advisor. She warned the president against the proposed Proclamation. She documented the weakness of the rebel forces around Richmond. The political and military consequences would be disastrous. If the president would act with caution, he would become "great next to Washington." Then came a significant reference to "the mediums which prevent the transmission of truth." We are told "Pa folded up the memorandum" and filed it away. He wrote on the back of the memo the name of the sender, the date, and the three words, "discusses public affairs." This memo can be found in the Library of Congress.[22] Thus, there can be little doubt that the role of mediums, in promoting the Emancipation Proclamation, caused a trusted advisor some concern.

Pa was all for emancipating the slaves, for ending the war and preserving the Union, but not in that exact order! To achieve all three goals was almost a "mission impossible"!

Pa was mindful of the Declaration of Independence. He applied its principles to the question of slavery and the saving of the Union when he said, "as a nation, we began by declaring 'all men are created equal.' We now practically read it 'all men are created equal except Negroes.' When the 'Know-Nothings' get control, it will read 'all men are created equal except Negroes and foreigners and Catholics.' When it comes to this, I shall prefer emigrating to some country where they make no pretense of loving liberty — to Russia, for instance — where despotism can be taken pure and without the base allow of hypocrisy."[22a] He pondered long and hard the idea of liberation with compensation. He understood that "liberation of slaves was the destruction of property" as seen in the South. He submitted, much to the distress of Congress, a plan for the deportation of slaves plus compensation to slave owners. The deportation would not be compulsory. "Only those freed men who desired would be colonized."[23]

Less and less Pa looked to Congress for advice and consent. This was no less true of his cabinet. As Pa put it; "things had gone from bad to worse, until I felt we had reached the end of the rope . . . the plan we had been pursuing must be changed. We must alter our tactics or lose the game. I am now determined upon the adoption of the Emancipation."[24] Pa was approaching his hour of decision.

Father was listening more and more to his Progressive Friends. One of Pa's more caustic critics mentions the Progressive Friends as a "new name for his kind of spiritualism." Father was by no means neglectful of his spiritualist friends . . . as may be seen in some of his appointments.[25] Who were his Progressive Friends? Their identity is not too clear. Father saw to this. It is clear that they did everything to promote the Proclamation . . . to make possible the impossible . . . to emancipate the emancipator. On June, 20, 1862 we learn that the Progressive Friends presented the president a "memorial praying for the emancipation."[26] A reliable source reveals the names of a group known to Father as his Progressive Friends.[27]

Among the names was that of Oliver Johnson. This particular group of Progressive Friends were said to be Quakers. As for Pa, the Quakers were among those Progressive Friends who had the 'inside track' to the White House. When the group presented the "memorial advocating the emancipation," Pa made it clear that he had not yet seen it and was not prepared to comment. He listened attentively while Oliver Johnson read it aloud and then assured them he was "seeking light" to do his duty in the position to which he had been called. That very morning Pa had signed a bill "freeing slaves in the territories."[27]a From this same Oliver Johnson, we learn that a British anti-slavery orator, George Thompson, delivered an address in the House of Representatives to a packed house. The date was April 6, 1864. Mr. Thompson next paid his respects to the president. Then, referring to the Emancipation Proclamation, Pa explained, "in our case, the moment came when I felt that slavery must die, that the nation might live."[27]b

There was a Progressive Spiritualist Convention which met annually throughout the state of Missouri. They considered Pa to be one of them in spirit, but often their enthusiasm was a source of embarrassment to Pa.[28] The Progressive Friends could have had some connection with a publication called *The Progressive Thinker.* Pa was content to label those who went along with his ESP thinking, as his Progressive Friends.[29] Progressive Friends was a term Pa employed, freely sometimes, secretly and with good reason — some of these Progressive Friends held various departmental positions in the administration!

Then there was the orthodox church delegation. They too, called upon the president to issue the Proclamation. Pa was inclined to lose patience with their type. "I hope it will not be irreverent for me to say that if it is probable God would reveal his will to others, on a point so connected with my duty, it might be supposed He would reveal it directly to me; for unless I am more deceived in myself than I often am, it is my earnest desire to know the Will of Providence in this matter."[30]

For those who thought of themselves as the high priests of organized religion, Pa reserved his strongest language. "What good would an Emancipation Proclamation from me do, especially as we are now situated? Would my word free the slaves? I cannot even enforce the Constitution in the rebel states. I do not want to issue a document that the whole world will see must necessarily be inoperative, *like the Poe's bull against the comet!*"[31] Pa went on . . . "and suppose they could be induced by proclamation of freedom from me to throw themselves upon us; what would we do with them? How can we feed and care for such a multitude?"[32]

When surrounded by his confreres, Pa would speak in another tone. "God selects his own instruments, and sometimes they are queer ones; for instance, He chose me to see the ship of state through a great crisis."[33] Pa was able to detect and accept the sources of wisdom from 'out of this world.'

A constant dilemma was that the Proclamation did not apply to some 800,000 slaves in the border states.[34] Slavery would never have been permitted to enter this or any other country if Pa had had his way. "Whenever I hear anyone arguing for slavery, I feel a strong impulse to have it tried on him personally."[35] The Proclamation at best was a poor compromise. Pa's primary interest was in equality and freedom. "There is no freedom for the free, without freedom for the slaves." That was Pa. He saw the Proclamation as a first step in the direction of freedom.

Father's personal emancipation emanated from my death. Later, his death would lead to the passing of the 13th Amendment and the emancipation of the slaves throughout the United States.

One of Pa's many Negro friends was the orator, Edward Douglass who said, "I base no man's right on his color or plead no man's right because of his color. My interest in any man is objectively in his own manhood, and subjectively in my own manhood."[36] Pa could not have agreed more, but he was president and put it this way; "I'm naturally anti-slavery. If slavery is not wrong, nothing is wrong . . . yet I have never understood that the presidency conferred upon me an unrestricted right to act offically upon this judgment and feeling."[37] He continued to seek for guidance, above and beyond the call of duty. To suggest the Proclamation was forced upon Pa by circumstances is a half truth. What forced Pa, were forces deep within his own life.

There are those who would remind us that both Ma and Pa came from the border state of Kentucky — but so did Jeff Davis![38] This implies a prejudice. One day Pa felt obliged to appear before a congressional committee investigating the conduct of the war. In a slow, solemn, measured beat, he spoke his mind: "I, Abraham Lincoln, President of the United States, appear of my own volition before this committee of the Senate to say that I, of my own knowledge, know that it is untrue that any of my family hold treasonable communication with the enemy." We are told the Senate committee sat speechless. The president walked out in quick silence.[38a]

No one understood better than Pa that the presidency extended north, south, east and west. He had this in mind when he wrote his close associate, Senator Browning: "I think to lose Kentucky is nearly the same as losing the whole game."[39]

Upon our arrival in Washington, we were ostracized as Southerners and Republicans."[40] Pa was, of course, a Quaker at heart and in heritage. The Quaker philosopher, Rufus Jones, vividly recalled that "in 1861 the grandson of the first Quaker was drafted." When the boy refused to take up arms, he was taken before his army colonel and informed he would be shot. The case was reported to the president, to whom the lad responded, "thee didn't think I was afraid, did thee?" That was enough for Pa . . . "Trump up some excuse. Send him home. You can't kill a boy like that. The country needs all the brave men, wherever they are. Send him home!"[40a]

Before a group of peace commissioners, Pa indicated it was not proper for him to deal, in person, with the rebels. One commissioner took exception. Had not King Charles done so? Father responded by saying, "I don't profess to be posted on history . . . all I distinctly recollect about King Charles I is that he lost his head!"[41]

As commander-in-chief, Pa was obliged to prosecute the war. He snapped back at one politician who criticized his handling of the war, asking; "would you have me drop the war where it is? Would you prosecute it in the future, with elder stalk squirts charged with rose water?"[41]a The fact that the spiritualists tended to support the abolitionists only intensified the slander.

As peacemaker, we see that he was no less determined to prosecute the peace. He sent the powerful anti-slavery voice of Henry Ward Beecher to England to plead for patience and understanding. The British response was affirmative.[42]

Pa was caught up in a paradox. His cosmic consciousness was severely tried. During the Battle of Gettysburg he wrote a letter to General Meade. He did not, or could not, send it. It read in part; "I do not believe you appreciate the magnitude of the misfortune involved in Lee's escape. He was within your easy grasp, and to have closed upon him would, in connection with our late successes, have ended this war. As it is, the war will be prolonged indefinitely . . ."[43]

The very thought of the Proclamation, meantime had plunged "much of the nation in despair." The South struck at the North harder than ever — and with success. The North called for the resignation of the president. It has been claimed that Pa even threatened to take his life. He is quoted as saying, "I shall never be happy again. My life springs are wearing out, and I shall not last . . . I long ago made up my mind that if anybody wants to kill me, he may do it. How hard it is to die unless I can make the world understand that I would be willing to die, if I could be sure I am doing my work toward lifting the burdens from all mankind."[44]

Members of his own party tried to break up his cabinet. One day Pa turned to a friend saying, "we are on the brink of destruction. It appears to me the Almighty is against us. I can see no ray of hope."[45]

On September 22, 1862 Pa received a call from the military governer of North Carolina, Honorable Ed Stanley. As they pondered over the Proclamation, Pa revealed he had prayed; "If it be possible, let this bitter cup pass from me." Then Pa added, ". . . my prayer has not been answered."[46] When cabinet member, Montgomery Blair, brought up the issue of the border states, Pa replied, "the difficulty was as great not to act, as to act!"[47]

On August 14, 1862 Pa spoke to a group of educated Negroes saying, "even when you cease to be slaves, you are far from being on an equality with the white race." Then, in disparagement he declared, "it is best for us both to be separated."[48]

One citizen wrote a letter-to-the-editor maintaining the president was acting wisely in an impossible situation.[49] His predicament became increasingly evident. Father always felt that had the Southern states not insisted on secession, slavery would ultimately become extinct, a victim of its own inherent evil.[50] To a friend he remarked; "we've both been wrong,

North and South, about slavery. No use to blame it all on the South. If both sides had been willing to give in a little, we might have worked it out . . ."[51]

No matter how controversial the issue, political or psychical, Pa could see it from all sides. It was the magnanimity of the man, plus his spirituality. One commentator summed it up when he said, "Lincoln proclaimed that liberty for every man must be established in himself . . . seeking his freedom through himself."[52] For Father, "freedom" was something fragile . . . "to be handled with prayer." Whether in politics or spiritual pursuits, Pa knew that too often the same words, liberty of freedom, could incite one group and unite another. He was quite aware that language often became a barrier to the truth. As late as April 18, 1864 Pa commented, "the world has never had a good definition of the word liberty. The American people just now are much in need of one. We all declare for liberty. In using the same word, we do not mean the same thing."[53]

An author who wrote on the spiritual life of Father tried to see the Proclamation as Pa saw it. ". . . the slaves are emancipated, but the Negroes are not freed; nor are they yet freed into the equality of opportunity, which should inform a great nation's life."[54] One Lincoln student rather begrudgingly concluded; "the most Lincoln would approve was the bestowal of suffrage on a few superior Negroes, leaving the rest to be gradually educated into citizenship."[55]

Meanwhile after an interview with an editor and authority on the occult, a United Press correspondent sent out a news release dated April 21, 1863 claiming, "it is known from letters recently found that Lincoln consulted spiritualists (mediums) frequently about the opposition, he was meeting, to the Emancipation. They always encouraged him to follow through."[56]

At the close of the war, and at his last cabinet meeting on the morning of his assassination, Pa was at ease. He assured General Grant, in an aside, that all was well. Pa had, as we shall learn, one of his precognitive dreams on the previous night. He placed some confidence in both precognition and predestination.[57]

2
Emancipated Guidance

Emancipated guidance has a double connotation. It applies in particular to the type of guidance which set Pa free and to that which was ultimately to set others free. It is a mystical-spiritual-psychical guidance, sometimes referred to as the Communion of Saints. Such phraseology holds more than conventional religious implications.

If anyone needed guidance it was Pa. In the days of the Lincoln-Douglas debates, his ambivalence on the slavery issue was pronounced. In Chicago he would argue that slavery was an evil. He took his clue from the Declaration of Independence. In Charleston he retreated saying. "I am not and never have been in favor of bringing about in any way an equality, political or social, between the black and white races.[1] It was an open secret that he was receiving and accepting guidance from psychics, sensitives or so-called spiritualists. The national turmoil which preceded and followed the Emancipation Proclamation produced in Pa an ever greater reliance on spiritistic guidance and communication. Supportive evidence is considered by one historian as first hand and valuable.[2] Verification comes from friend and foe alike. The Spiritualists and non-Spiritualists agree.[3]

The *Encyclopedia of Psychic Science* edited by Dr. Nandor Fodor states that "Senator Thomas Richmond by his experience through mediums, J. B. Conklin, Mrs. Cranston Laurie, and Nettie Colburn as well as Dr. Farnswo th's predications influenced a change in Lincoln's attitude which produced the Anti-Slavery Proclamation."[3a]

The absence of material in Pa's own hand and signature is explainable, but none-the-less regrettable, although there is some indication that shortly before his death, he intended to rectify this. In the early days Pa had said to Joshua Speed, "I have always had a strong tendency toward mysticism . . . I have had so many evidences of God's direction, so many instances when I have been controlled by some other power than my own will, that I cannot doubt that this power comes from above. I frequently see my way clear to a decision, when I am aware that I do not have sufficient facts upon which to found it."[4] This mysticism, which was so much a part of Lincoln, was found eloquently described by Albert Einstein in a *Mt. Toby Friends Newsletter* issued in September, 1973: "*The most beautiful and most profound emotion we can experience is the sensation of the mystical. It is the sower of all true science. He to whom this emotion is a stranger, who can no longer wonder and stand rapt in awe, is as good as dead. To know that what is impenetrable to us really exists, manifests as the highest wisdom and the most radiant beauty which our dull faculties can comprehend in their most primitive forms . . . this knowledge, this feeling is at the center of true religiousness.*"[4a]

In the old days "a new frontier and one of prime significance"[5] had been opened for Father, which was to gain scientific sanction in the years ahead. Researchers along the frontiers of the spirit contend "there is satisfactory scientific evidence for the survival of personal consciousness."[6] In receiving and accepting guidance from the unseen world, it was the personal experience, not scientific evidence, which meant most to Pa.

The innumerable cross references to both the Maynard and Hall publications contained in the Simon P. Kase booklet, *The Emancipation Proclamation: How and By Whom It Was Given To Abraham Lincoln*, make it a substantial study of Pa's emancipated guidance. One must comprehend guidance in its larger context. Such enlightened guidance includes the Eternal and all the infinite sources from the spirit world.

A rather disarming Kase story, which had a direct bearing on the issuance of the Emancipation Proclamation, may have been discounted by some, due to the stigma associated with séances. As it relates to the emancipated Lincoln the significance of the Colonel's testimony cannot be overemphasized. There is no reason to doubt the Colonel's honesty and sincerety. Assuming the accuracy of the details, the document would seem to be worthy of careful consideration.[6a] Kase was a railroad executive, distinguished business leader and churchman. His visits to Washington were quite frequent and although he was well acquainted with congressional committee leaders who were quick to seek his council, he had never met the president. Kase had nothing to gain and probably everything to lose by publicizing his encounter. It seems the Colonel was walking along a Washington street when he noticed the name Conklin on the door of a residence he had resided in some 11 years previous. Kase had met a sensitive by the name of Conklin who was known for his proficiency in automatic writing, some two years earlier. Suddenly, as the Colonel walked on, he was startled by a "voice at his right side" urging him to "go see him; he is in the same room you used to occupy." Kase entered the house and found Conklin completing a letter to the president, and which Conklin was to insist Kase had come to deliver. The Colonel, however, was equally insistent this was not the case. He neither knew the president, nor the contents of the letter, but he now heard the same inner voice he had experienced in the street urging him to "go see what will become of this." He finally undertook to deliver the letter and, much to his surprise, was admitted to the president's office . . . a stranger without a previous appointment! It seems when 'Kase' was announced to Lincoln, it was mistaken for 'Chase', the secretary of the treasury with whom the president anticipated a meeting. When Pa was handed the message, he was mystified. This was no less true when he read it. As Pa read it aloud, he learned that Kase knew nothing of the contents. They were both dumbfounded to learn, "I have been sent from New York City by spiritual influence pertaining to the interest of the nation. I can't return until I see you. Appoint the time." Signed: J. B. Conklin.[7] Even as Kase had met Conklin in New York City, so also was Father to meet him there some years later; most probably on one of his visits to Henry Ward Beecher in Brooklyn.

Some will say Pa received and accepted only what he wanted. Others will maintain the psychics played up to Pa and his Proclamation, but even Herndon used to say Pa was a born analyst and realist. There is nothing peculiar about people hearing what they want to hear.

A Lincoln historian holds that Kase, along with Nettie Colburn and Hall provide the "real and only substantial foundation" concerning spirit communication relating to the formation of the Emancipation Proclamation.[8]

Kase added in his account of the incident that Pa agreed to give Conklin an appointment in writing. This was after the Colonel had respectfully declined the Lincoln request to convey a message to Conklin. At a later time the Colonel was in the home of Mrs. Laurie where, to his utter astonishment, he found the President, Mrs. Lincoln and an honor guard. It was on this occasion that the gifted Nettie Colburn delivered a spirit message on the Proclamation. As for Pa, it led to the emancipation of the emancipator as well. It was not merely the spirit message but the spirit of the message which gripped Father.

In a calm, conversational style, the Colonel explained his presence at the Laurie home. He happened to be seated one afternoon in the gallery of the House of Representatives, when an elderly lady handed him a card. On it was the notation, "call when it suits you."[9] The Colonel spotted his friend, Judge Wattels, and showing him the card, the judge recognized the name Laurie. Indeed, Wattels had been at her Georgetown residence on several occasions. He told Kase about the daughter of Mrs. Miller, who had played a grand piano "with her eyes closed," whereupon "the piano rose from the floor!" "They call it Spiritualism," volunteered the judge, who might have been referring to a clergyman who had had a similar experience. He understood it as a psychic phenomenon called levitation,[10] wherein musical instruments have sometimes been involved.[11] Judge Wattels agreed to accompany the Colonel on his first visit to the Laurie home! In the Colonel's account of the crucial sitting, he claimed that, "after speaking and passing the courtesies of the day, perhaps ten minutes intervening, I saw a young girl approaching the president with measured step, with her eyes closed, and walking up to the knees of the president, accosted him as follows: 'Sir, you have been called to the position you now occupy for a very great purpose. The world is in universal bondage; it must be physically set free, that it may mentally rise to its proper status. There is a Spiritual Congress, supervising the affairs of this nation, as well as the affairs of Congress in Washington. This Republic is leading the van of Republics throughout the world'."[12] She continued for a full hour. She dealt in specific manner with the Proclamation. Her language, according to the Colonel, became sublime. Finally, as she "came out of her trance, she ran off, frightened to think she had been talking to the president."[13]

Miss Colburn had come to Washington for a visit with her brothers who were in an army hospital. Nettie Colburn Maynard's personal narration of numerous meetings with the president, as we know, appeared in book form. The Colonel confirms in essence the Colburn account. The denial of Miss Colburn (Mrs. Maynard) that she influenced the president's position relative to the Proclamation is understandable. She was in trance. She was not functioning on a conscious level. It is claimed that those present were not even aware she had the Proclamation in mind. There was no doubt in Pa's mind, nor in that of the Colonel's. Kase has said; "Thus it was that the president was convinced as to the course he should pursue. The command coming from the All-seeing Spirit through the instrumentality of the angelic world was not to be overlooked."[14]

Lest we rush to label this somnambulism or a case of hysterics, we should note these several other factors. The business directory of his home town, enumerates the Colonel's achievements and calls him a "remarkable man." No where does it mention his religion, except as an elder in the church. He had informed Pa that he always "condemned spiritualism as the veriest humbug of the day."[15] A merchant friend in Philadelphia urged him to look into the subject. Later they were to visit a sensitive. Kase was sufficiently impressed to lose much of his prejudice. He explained all this to Pa at their first meeting.

At the conclusion of his printed booklet, Kase referred to himself as a 'modern spiritualist' — whatever that may mean! At no point in his account, however, does he use the term spiritualist to describe Father. Whether Spiritualist or non-Spiritualist, Kase has preserved for posterity a personal experience related to Pa and the proclamation. The Colonel's first visit to the Laurie residence was followed by others where again he would meet both the president and first lady. The Colonel's own last words in defense of his

General Daniel E. Sickles

stand advanced the thought that, "in this enlightened age, government aid is not given to any special theology, and no attempts to concentrate a sectarian alliance under the name of 'Spiritual' will ever succeed in our great and glorious nation."[16]

General Sickles was often present at the private séances in Georgetown. We have already discovered how near he was to Pa. At one séance, he would hear speak of "the sweet and comfort that came into his soul." The séance supported the Emancipation.[17]

Another sidelight at the Emancipation séance referred to Daniel Webster. The "peculiar method of address" through the child medium reminded Father of the famous orator. His painting was visible on the room of the Laurie home. For Pa, it all pointed to the Proclamation.[18]

Receiving guidance was not something confined to a séance. Father was constantly aware that he "was being controlled by some other power." "That the Almighty does make use of human agencies, and directly intervenes in human affairs, is one of the plainest statements in the Bible. I have had so many evidences of His direction, so many instances when I have been controlled by some other power than my own will, that I cannot doubt that this power comes from above . . ."[19] Pa was speaking to his Registrar of the Treasury, L. E. Chittenden.

From an avowed and respected Spiritualist, we have further testimony that, "Lincoln was advised by at least some of our nation . . . under their guidance Lincoln issued the Emancipation." This same gentleman further referred to his personal acquaintance with Pa, and Senators Wade, Wilson, Howard Howe, and many others.[20] Another recognized Spiritualist has claimed it was twenty years after he met Kase, that he first learned of the Maynard book.[21]

3

Binding Up The Wounds

Those final three years, between my death in 1862 and Father's passing in 1865, with the war dead mounting, provided a climate for a healing ministry which Pa had not anticipated. When General Sickles' right leg was shattered at Gettysburg, Father was at his bedside. Pa described his fervent prayer before the battle and then repeated what the General already knew, saying: "Sickles, I have been told that your condition is perhaps serious. I am in a prophetic mood today. You will get well."[1] The doctors had given the General one chance in five hundred to recover.

Father prophesied the General's complete recovery. Within a few months Sickles was attending Father's favorite church in Brooklyn, New York. Henry Ward Beecher was the pastor.[1a]

Father was always reluctant to admit he had gone to his knees over the battle of Gettysburg.[2]. At one séance Pa had Sickles and Gettysburg on his soul. He prayerfully told the General "that is why I had no fear about you."[3] Mother, you may remember, devised a test at one séance for her sensitive young friend Nettie Colburn, involving the General. He was in her mind and heart. Nettie passed the test.[4]

Another instance of healing concerned a 20 year old Union Officer, Major Charles H. Houghton. As in the case of Sickles, the president had visited him at the hospital. When father took the dying man's hand in his, the young Major's eyes began to open. Pa asked the nurses if he might see the wound. Father's healing spirit took hold. Father sobbed: "Oh this war; this awful, awful war." Then he took Houghton's face between his brawny hands and uttered, "my boy, you must live, you must live." Houghton responded saying, "I intend to, Sir." That was it! The young Major lived.[5]

The Chief Surgeon on that occasion was Dr. MacDonald. Pa inquired of him: "Was this the man who held Fort Haskell? The surgeon nodded in the affirmative. The president then motioned for a chair. He sat at the head of the cot. He laid his 'stovepipe' hat on the floor. His clothes were dusty and disheveled. He asked to see young Houghton's wound. The surgeon and the nurse tried to dissuade Pa. What he saw caused him to fling his lanky arms upward and groan. Then followed the healing treatment."[5a] This is the Major's personal account.

Since Father's day, the medical profession has been making studies of "magnetic healing" through touch. "The energy field around the body and interpenetrating the body" has been the subject of examination.[6] "As early as 1856," Judge Whitney, Father's legal associate, recognized in Lincoln a "prodigy of local force."[7]

Father's healing efforts also took the form of reconciliation between the North and South. He pleaded; "Let us all join in doing the acts necessary to restoring the proper relationship between the states."[8] One notable psychic researcher has stated: "If any message from the spiritual world can be accepted because of its frequent repetition, it is that human brotherhood, human love, alone guarantees salvation."[9] Four days before Pa's assassination, he was being serenaded at the White House. General Lee had surrendered. Pa saw an opportunity to perform "an act necessary" to reconciliation. He addressed the serenaders: "I see you have a band. I propose now that you play a certain air or tune. I have always thought *Dixie* one of the best tunes I have ever heard."[10]

Under the pressure of official life, Pa was not as conscious as he might have been of the unseen healing forces at work. His friend, Nettie Colburn, was to refresh his mind. At their last meeting the young medium announced her father was ill and she was leaving town. She would not be at Lincoln's second inauguration. Pa asked if "our friends from the upper country could

Nettie addressing Mr. Lincoln

not indicate whether his illness was critical." The reply came, "they had indicated her father was not receiving the correct treatment. Her presence was needed if a cure was to be effected."[11]

In his first inaugural address, Pa had a paragraph to which his Secretary of State Seward may have contributed. Pa welcomed it as expressive of his own feelings. "The mystic chords of memory stretching from every battlefield and patriot grave pass through all the hearts and all the hearths in this broad continent of ours, and will yet again harmonize in their ancient music, when breathed upon by the guardian angel of the nation."[12] This healing paragraph did not lessen the tension of war. Yet in the light of time and eternity, who is to judge? Lincoln still lives!

The man who led Pickett's charge for the Confederacy at Gettysburg had been a friend of Father's since Springfield days. Father had assisted in bringing about George Pickett's appointment to West Point. At one point Pa was hard on the heels of the Union Army, with an act of healing as it entered Richmond. He knocked at the door of the Pickett residence. Mrs. Pickett answered the door. Was George at home? Yes, he was! Pa offered to hold the Pickett baby. His offer was accepted and Mrs. Pickett went after her husband. Pa had urged her to simply announce that his "old friend," Abraham Lincoln, was calling.[13] At Gettysburg, Pa had spoken to the

Confederate force, as well as the Union Army, when he prayed that "this Nation, under God, might have a new birth of freedom."

With the second inaugural address, who can forget Pa's healing tongue? *To bind up the nation's wounds, to care for him who shall have borne the battle, and for his widow and orphan – to do all which may achieve and cherish a just and lasting peace among ourselves and with all nations.*[14] This was not merely a piece of rhetoric. The London *Spectator* called Pa's second inaugural address "by far the noblest which any American president has yet uttered." But the Chicago Times gave Pa the usual treatment from the American press: "We did not conceive it possible that even Mr. Lincoln could produce such a slipshod loose-jointed, so puerile, not alone in literary construction but in its ideas, its sentiments, its grasp. By the side of it mediocrity is superb."[14a]

Another healing, the "Proclamation of Amnesty and Reconstruction," was requested of the Congress by Pa. It granted "full pardon with the restoration of all rights of property, except as to slaves."[15] The magnanimity of this message brought release to the captives and relief to the down-trodden. Some members of the cabinet and of Congress were incensed, Stanton in particular. That the president was treating the enemy as if they were friends, was thought stupid or traitorous. But Pa had a higher sensory

Secretary Stanton
Edwin M. Stanton

perception of national goals.[16] A "policy of pardon" became an "absolute necessity" for Pa as the war drew to a close. When Ma referred to Washington as "that city full of enemies," Pa promptly spoke his mind. "Enemies, never again must we repeat that word."[16a]

It was after the battles of Gettysburg and Vicksburg that Pa called upon "The Holy spirit to subdue the anger which has produced and so long sustained a needless and cruel rebellion, to change the hearts of the insurgents, to guide the counsels of the government with wisdom adequate to so great an emergency, and to visit with tender care and consolation throughout the length and breadth of our land all those who through the vicissitudes of marches, voyages, battles and seiges, have been brought to suffer in mind and body, or estate, and finally to lead the whole nation through the paths of repentance and submission to the Divine Will, back to the perfect enjoyment of union and fraternal peace."[17] Pa was not simply a peace-talker. He was a peace-maker. Nothing could be more anomalous than Pa cast in the role of commander-in-chief. He was out of character. As early as 1858 on Sept. 11, he revealed his revulsion against military force. "It is not our frowning battlements . . . our bristling sea coasts . . . these are not our reliance against tyranny . . . Our reliance is in the love of liberty, which God has planted in our bosoms."[17a] The incongruity of this position only increased his determination to make peace . . . a lasting peace, based upon justice and amnesty. "I fear it will be difficult for the whole world to understand how fully I appreciate the principles of peace, inculcated everywhere by the Society of Friends."[18] Father was accused, with some justification of "being more generous to his enemies than his friends."[19]

The triumphant re-election in 1864 produced a few extemporaneous remarks from Pa relevant to the spirit which pervaded his whole being: "For my part I have striven, and still strive, to avoid placing any obstruction in the way of peace. So long as I have been here I have not willingly planted a thorn in any man's bosom.[20]

The abolitionists plagued Pa. He admired John Brown, yet he could not support him. Even Horace Greeley with his *Prayer for Twenty Million People* played into the hands of these extremists. Father sincerely believed if slavery were contained, it would in time "pass away" and the nation would be set free.[21] Between John Brown and Horace Greeley, the abolitionists went after Father with a vengeance. But Pa maintained his ground. "He did not wish to encounter (the Greeley faction) before the proper time, nor at all, if it could be avoided."[22]

Pa replied to Greeley in the August 23, 1862 issue of the *National Intelligencer.* Pa made it abundantly clear that his first aim was to heal a broken and divided nation. He purposely deleted one passage from the printed copy. It was a typical Lincoln line which Pa felt did not add to the dignity of his office. It did, however, convey his concern for "binding up the wounds." "Broken eggs," the line read, "can never be mended. The longer the breaking proceeds, the more will be broken."[23]

In war, as in peace, one of Father's ablest antagonists was George B. McClellan who, for a time seemed certain to succeed Pa in the 1864 presidential contest. A few days before the national election, Pa wrote himself a note. He hid it in his desk. By November 11, 1864 Pa was firmly reestablished in the White House for another four years. At a regular meeting of his cabinet, he then shared the contents of his hidden memo. It was outdated, but not out of order. It was read to a cabinet infected by grudges and petty politics, unable to forgive or forget. The outdated memorandum read: "General, the election has demonstrated you are the stronger, have more influence with the people than I. Now let us, together — you, with your influence and with the executive power of the government — try to save the country. You raise as many troops as you possibly can for the final trial. I will devote my energies to assisting and finishing the war."[24]

It has been suggested, "if Washington was the Father of our country,

Lincoln was the Saviour." As we have come to see, Pa felt a nearness to our first president. There was a common psychic and political bond.

It did not take a 'great physician' to see that "the North shared the

South's guilt in having permitted slavery to be established in the nation."[25] It was an inability to grasp the reality of their guilt, as Father saw it, that drove the abolitionists to extremism. From the beginning, Pa spoke to their sickness. On March 4, 1861 his familiar words rang out, but fell mostly on deaf ears. "We are not enemies but friends. We must not be enemies. Though passions have strained, it must not break our bonds of affection."[26]

In later years came the Gettysburg Address. The *Springfield Republican* of Massachusetts urged the people to read it. "Strong feelings . . . were its parents" read the editorial line. Most other leading newpapers, however, omitted any reference to Pa's greatest healing message, and printed instead such commentary as: "We pass over the silly remarks of the President. For the credit of the nation, we are willing that the veil of oblivion shall be dropped over them."[27] For a time, a veil of oblivion did fall over the Gettysburg Address. Father felt it would, yet he never gave up.

IMMORTALITY

With the war nearing an end, a luncheon and reception were held at the White House. The Union General, Weitzel, asked Pa what should be done with the conquered people. "If I were in your place, I'd let 'em up easy." Pa repeated, "Let 'em up easy."[28] That was far from reflecting the view of the cabinet or Congress.

Shortly before his assassination, a Southerner, stopped by Pa, greeted him by saying: "I love the southern people, more than they love me. My desire is to restore the Union. I do not intend to hurt the hair of the head of a single man in the south, if it can possibly be avoided."[29] This kind of talk made no sense to Stanton and others. Their hate for the enemy was all consuming and left little room to heal the breach.

Pa, the peacemaker, extended his ministry to the Pueblo Indians. The Pueblo tribes had remained neutral throughout the war. In 1863 Pa presented 19 Pueblo governors in New Mexico with silver studded canes. The Pueblos continue to cherish these symbols of peace and good-will.[30] This aspect of Pa's life was a religion. During October 1862 a military tribunal condemned 307 Indians to death because of a full scale Sioux uprising. Lincoln later decided that only 38 of the condemned group were guilty of "having murdered unarmed citizens." The unfortunate affair had been the result of food riots "in which about 450 settlers were slain."[30a]

A young law student in the offices of Lincoln and Herndon was Henry B. Rankin. He said to know Lincoln "was a kind of religion."[31] There were those who denied Lincoln had any religion. Theologically, such a charge bore some truth. One biographer wrote: "If Lincoln was no professing Christian, neither was he in any sense an atheist."[32] It was presumed the surrender of the Confederate forces would occur around April 11 or 12, 1864. General Grant and his cohorts appeared intent upon "the capture of Jefferson Davis and his cabinet. Pa repeated over and over a scriptural passage he had used in his second inaugural: "Let us judge not that we be not judged."[32a]

Pa was drawn to The Young Carpenter, The Great Physician, The Healer, The Communicator, with The Creator and His Creatures as a Master Guide. He was not a person, as Pa understood, who wanted to be defied, worshipped or glorified by his followers. He wanted only that they who followed him should seek to exemplify (not imitate) his life of service and sacrifice. He was, for Pa, the Supreme revelation of a Divine plan and purpose. Pa saw a vast distinction between the historical person and the theological interpretation.

4

The Hour of Decision

"To every man and nation comes a moment to decide . . . for the good or evil side."[1] When that moment came for Pa, he was ready. He had experienced the "truth that sets men free." His attendance at séances had not been in vain. His motive in meeting mediums had not been to receive messages from me or any other person. Nor was it to uphold his conviction in the continuity of personality. It was to bolster his belief in the bulwark of his high office. The burning issue was the timing of the Emancipation Proclamation. "God spoke to Moses through the burning bush. He speaks to us through burning issues."[2]

Ralph Waldo Emerson urged Father "not to let the dying die . . . until you have charged their era with the message."[3] The pressure had built up for the Proclamation. Generals Fremont and Hunter threatened to issue their own proclamations. "Lincoln's firmness in revoking Hunter's own proclamation brought praise from California . . . it is high time the 'proclamation mania' from our Generals should be crushed."[4] Father removed both Hunter and Fremont from command. He reminded them there was but one commander-in-chief. Pa had first urged Fremont to modify his stand. The General refused and Pa was put on the defensive. The demand for a proclamation was wide spread.

Fremont became a national figure and was later to become a Republican candidate for the presidency. This was not, however, before the tide turned.[5] The extremists groups were demanding immediate action. Father's friend, Senator Browning, had warned that Fremont had succeeded in bringing "the issue of the emancipation out into the open."[6] As early as July of 1862, Senator Sumner had announced "the moment had come" to issue the Proclamation. Pa did not agree.[7]

Late in the day on September 10, 1862 Mrs. Jessie Benton Fremont arrived in Washington. She had been on the road several days, enroute from St. Louis. At the request of her husband, she was determined to see the president. Pa put her off several days. He knew her mission. She was there to plead for the prompt issuance of the Proclamation. Pa listened in patience, then laconically replied, "You are quite a female politician!"[7a]

Fremont was a Senator and an experienced overland explorer. In his diary containing records of his explorations, Fremont indicated he was dying of starvation in the desert. The incident was to have psychic repercussions. In a biography of her father, his daughter wrote that at the very moment her father was in the desert on the verge of collapse, her mother, at home, experienced a sense of utter starvation. "Mother had gone to get wood. As she knelt to pick up a stick she felt an invisible hand on her shoulder. She heard the laughing voice of her husband whisper 'Jessie.' Then she regained her strength, free from fear."[8] This episode may not have been known to Father, yet he could understand.

General J. C. Fremont, a former instructor in mathematics at the United States Naval Academy from 1833 to 1835, in a statement dated July 15, 1889, confirmed his predicament in the desert as it appeared in the vision his wife experienced. As late as February 12, 1889, just 80 years after the birth of Lincoln, Mrs. Fremont, then in Los Angeles, responded in detail to inquiries concerning her psychic experience. Later her sister, Mary Benton Warren, was to corroborate her story.[8a]

The news media continued to play upon the psychical element in Pa's life. The *Washington National Intelligencer* of September 26, 1862 referred to the "anti-slavery astrologers."[9] Then the day came when he saw his way clear. "My duty is plain . . . it must be done. I am driven to it . . ."[10] such comments were made light of in the press. To his Secretary of the Treasury, Salmon P. Chase, not always one to be relied upon, Father confessed he had made "a solemn vow before God." If General Lee was driven back from Pennsylvania, he would crown the results by a declaration of freedom to the slaves.[11] Pa was not one to bargain with the ruler of the Universe. As we know, "he had a strong leaning toward predestination or the doctrine of necessity." One author explained; "It is a matter of history that he told the Cabinet he had promised his Maker to issue the Emancipation. It was no idle remark."[12]

President Lincoln, writing the Proclamation of Freedom.
Painting by Blythe—January 1, 1863

The Lincoln Life Foundation has uncovered a reproduction of a painting by David Gilmore Blythe of, "President Lincoln Writing The Proclamation of Freedom January 1, 1863." The painting shows Pa with pen in hand, and the Bible in his lap, musing over the Proclamation. He is surrounded by books, papers, plaques, statues, etc. He sits in an old chair, with one slipper on, and in shirt sleeves.[12a] The room, possibly in the Soldier's Home, remains in disarray. The American flag is half draped over a window.

The Foundation solicited interpretations and impressions from Lincoln scholars and other sources. "He is attuned to ideals, ideas and language, closely related to what he has read in the Bible," responded one historian. A staff member of the National Archives and Record Services thought "Mr. Lincoln saw himself in his time of torment, striving to arrive at the right decision . . . Lincoln was at this moment closest to greatness, without knowing it . . . the President has raised one corner of the flag at the window to give him light as he considers the petition of the people, the Quakers, the conscientious objectors, the draft riots, the division within the churches."[13] Blythe's painting captures something of a mystical-psychical mood or atmosphere. Perhaps it was this mood reflected which caused Elbert Hubbard to suggest; "When Lincoln freed the slaves he freed himself." It was so true!

The Proclamation itself proved a step in the direction of freedom and equality for black and white alike. Initially, it was not even a "philanthropic gesture to benefit the enslaved Negroes, but rather a war-time measure intended to weaken the insurgent states."[14] What brought immediate satisfaction to Father was the fact that he was able to issue the document, on the strength of enlightened council, from a higher plane.

Pa would lose his patience with some religious delegations. Before they left the White House he assured them "that the subject is on my mind by day and night more than any other."[15] The depth of Father's devotion to duty cannot be fully comprehended unless seen in terms of Divine Intervention. Pa wrote one meditation which bears the inscription "not to be seen of men." It begins with the words, "The Will of God Prevails." Colonel McClure heard Father speak of the "One Overruling Power of the nation and the world . . . that he was an instrument in the hands of Divine Providence."[16] On April 4, 1864, Pa addressed a personal letter to Mr. A. G. Hodges of Kentucky. In his final paragraph he wrote; "If God now wills the removal of a great wrong, and wills also that we of the North as well as of the South shall pay fully for our complicity in that wrong, impartial history will find therein new cause to attest and revere the justice goodness of God."[17] Such a faith was neither acceptable nor understandable to the Congress or the cabinet.

With my death, Pa took his "first measurable step to monumental fame. He was long prepared and here resolved on the violent subject of Emancipation."[18] No one who knew Pa can doubt that even before my death his spiritual-psychical nature participated in the preparation of the Proclamation. His consciousness was centered in his psyche. Among the writings of an analyst of the psyche, Carl Jung, appears this descriptive paragraph: "In the initiation of the living, the beyond is by no means the realm of the dead, but a reversal of attitude, i.e., a psychological beyond or, in Christian terms, a redemption of the bonds of this world. Redemption is a release and a liberation from an earlier state of darkness and unconsciousness, and the attainment of a state of enlightenment of detachment, of victory and of triumph over given facts."[18]a

Pa labored over various drafts of the emancipation document. On September 22, 1862 he was making up his mind; collecting his thoughts. "What I did, I did after very full deliberation, and under a very solemn sense of responsibility. I can only trust in God. I have made no mistake. . . . It is now for the country and the world to pass judgment on it."[19] Secretary of the Navy, Gideon Wells, wrote in his private diary; "We had a special Cabinet meeting . . . the subject was the Proclamation. . . . For several weeks the subject has been suspended. The president says he never lost sight of it. He wished his paper, announcing his course to be correct. He would countenance no attempt to change his determination. For that he was fixed."[20]

Pa's determination was influenced by his Progressive Friends as well as the impact made by young Nettie Colburn. As we know, Father employed the term Progressive Friends to avoid undue speculation as to their indentity.

Pa continued to seek guidance, not alone on his Proclamation, but on plans for reconstruction. He was most concerned about the "after consequences of a wholesale emancipation of four million people, who for a period of nearly two centuries had been in the most absolute bondage." "If my life is spared, and we should devolve, in connection with the National Legislature, the solving of this important problem, I am free to say right here, in my opinion, the blacks should be regarded in the same light as any infant son just born, and necessarily dependent upon its parent for the most careful nurture; that the benign spirit of education must form the chief cornerstone of their nurture; that in this most important matter, they must be taught to crawl before they are permitted to stand upright and walk."[20]a

There are today some Negro leaders who raise the question as to whether Pa was a 'white supremist'. They claim that Pa "shared the racial prejudices of most of his white contemporaries."[21] Such a charge reveals a far deeper prejudice than Pa appears to have harbored. No one knowing the depth of Pa's feeling and thinking could make such a claim. A leading newspaper editorial, responding to this charge, concluded; "Lincoln may well have shared in the prejudices of his time. Who doesn't? Yet the fact remains that without him the Emancipation Proclamation would not have been issued on New Year's Day of 1863."[22] No one more effectively answered the charge against Lincoln than his black contemporary Fred Douglass, who claimed; "in all my interviews with Mr. Lincoln, I was impressed with his entire freedom from prejudice against the colored race. He was the first great man in the United States that I talked with freely, who in no single instance reminded me between himself and myself, of the difference of color. I thought that all the more remarkable because he came from a state where there were black laws."[23]

Pa lived long enough to see the House of Representatives pass a resolution calling for a constitutional amendment to grant freedom from slavery throughout the United States. The consummation of that amendment by a two-thirds vote of the states, did not come until after his death.[24] By the Proclamation alone, it is estimated that Pa freed four million slaves.[25]

Reconstruction without reconciliation made little sense to Pa. Warring brothers must be united once more when war was done with. For this effort there were few better public relations men than Lincoln. The humanitarian once pardoned a Confederate soldier who confessed he "had run the blockade from Richmond." Pa grasped the Confederate soldier's hand with these words: "I am happy to know I am able to serve an enemy."[26] Pa had learned not simply to love, but to serve the enemy if peace was to be restored and to endure. Love drained of service is sentimentality. Love for Pa was not synonymous with like. Pa could love and yet not like the enemy, who was, after all, of one nation however divisive it would become. Pa had a higher sense of oneness with all things. He had a way, as we have seen, of handling those who came to the White House insisting they had a "recommendation from the Divine Master." He would inquire, "is it not odd that the only channel He could send it by was the round about route (as in one instance) from the awful City of Chicago?"[26a] Pa's cordial reception given an elderly Quaker member of the Society of Friends in September, 1862, was acknowledged by mail: "I am glad of our interview and glad to know that I have your sympathy and prayers."[27] Whoever and whatever could aid in the restoration of the Union and the dignity of all its citizens would have Pa's devoted and prayerful attention.

As a young boy back in Springfield, Pa had discussed the danger of secession with me. He concluded then, "independence is in our blood — so also is states rights."[28] That was fine for Springfield. In Washington it was a different story. "My primary object is to save the Union, and is not to save or destroy slavery."[29] But one Lincoln observer has argued; "If the Civil War had been short (as many believed) it would have ended without the emancipation of the slaves." As we know, "the Constitution gave neither the President nor Congress any power to abolish slavery."[30]

The great carnage of war and catastrophy brings always in its wake a new set of national resolves . . . a reexamination of human purpose and values spurts from an awareness of the "valley of the shadow of death." Carl Jung has said, "I am convinced that it is hygienic — if I may use that word — to discover in death a goal toward which one can strive, and that shrinking away from it is something unhealthy and abnormal which robs the second half of life of its purpose."[31] Pa began to conduct the war "on the theory that it was waged for the restoration of the Union, under the Constitution, as it was at the outbreak of the secession movement."[32] Out of "Lincoln's War" would come a reassessment of human worth and dignity.

Father's inner resources were put to the test within his own political party. The Republican National Committee found itself torn asunder by the emancipation. Pa, who was up for reelection, healed the breach by persuading the committee that the priority was the preservation of the Union. An outstanding British biographer states: "Lincoln won a complete spiritual victory over the National Republican Committee."[33] Such a perspective brings into focus the spirit of the president in the shape of things to come. Yet there were those who were sure that Pa, once "the great enemy of slavery" had surrendered.[34]

Pa was aware that his policy might have prevented his reelection. At the age of 23, he was a candidate for the legislative branch. One campaign speech ended; "If the good people in their wisdom shall see fit to keep me in the background, I have been too familiar with disappointment to be very much chagrinned."[35]

His determination to preserve the Union first was decisive.[36] "What I do about slavery . . . I do because it helps to save the Union."[37] The die was cast. Pa was sure of himself. He was functioning from within!

In August of 1863 John Hay wrote Nicolay: "The tycoon is a true whack. I have never seen him more serene and busy. He is managing this war, the draft, foreign relations, and planning reconstruction of the Union, all at once. I never knew with what a tyrannous authority he runs the Cabinet, until now. The most important things he decides, and there is no gavel![38] Little did they realize the psychic springboard of Pa's "tyrannous authority." If they had, they would have been shocked! Secretary Seward wrote to his wife, "there is but one vote in the Cabinet, and that is cast by the President."[39] For too long Pa had waited upon his cabinet and the Congress to act. A new Lincoln, a man of destiny and action, emerged.

Pa was possessed! The practical application of his spiritual-psychical nature at either a séance or at a session of his cabinet, accounts, in part, for his personal liberation and triumph. The unfoldment of his inner resources neither began nor ended with my passing. His emancipation emanated, in some measure from my release, and led to the release of millions from bondage. Pa did not run to mediums. He simply became more conscious of his own sensitivity, and sought to make himself available as a channel or medium through which information, instructions from the Eternal . . . from the Cosmos . . . from discarnate beings of good will, could be received and transmitted.

General O. O. Howard was quoting Father when he said, "many free countries have lost their liberties, and ours may lose hers. But if she shall, may it be my proudest boast, not that I was the last to desert, but that I never, never deserted her."[40] That was more than partriotism! At Newark, New Jersey, Pa reiterated, "I am sure I have not the ability to do anything unaided by God," And again at Philadelphia; "I have said nothing that I am not willing to live by, and if it be the pleasure of Almighty God, to die by."[41] Father became more firm in his dependence upon his Maker, in his stand in matters of vital importance. The Emancipation was one such matter. A Congressman referred to Father as "firm as a rock."[42] During those days of decision, the Attorney General characterized Pa as "the master mind of the Cabinet,"[43] while Father knew his wisdom was 'not of this world!' A British Lincoln enthusiast, K. C. Wheare, wrote that Pa was a "supreme example of solitary action in the formulation and announcement of his policy on the Emancipation."[44]

Lincoln was alone, yet not alone. He was surrounded by a "great cloud of witnesses." Some historians like to portray Pa as a victim of circumstances during those darkest days. His was not a "strength born of desperation," but rather, a divine inspiration that made him say, "it had got to be!"[45]

My death was far more than a memory in Fathers mind. It was a stimulant to his acceptance of bodily survival and spirit communication. His artist friend Carpenter confirmed this. It was evident in the effective manner in which he personally and confidentially drew up the Emancipation Proclamation. One Saturday he completed a second draft of the document at the Soldiers Home. The following Monday, the Proclamation was published.[46]

In the meantime he had called the cabinet together, but "not to ask their advice."[47] It was to insist "that once adopted, debates must end, and all agree and abide." When Seward was all for altering one word, Father, "his head bowed, murmured to himself, 'one war at a time, one war'."[48] Pa's attitude, as he approached the consummation of the Emancipation for himself and others, is best summed up by historian, Randall: "If these deliberations had given him humility and a sense of association with Divine Purpose, they had also given executive confidence. In reaching his important decision there is ample reason to believe that Lincoln had not only endured anxious hours, but had undergone a significant inner experience, from which he emerged with quiet serenity."[49] The nature of this inner experience is apparently illusive to most Lincoln writers.

Secretary of the Treasury Chase, just before Father called the cabinet to consider the Proclamation, submitted a revised version. It included the sentence; "And upon this act, believed to be an act of justice warranted by the Constitution, I invoke the considered judgment of mankind and the gracious favor of Almighty God."[50] This struck Father as the right note. He acquiesced and the phrase was included in the document.

As Pa signed the Proclamation, he commented; "If my name is ever remembered, it will be for this act. My whole soul is in it."[51] With those words we cannot forget that throughout the ordeal, leading up to the historic moment, Pa had consulted mediums. None, however, made quite the impact which issued forth from Nettie Colburn's gifts of the spirit. The evidence for her contribution is quite conclusive, and with it much of the president's "hesitation and doubt vanished."[52]

5
Liberation In Death

What Pa had ultimately experienced in my death, was to be verified in his own death. Some would look upon the year of the Emancipation as the beginning of the end, while Father was to look upon it simply as the beginning. "It is a well-known fact that the highest summit of life is expressed by the symbolism of death. For creation beyond oneself means one's own death. The coming generation is the end of the preceding one."[1] Pa's life and death gave validity to this declaration by a psychic a researcher.

During these final three years, as we have seen, there was a dire demand for council, beyond the confines of the physical. Pa's participation in séances was never to prove anything, but rather as captain of the ship of state, he sought direction. As these pages have attempted to show, personal survival and spirit communication with the departed were accepted by Pa as fact! For him, it followed that death on the earth plane was but the end of one phase of life eternal. "Death after all was a form of birth, releasing the soul or spirit from the womb of earthly life." Psychics speak of a spiritual umbilical cord that unites the spirit to the body.[2]

Personal survival became a personal experience. One scientist, a philosopher, has said; "The evidence I regard as scientifically proving survival . . . the evidence is so strong I do not hesitate to say that the proof is even equal or superior to that of evolution."[3]

Pa seemed always to have a speech ready in commemoration of George Washington's birth. His nearness to Washington, as previously mentioned, included the psychical. Pa spoke in the City of Brotherly Love, some years before his death, in celebration of Washington's Birthday. He said, "I would rather be assassinated than to surrender the principle that all men should have an equal chance."[4] Pa was made increasingly conscious of this declaration as the war dragged on. It haunted him, nagged him like a bee-sting that may have strangely prophesied his own end. Julia, the house girl, tells us that Ma laughed at Pa's premonitions. But Pa remained convinced. "His prescient soul saw it somewhere, somehow, sometime. . . ."[5] His premonitions, thereafter, took the form of precognitive dreams of his death. This is not to suggest an obsession. Yet the "suffering, misery, squalor and foulness which accompanied war" was ever with Pa.[6] The poet,

Longfellow, was born on this plane just two years before Father. He gave expression to a truth which held Pa steadfast:

Life is real! Life is earnest!
And the grave is not its goal;
Dust thou art to dust returnest,
Was not spoken of the soul.[7]

This was one of Lincoln's favorite verses.[7a]

The sting of death for many is the dread of death. This can be equally true for those who are left behind. Ma and Pa can testify to this. An experienced psychic suggests there would be a "general emancipation from the searing grip of the most fearsome of all dreads, if people would (as Pa did) accept the essential fact of survival."[8]

Pa's death was prophesied by himself and others many times. One commentator has said "his seer-like quality of soul swayed Lincoln toward the end, softening all that was hard in him, and hardening all that was soft.[9]

One week after Father's assassination, a United Press correspondent reported that at Ma's suggestion, Pa attended a séance at which he was seen "emerging in a pool of blood." The séance took place two days before the assassination.[10] Predictions of his sudden death were prevalent even before he became president. In a letter dated December 11, 1860 from Cleveland, Ohio, a young female clairvoyant saw "a conspiracy . . . to murder Pa."[11] This sort of mail did not perturb Pa. His "confidence in immortality grew stronger, though his mind, at times, "dwelt on death." Senator Sumner referred, you will recall, to Father's favorite passage from Shakespeare dealing with the death of Duncan.[12] Lamon reported that his continued warning to Pa once met with the response: "I long ago made up my mind that if anybody wants to kill me, he will do it. If I wore a shirt of mail and kept myself surrounded by guards, it would all be the same.[12a] This may have been a reflection of Pigeon Creek predestination.

On the very night before his assassination, we are told of Pa's dream presentiment. He had proceeded with some reluctance to Ford Theatre.

On the morning of that fatal day, General Grant had been at the cabinet meeting. Pa was overheard then to say "something serious is going to happen." Grant, for reasons best known to himself, declined Father's invitaton to attend the theatre.[13]

Between the inauguration in March and the assassination in April of 1865, Pa chatted frequently with Ma about his interpretation of the biblical emphasis on dreams. "If we believe the Bible, we must accept the fact that God and His angels come to men in their sleep and make themselves known in dreams." He would then mention the 28th Chapter of Genesis . . . "it relates the wonderful dream Jacob had," he would say. It was then Father confessed to a dream he had had ten days previously. Mother exclaimed: "That is horrid! I wish you had not told it." Pa saw his "corpse wrapped in funeral vestments . . . his face was covered . . . people were weeping pitifully." The casket was surrounded by a guard of honor in the East Room of the White House.[14]

Father, the seer, the prophetic psychic, was clearly clairvoyant and precisely precognitive during those weeks preceding Good Friday in 1865. Pa's bodyguard, Lamon, prided himself on knowing more about Pa's presentiments or premonitions than most people. What is recorded are somewhat amateurish first-hand impressions pertaining to Pa's precognitive side: "With the firm conviction which no philosophy could shake, Mr. Lincoln moved on through a maze of mighty events, calmly awaiting the inevitable hour of his fall by a murderous hand." Lamon, who was not too far from accepting Pa's philosophy himself, continued; "Long before Lincoln's admission to the bar or his entrance into politics, he believed he was destined to rise to a great height; that from a lofty station to which he would be called, he would be able to confer lasting benefits on his fellowmen. He believed also from a lofty station he would fall."[15] Much of this was Lamon, rather than Lincoln talking.[16]

One day the artist Carpenter assured Pa his efforts would be rewarded. Pa mused; "I may never live to see it. I feel a presentiment that I shall not outlast the rebellion. When it is over, my work is done."[17] Carpenter named others, including Harriet Beecher Stowe, to whom Pa made similar statements.[18]

Father Charles Chiniqiquy could not refrain from getting into the act. This dear soul, you will recall, was Pa's Catholic Priest friend from Springfield days who was ultimately to turn Protestant. He claimed Pa unburdened himself one day. Pa, may well have confided in his friend. He alleges Pa confessed; "Do you know that there is a still but solemn voice, which tells me that I . . . will cross the Jordan and dwell in the land of Paradise, where peace, industry, happiness and liberty will make everyone happy . . ."[19] but the words seem somehow more ministerial than Lincolnian.

My brother Robert recalled that Father had asked him to attend the theater the evening of the assassination. The fact that he had declined became something of an obsession for Robert. "He was sure he might have saved Pa, had he accepted."[20] Father understood Robert better than Robert did. In what proved to be his last session with Nettie Colburn, Pa was told that his spirit friends "reaffirm that the shadow they have spoken of, still hangs over you." Pa became impatient: "I have letters from all over the country from your kind of people — mediums, I mean — warning me against some dreadful plot against my life."[21] As Father bade farewell to Nettie and her girl companion that evening he expressed a desire to see them "next fall." They responsed, "we shall certainly come if you are here."[22]

When Pa bade farewell to his neighbors in Springfield at an earlier time he spoke these memorable words: "I now leave, not knowing when or whether *ever* I may return . . . trusting in Him who can go with me and remain with you, and be everywhere for good, let us confidently hope all will be well."[23]

Negro leader, Frederick Douglass had written, after attending Pa's second inauguration, "I felt there was murder in the air. I kept close to his carriage on the way to the Capitol. I felt I might see him fall that day. It was a vague presentiment."[24]

Although it was Good Friday Eve, Ma, probably for Pa's sake, wanted to see the play, *The American Cousin.* It was a comedy which Pa much preferred.

Pa had once explained his interest in the theater to a visiting Union Officer, saying: "My earbones ached to hear a good peal of honest laughter." And to a writer for *Putnam's Magazine* he said, "I sometimes go to amusements much against my inclinations . . . I laugh because I must not weep. . . ."[24a]

On that evening, however, he was not inclined to go at all, but Mother urged him on. "All right, Mary," he said, "I'll go, but if I don't go down in history as the martyred President, I'll miss my guess."[25]

Pa wanted to die for a worthy cause and when death came, he wanted it to be quick. With the approach of Good Friday, he told of being on his knees and reading the story of Gethsemene. "I am in the garden of Gethsemene now. My cup of bitterness is full and running over, now."[26] Pa did not take all his premonitions as inevitable. When Lamon was alarmed, Pa called it "downright foolishness"[27]

Gideon Wells recorded the scene in "the house across the street" on that Good Friday night. "His features were calm and striking. I had never seen them appear to greater advantage." In death, Father was taller than ever. They were obliged, because of his height, to lay him diagonally on a bed soon to become blood stained.[28] Another description of Ford Theatre after the fatal shot has been handed down to us from Park Service Historian, John Lissimore: "They maneuvered his long body into this cramped hallway. They took him up this aisle holding back the frenzied crowd, then down these side steps and across the street to the Peterson House."[28a] If Father appeared "calm and striking," and to "greater advantage" than ever, it could be described as the emancipation of the emancipator.

Among the cabinet members around the death bed in the small, crowded room, was Stanton, who remained slave to his own hate and fear of the enemy. Reconciliation held no place in his objectives. He became suspicious of Pa's plans. He was out to get "those terrible rebels, those cutthroats, who were creeping everywhere." His "phobia made him a wild thing." He became more and more incensed at the "Lincoln Policy of mercy toward the Southerners."[29] Some would implicate the intemperate Secretary of War in the Lincoln murder plot. His irrational acts following the assassination have made him more suspect, but the evidence appears circumstantial.

Hans Holzer, psychic researcher and author has said: "As I began my investigation, my own feelings were that an involvement of Stanton could be shown."[30] Biographer Barton, however, sees Stanton as an admirer of Father, even though he was a divisive element in the administration. At the last cabinet meeting on the morning of Good Friday, Barton quotes Stanton as saying, "he (Lincoln) manifested in marked degree the kindness and humanity of his disposition . . . the tender, forgiving spirit that so eminently distinguished him."[31] How much of this is Barton or Stanton is difficult to ascertain.

Pa had sought earlier to persuade Stanton that if the reconstruction of the South were to become a reality, then reconciliation was essential. If Father could forgive Stanton in life, as he did many times, certainly he could in death.

It was Edwin M. Stanton who once spoke of Pa as "the original gorilla." And for the disaster at Bull Run he blamed the "imbecility of the administration." At one point Stanton harbored the hope that "Jeff Davis might turn out the whole administration." At another he was all for "prolonging the war" to aid the abolitionists who wanted nothing less than "disfranchisement of the South." His "contempt" for Pa was no secret. Stanton has been described as "domineering, brusque, cruel and insolent." In his chapter on the 'Case against Stanton,' author Otto Eisenschmil made it clear that Stanton was "one man who profited greatly by Lincoln's death."[32] Speculation, however, as to Stanton's involvement in Pa's assassination continue to bring denials from some Lincoln students.[33]

"Half insane son of an insane father," John Wilkes Booth, was observed in suspicious operations during Pa's second inauguration. Many a premonition was verified when the police ejected him from the crowd. It had occurred last, just one month before the Ford Theatre shooting. Indeed Ma and Pa had attended Ford Theatre some ten days before Pa gave his Gettysburg speech. They had been accompanied by Nicolay and Hay to a play having the suggestive title *The Marble Heart.* The leading actor was John Wilkes Booth![34]

On the occasion of Father's last visit with his devoted stepmother she had a foreboding. She claimed "something told me that something would befall Abe, and that I would see him no more."[35] Brand Whitlock, a Lincoln biographer wrote of "the tragedy to which destiny plainly marked him."[36] Whether destiny or predestination, it was all the same to Pa. When his disbursing officer Col. William H. Crook, who had served at the White House for 50 years, begged Pa not to attend the theater, father retorted; "Go home and rest!"[37]

Pa and Ma had been for a carriage ride on the afternoon of the assassination. During the ride Pa confided, "We must both be more cheerful in the future. Between the war and the loss of our darling Willie, we have been very miserable."[38] The mention of my name, Willie, was too much for Ma.[39] As for Pa's cheerfulness, can we not conclude that it emanated in part from the sense of liberation? Was he not experiencing the larger life he had so often explored? For my mother, Pa's moments of bouyancy on this fateful day continued to be nothing more or less than a "portentous joy".[40] Dr. Miner, our Springfield pastor, tells us that my father had claimed this final day was "the happiest day in his life." He radiated a sense of renewalment.[41]

Sometime after the Ford Theatre tragedy, one of father's innumerable critics spoke his mind. "When J. Wilkes Booth performed his mission. It was all at once discovered that Abraham Lincoln was the greatest man the world had ever produced. . . .[42] While this bit of cynicism has an element of truth, it was directed not alone at the president, but at the ESP activities in the White House. A post-mortem admission by one of Pa's private secretaries, not friendly toward the psychic realm, conceded in a moderately toned letter addressed to my brother Robert, that Pa was probably "greater than even we imagined while he lived."[43]

A soliloquy, illumined by an imaginative insight, appears in the play, *The Haunted Biographer.* The author, Gamaliel Bradford, many years after Pa's death, has him saying to John Wilkes Booth; "The smoke of your pistol blew a halo round me, I confess, without that, only God knows how it would all have ended. If poor Woodrow Wilson had had someone to do for him what you did for me, he might have counted in history, as I do. That's why I want to do something for you, John."[44] Pa would have been far more impressed by this sort of eulogy than by much of the maudlin sentiment which attended the assassination.

One quizzical observer wrote: "There must have been a great many people with some supernatural force, some divine guidance that was behind Lincoln's rise."[45] Such an appraisal certainly contains more than an element of truth.

Some northern preachers promptly labeled Easter, 1865 as 'Black Easter.'[46] All due respect to the northern preachers, but Pa could not concur with their opinion.

Pa had made arrangements, or so it seems, to become a member of the New York Avenue Presbyterian Church of Washington D. C. on that Easter Sunday. His friend Dr. Gurley was to preside. Father had anticipated he would carry on in his new found freedom, so now, for the first time since coming to Washington, he wished to become a member of a traditional church[47] . . . a church so in need of his mystical-psychical approach to life. The British biographer Nathaniel Stephanson had occassion to write of my father; "Though little of a theologian, he appreciated intuitively some metaphysical ideas."[48]

Among numerous biographers there is agreement that in the "flitting thoughts" on Pa's mind, as he sat in the Presidential Box at Ford Theatre on that Good Friday evening 1865, was his hope that he might visit Palestine. John Wesley Hill has him exclaiming to Mother, "There is no place I wish to see more than Jerusalem." Mary heard him utter "Jeru-" when "the senseless bullet . . . sped surely to its mark." Later Pa's friend Pastor Miner, in a conversation with Mother remarked; "The man of God started for Jerusalem but it was *Jerusalem the Golden, the Home of the Elect.*"[49]

There is no death! Our stars go down
To rise on some fairer shore;
And ever near us, though unseen,
The Fair immortal spirits tread;
For all the boundless universe
Is LIFE; there are NO dead.
Lord Lytton 1863[50]

THE ASSASSINATION OF PRESIDENT LINCOLN

We know that the serious science of astronomy grew out of primitive astrology; that the modern marvels of chemistry developed from the alchemists of the Middle Ages; but we are reluctant to admit that such stuff as dreams and 'hunches' and 'intuitions' may be the precursors of a new psychology that goes far beyond anything yet apprehended by man.

Sidney Harris, Philosopher Author Journalist
Independent Press-Telegram, July 22, 1969

EPILOGUE

Over the years, time has proven a valid vindicator, if one is required, for Lincoln's psychical-mystical life. A distinguished company of men and women have stood up to be counted. Some of their names have appeared in this book.

Today Lincoln is surrounded by a great 'cloud of witnesses' who have experienced the reality of spirit communication. The illustrious in science and religion, men known for their statesmenship and churchmenship, have come to see personal spirit survival as basic to personal spirit communication.

Willie's account has indicated that the psychical is no respector of persons! His own paternal parent illustrated that psychic phenomena operates, more often than not, among the less distinguished members of society. "It does not necessarily impart to an 'occult' incident more weight because it was experienced or related or credited to a person whose name is prominent for one reason or another."[1] Irrespective of another's reputation, some people are so constituted they cannot see or hear beyond the confines of their own constitution. Lincoln might call them the strict constitutionalists. They gave him trouble in politics and in his psychic activity. They insist on more convincing evidence. The more evidence they obtain the more they demand. They are among those who refuse to accept what evidence there is because acceptance would mean *change;* and change involves self-surrender!

Willie quotes Sir Thomas Huxley to this effect: The failure to 'lose self' becomes a deterrent to psychical research. Often the absence of spontaneous psychic experience among the prominent or less prominent, can explain a disinclination to discover or admit the evidence. One who has studied a list of notable witnesses of psychic occurrences reports that, "with a single exception I cannot remember any person of prominence in professional psychic research who is generally regarded as scientific in his modes of approach, and who had admitted having had in his own person a spontaneous psychic experience."[2]

Several illustrious statesmen have, in their day, served to verify Lincoln's psychic life. Arthur James Balfour has been called "A Statesman Clairvoyant."[3] The title could apply to Lincoln! In 1894, Lord Balfour, a former British Premier of distinction, became president of the Psychical Research Society. In his presidential address he stated: "*Even if we cannot entertain any confident hope of discovering what laws these half-seen phenomena obey, at all events it will be some gain to have shown, not as a matter of conjecture or speculation, but as a matter of ascertained fact, that there are things in heaven and earth not hitherto dreamed of in our scientific philosophy.*"[4] Sir William Barrett, the British scientist, reminds us those were "... the words of a statesman, not of a dreamer or a fanatic. They express the opinion of a singularly acute and philosophic mind."[5]

Canada has produced another great statesman, William Lyon MacKenzie King. An article on his psychic life bears the title, *Statesmen's Otherside.* "As a result of years of careful personal inquiries he came to accept human survival as a demonstrable fact ... he never ceased to be critical in appraising the evidence. He did not act on Spiritualistic faith. . . ."[6] Another psychic-minded statesman was Air Chief Marshall, Lord Dowding. Like Lincoln, he was faced with the task of saving his country. The circumstances were vastly different but the goal was the same. Both men became confirmed practitioners of spirit communication based on personal survival. In the midst of America's most destructive and divisive conflict, Lincoln, unlike Lord Dowding in his day, could afford the luxury of boasting emphatically, even whimsically before his severest critics; "All the armies of Europe, Asia and Africa combined ... could not by force take a drink from the Ohio, or make a track on the Blue Ridge, in a trial of a thousand years."[6a]

Lord Dowding, the obstinate Scot, saw England about to crumble with the fall of France in World War II. He succeeded in securing "every plane and pilot" for the Battle of Britain.[7] Winston Churchill opposed his Chief Air Marshall. Finally the Premier promoted the Dowding plan. But he failed to promote the man who had the vision. Dowding died an 'unsung hero.'[8] Notwithstanding, every United States President since the Civil War has praised Lincoln for "the clarity of his vision." In a recent *New York Times* editorial, the columnist declared; "This is precisely the issue at the present time."[9]

A world churchman, mentioned by Willie in the course of relating his father's psychic life, is Rev. Henry Smith Leiper. This distinguished man testified to "his personal involvement with those who have passed beyond the visible world." He does not have the "least doubt about the validity of these experiences." He is quite ready to concede, "that as in every other field of human activity, there are fakirs to be encountered here and there."[10] A close friend of Reverend Leiper, another foremost world churchman, was Sherwood Eddy. These two men have been most active in the work of the Spiritual Frontiers Fellowship. Their lives serve to vindicate the effective role of the psychic when combined with the spiritual in the shaping of a new and better world. Such was the pragmatic, psychic aim of President Lincoln. He would be quick to warn that the Spiritual Frontiers Fellowship will be most fortunate if, over the years, it does not succumb to the evils of organized religion. Nothing could more effectively defeat its purpose and principles.

A great pragmatic philosopher and psychologist was William James of Harvard. His keen mind as applied to the psychical was difficult to match. Not too many years ago he wrote; "Hardly have the facts called 'psychic' begun to be scratched for scientific purposes. It is through following these facts, I am persuaded, that the greatest scientific conquest of the coming generation will be achieved."[11] In this same vein we hear again from one of the more shrewd commentators of our day, Sidney Harris: "*Our progress in science and technology has come because we have increasingly understood the forces of nature; but we have made little progress in serving the deeper needs of man because we have refused to understand the intricate and subtle workings of the mind and spirit.*"[12] It was the subtle workings of the mind and spirit that Lincoln understood and applied so well.

Those not much credited for their pragmatism or realism are the poets. Lincoln and his son Willie each displayed poetic gifts. The line between the poetical, the mystical and the psychical is often difficult to distinguish. This was true of Henry Wadsworth Longfellow, as noted by Willie. The British Poet Laureate, Lord Alfred Tennyson, bore testimony to the significance of the psychical as related to the spiritual. American poet, Robert Louis Stevenson, was another witness to the truth which Lincoln upheld. Some of the great among the 'men of letters' is French philosopher, Henri Bergson, and an Oxford Professor of Literature, Doctor L. P. Jacks. These men gave support to spirit communication based on spirit survival.[13] A classic in this field is, *The Survival of Personality After Bodily Death*, by Professor F. W. H. Meyers who, with Mr. Edward Gurney, was a Fellow of Trinity College, Cambridge, England. Along with Mr. Lincoln, each deserves a place on the psychic roll of honor. They are not men to be taken lightly. None were disposed to inflict his views upon the others. Most were willing to share, although some were secretive as to their psychic experiences. On August 8, 1938, the Prime Minister of Canada was apprehensive of his position as it pertained to the psychical in his life, as was Lincoln on occasions. MacKenzie King wrote to a friend; "For reasons which you will appreciate, it has seemed to me inadvisable to become too actively identified with psychical research work. What I really mean to say wa (sic) too actively identified in the public mind."[14] Many a public figure has awaited retirement before revealing the source of his strength. This tendency toward secrecy has slowed down the advance of psychical research and development. Meantime, the stature of many a person has been enhanced by some psychic experience, perhaps of spiritual healing, shared to the benefit of others. For this reason, among others, WILLIE SPEAKS OUT!

Our friend, the great psychic or sensitive Arthur Ford, has said, "The day of professional mediums is almost over. . . . The phenomena should be a means to an end. The end should be spiritual understanding and a way to serve our fellowmen in a better way."[15] He concludes we are living in a new age. "The mark of a new age is not that it has the answers, but that it is asking the questions."[16] Reverend Ford, who gave direction to the writing of this book, emphasises the psychical as a means "to spiritual understanding and a better way to serve our fellowmen." He strikes a responsive chord in Lincoln. Some of the searching questions to which Ford alludes have been thus phrased: "*Is man moving out a little beyond the limitations of his five senses? Is this development an extension of the five senses in its own direction of contact with environment toward what we would call supersensory levels? Is man beginning to experience a 'mutation in consciousness' and developing a 'sense of frequency' which could give him a more direct experience of his real environment?*"[17]

Then follows the observation: "Our neuroanatomists suggest that the brain of man has areas which may not as yet be in function, but that these areas are provided by nature for future stages of development."[18] Was not Abraham Lincoln among the vanguard of those pointing the way and providing direction to such thinking? Moreover, did not his life show that our present system of education from early childhood, instead of encouraging such questions, neglect them and thus nullify their validity? There are exceptions appearing at the college or seminary level. One Lincoln student cited two colleges.[19] Reverend Ford, who has addressed seminary students, made specific reference to "one of the finest examples" — a Jesuit College.[20] William James, the psychologist, once commented that "souls have gone out of fashion." During his day the distinguished professor of psychology and educator, William McDougall, supported the soul theory.[21] As this book has indicated, psychology was initially concerned with the study of the soul or the psyche. A recent *News Letter* from the Spiritual Frontiers Fellowship reports that its vice president is teaching a college course in 'psychic phenomena.[22] Lincoln would have agreed with the cynical comment, "we stop learning when we go to school." He might relate some of the current campus unrest to the lack of courses and teachers which challenge the imagination. George Eres, a science-fiction writer of some reputation has asked; "Why bother being alive? Why be born upon this earth if we must die? What are our chances of survival?" He answers his own questions by stating; "Once we make it to the moon, once we touch down on Mars . . . and to the other planets revolving around the stars . . . we become the 'thing' we have been always wanting to become and that is immortal!"[23] There is little creativity or invention in education without imagination. That was

Lincoln's experience.

In 1858 Horace Bushnell published a book which "anticipated psychical research." Lincoln was, in a measure, vindicated by this outstanding theologian and one of his contemporaries.[24] A Lincoln scholar, Paul Graebel, suggests that the "newest discovery in the field of Lincoln lore gives us cause to research into the religious attitudes of the man."[25] The increased research should reveal the psychic depth of his spiritual life. In this admittedly controversial documentary study, "we have moved from séances in darkened rooms to the light and quiet of the Library of The Society of Psychic Research."[26]

Lincoln was called most everything but a fanatic, if a fanatic is defined as "some person who is enthusiastic about something that you are not interested in!"[27] But to many people Lincoln was fanatic. The author of this quotation speaks of Lincoln's condition: "A great many churches are concerned only with keeping a roof over the head of God but the fanatics are trying to knock the roof off and find God everywhere."[28] If Lincoln's attitudes toward the church demand any vindication, it can be found in such a declaration.

The names of leading statesmen, scientists and clergymen have come to the defense of Lincoln's spiritual-psychic stance in this study. One such scientist concluded; "Although many eminent scientific men in the past and in the present generation . . . have testified to the importance and genuineness of this phenomena, *official science still stands aloof.*"[29] The psychical-spiritual path which Lincoln followed involved pain and patience. "Surely when the sublime truth becomes realized in the world (it is sure to come) — it is only a question of time among well-thinking and intelligent people — then will the millennium dawn."[30] This summation was submitted by Lincoln's friend and business leader, Colonel Kase, who attended the séance at which the Emancipation Proclamation was prophesied. A book which proclaims *Spiritual Breakthroughs for Our Times,* is a clear vindication of the spiritual-psychical life, such as that of Lincoln. "Under the breakthrough, the outlook of the entire field (the spiritual-psychical) was transformed. With surprising suddenness, impeccable names sprang into prominence, as if they had been there all along, waiting only to be recognized. . . ."[31]

The testimony for the defense, if a defense is required in the case of Lincoln, is strengthened as the years go by. The Herndons lose their hold on Lincoln. "It was the fault of Herndon that he had no soul, no mind, no eye for the really remarkable qualities of Mr. Lincoln."[32] Since 1963 the Russians have become more prominent in psychic research. Russian scientist Vasiliev has written; *"Should one or should not one accept telepathic phenomena as definitely true? One thing is obvious: they can no longer be ignored, they must be studied . . . it is necessary for people in the Soviet Union to know what has already been done and what is being done abroad and above all, we must conduct our researches in this matter.'*[33] This commentary would cause Lincoln to look up with contentment and confidence.

Back in his New Salem days, young Lincoln heard Dr. Peter Akers preach from a text in Zacharias 9:9,10. The discourse included these passages: "*If we interpret the prophecy of this book aright . . . there will come a decade about 1860 and 1870 . . . when slaveships like beasts of prey shall no longer prowl along the coasts of helpless Africa, a time when we shall no longer trade in the souls of men; but the whip, the manacle and unrequited toil shall be banished from our fair land.*" Then Dr. Akers added: "*Who can tell but that the man who shall lead us through this strife may be standing in our presence!*" When young Lincoln was asked to respond to the prophetic preacher, you may recall his comment, "it is wonderful that God had given such power to such men. I firmly believe his interpretation of the prophecy. . . . I was deeply impressed that somehow I should be strangely mixed up with these changes and revolutions he described."[34] Years later, by day and by night, Lincoln as president, was to become more, rather than less, prophetic. If it was an indication or a vindication of anything, it was the mystical-psychical nature of the man.

My notes taken at a recent lecture by Dr. Raynor Johnson, the celebrated British physicist, underscores two items. Dr. Johnson, who has turned his talents since retirement to the mystical-psychical, claims first; nothing happens by accident. Lincoln's preordained destiny would illustrate his point. Second, the soul on this planetary plane forever remains a prisoner of the ego. Throughout its earthly life the soul of Lincoln was finding release through his mystical-psychical nature.[34a]

The Publisher's Preface in the first edition is required reading for those who feel the Maynard account covering the Colburn séances is in need of vindication. This remarkable preface appears only in the first edition. The publisher disclaims any personal bias concerning the subject of spiritualism. He became "interested in the subject from a purely historical standpoint. . . ." He calls upon a wide range of witnesses to testify or verify as to the validity of the book and the author.[35] The publisher carries his case into the Appended Notes, and most of the testimonials are notarized. Much of this material comes from outside the Spiritualist camp. One letter is signed by "ten leading citizens." Another letter is signed by the head of Rogers Brothers internationally-known silver cutlery firm. One correspondent emphasizes over again that the child medium, Nettie Colburn, was quite unaware that the president was influenced by her 'control' as it pertained to the Emancipation Proclamation.[36] The Spiritualists continue to see the Maynard book simply as a vindication of their claims. One renowned Spiritualist answers his own question, "How many Americans realize that Lincoln was a convinced Spiritualist," by citing the case of Miss Colburn.[37]

As for the publisher of the Colburn account, he urges his readers to arrive at their own separate conclusions.[38]

In the preface, no mention is made by the publisher as to the loss of the original manuscript. The circumstances under which, after many years later, a second manuscript was made available, is also omitted. This is understandable. The publisher was not a spiritualist. He did not care to become involved in some rare aspects of psychic phenomena known as materialization. It would only serve to detract or discredit the essential facts, some of which were recalled through materialization. One is reminded of the TV broadcaster who introduces his 'mind reading' program with the words: "To those who believe, no explanation is necessary. To those who do not believe, no explanation is possible!" Dr. Raynor Johnson, has been mentioned in connection with the Maynard book and materialization. His conclusion was that "when we look at the names, the distinguished records, and the competence of the men who, after many years of the study of these things (materialization) testified to what their own senses had observed, we cannot, I think, do other than regard them as facts."[38]

Madison C. Peters, who defended Lincoln against the claims of the Spiritualist, wrote that "all his life Lincoln was a man who thought for himself. He would not allow the opinions of others to obtrude themselves on him; he investigated for himself. His intellectual honesty would not permit him to make pretense to faith or simulate what he did not feel."[39] Another biographer who would vindicate Lincoln against the charge that he was a Spiritualist concedes there is ample evidence that Lincoln "received and talked with Spiritualists," but nothing to connect him with their organization.[40]

One must not overlook the personal testimony of Lincoln's friend, Carl Schurz. The General had some profound psychic-mystic experiences. He writes there are "forces in and upon the human mind, the nature of which we cannot know. . . . The believer in Spiritualism may see in it striking proof of the truthfulness of his belief."[41] Vindication in the last analysis did not appeal to Lincoln. His position on all 'isms' has been made plain. Any further word would be repetitious. Such terms as extra-sensory perception would strike Lincoln as unnecessary. It simply constitutes an aspect of the mind and spirit, unused and undeveloped. What we now call extra-sensory becomes merely an extension of the sensory when it is exercised. Not vindication, but education could help if that part of the psyche is to be properly employed. From Carl Jung we learn "only that which is psychic has direct reality . . . the psyche is no exception to the general rule that the universe can be established only in so far as our psychic organism permits."[42] This interpretive study of Lincoln in depth tends to verify such conclusions.

There will be those who feel this book is not a vindication of Lincoln but rather a vindication of an interpretation. Certainly this interpretation of

Mr. Lincoln demands some criticism coupled with skepticism. Those who lend credence, if not substance, to Lincoln's participation in, and application of, the psychical as a vital phase of his spiritual and mystical life, are the very people who harassed Lincoln as a cultist or a victim of the occult. That was true of Hall and Herndon.

One can only draw his own conclusions as to the ultimate effect Lincoln's psychical-spiritual nature had upon the conduct of the war and the administration of his high office. That Lincoln accepted the concept of intercommunication between two worlds is, in this book, a foregone conclusion. The liberty or license taken in relating the recent strides in psychical research to Lincoln, in order to throw light on his spiritual-psychical life, would thus seem justified. Much of the advance in psychical research is still slow to be recognized in academic circles. Hence, the application to Lincoln may be disputed or doubted. The psychical as related to the spiritual, flourished during Lincoln's administration. The crises in the life of the president and in the nation were contributing factors. If this sounds like a vindication of psychical research, or the psychical as related to the spiritual in the life of Lincoln, it is both.

"Spirit messages" can also be a most controversial subject. Their inclusion in this book requires some explanation or justification. This applies to those "spirit messages" attributed to Lincoln since his death. They have been formidable and some of doubtful origin. Most of the "spirit messages" are found in private Lincoln collections or rare book sections. Presumably they have some historic and authentic value. They provide an insight into the Lincoln who lived and died and lived again. They are in accord with the concept of spirit communication based on personal survival, which was in the main stream of Lincoln's life,

One of the outstanding British scholars of current years is the translator of the New Testament from the Greek. In the course of his little book entitled *Ring of Truth*, Canon J. B. Phillips records a personal, out of this world, experience. It was clairvoyant. It came to him as a shock. He seeks to vindicate himself when he stated, "let me say at once I am incredulous by nature." He refers to the experience as "incontrovertible." The conclusion to his little commentary begins: "Prejudiced? Of course I am prejudiced!"[43] Lincoln, the lawyer, would hold that the burden of proof in any (psychic) case does not rest solely with the defendant. The plaintiff against the psychical must share in the responsibility of proof. Furthermore, one piece of incontrovertible psychic evidence can be sufficient proof. Lincoln might well have taken exception to the concept of proof as applied to the psychical.[44]

These same words could apply to the conclusions drawn in this study of Lincoln from another scholar, F. W. Meyers. Although not a translator of the Bible, he is a student of English and Greek literature. He made the statement: "I predict in consequence of the new evidence (psychical-mystical) all reasonable men a century hence will believe in the Resurrection of The Christ, whereas in default of the new evidence, no reasonable men, a century hence would have believed it."[45] This is both a prediction and a vindication to which Lincoln could give assent. In the lives of such men, the psychical had little or no place, except as it led to the spiritual. Although Lincoln avoided institutionalism of any kind, when it came to the spiritual, he was able to see that Spiritualism had served to keep alive the role of the psychical as an approach to the spiritual. In this context one can sympathize with the Spiritualists, who protest to the continued persecution to which they have been subjected.[46]

Much that has been controversial in this Lincoln account is fast becoming factual. A great psychic, for whom the spiritual is paramount, informs us that mediumship is fast becoming the common property of more people.[47] Lincoln became the medium, the channel, the instrument of spiritual guidance. Professional mediums sought Lincoln. Less and less did he seek them. Nor did he go in for messages from friends or relatives, or those who might simply foretell the future. At some private séances, he was aware that the incidental could prove fundamental. Professor Hyslop, a non-professional psychical researcher has written; "Trivial incidents are the best evidence of identity."[48] It was at the informal home circles where the 'pearl of great price' was discovered and preserved. Lincoln is hardly to blame for the very limited data descriptive of these precious moments.

As a culmination to this section on vindication, consider the interest that some of the biological-physiological scientists such as Edmund N. Sinnott are showing in the spiritual-psychical. "The biology of the human spirit will not be easy to investigate because experience rather than experiment is such an important part of it. For its development there may be required some tools that science does not now possess."[49]

In Lincoln tradition, a hometown poet Vachel Lindsey wrote *Abraham Walks at Midnight:*

> *It is portentous and a thing of state,*
> *That here at midnight in our little town*
> *A mourning figure walks and will not rest,*
> *Near the old courthouse, pacing up and down.*"[50]

* * *

The box at Ford's Theatre where Lincoln was assasinated
Washington D.C., April 1865.

The Peterson House, where Lincoln died.

BIBLIOGRAPHY

AUTHOR	TITLE	PUBLISHER	DATE
Abbott, William	Magazine of History, Extra 19	William Abbott New York, N. Y.	1912
Abbott, William	Magazine of History, Extra 85	William Abbott Tarrytown, New York	1922
Aikman, Lonnelle	"Ford Theatre Report in Memory of Lincoln"	National Geographic Vol. 137, No. 3 Washington, D. C.	3/1970
Aked, Dr. Charles F.	Lincoln and Gladstone	Lincoln Club Los Angeles, Calif.	1925
Allport, Paul	Abraham Lincoln	Harrison & Sons	
American-Japanese Society	Fourth Annual Contest	A. Lincoln Assn. Springfield, Ill.	3/1930
Angle & Miers	The Living Lincoln	Rutgers University Press New Brunswick, N. J.	1955
Angle, Paul	Abraham Lincoln	Rutgers University Press New Brunswick, N. J.	1947
Angle, Paul	The Lincoln Reader	Rutgers University Press New Brunswick, N. J.	1947
Angle & Sandburg	Mary Lincoln, Wife and Widow	Harcourt Brace New York, N. Y.	1932
Appleman, Roy E.	Lincoln's Own Words and Contemporary Account	U. S. Dept. of the Interior Park Service, Washington, D. C.	1942
Auder, O. F.	Lincoln Images (Part 1)	Augustine College Library Rock Island, Ill.	1960
Bach, Marcus	Inner Ecstasy	World Press Cleveland, O.	1969
Bach, Marcus	Foundation of Spiritual Understanding (Learning), Letter No. 20, p. 7	Palos Verdes Estates, Calif.	1969
Bach, Marcus	Spiritual Breakthrough For Our Time	Doubleday & Co. New York, N. Y.	1965
Baker, E. (Editor)	Lincolniana	Journal, Illinois State Historical Society, Vol. XLI	1948
Baringer, William	Philosophy of Lincoln	Falcon's Wing Press New York, N. Y.	1959
Barrett, J. H.	Life of Abraham Lincoln	Moore Wilstch Keys & Co., Cincinnati, O.	1960
Barrett, Sir William	On the Threshold of the Unseen	Kegan Paul Trubner & Co., London, Eng.	1920
Barton, William E.	A. Lincoln and Walt Whitman	Dobbs & Merrill & Co. London, Eng.	1928
Barton, William E.	The Life of Lincoln, Vols. I & II	Dobbs & Merrill & Co. London, Eng.	1925
Barton, William E.	The Soul of Lincoln	George H. Doran & Co. (formerly Doubleday Doran) New York, N. Y.	1920
Basler, Roy E. (Editor)	Collected Works of Lincoln, Vol. V	Rutgers University Press New Brunswick, N. J.	1953

AUTHOR	TITLE	PUBLISHER	DATE
Basler, Roy E. (Editor)	Collected Works of Lincoln, Vol. VII	Rutgers University Press New Brunswick, N. J.	1953
Basler, Roy E. (Editor)	Collected Works of Lincoln, (No Vol.)	Rutgers University Press New Brunswick, N. J.	1953
Bates, William	Religious Life of Lincoln	Little, Brown & Co. Boston, Mass.	1931
Baxter, Sir William	O. H. Browning, Lincoln's Friend and Critic	Indiana University Press Bloomington, Ind.	1957
Bayne, Julia T.	Tad Lincoln's Father	Little, Brown & Co. Boston, Mass.	1931
Bellman, Harold	Architects of the New Age	Sampson Log Marston London, Eng.	1923
Bennett, Charles A.	Philosophical Study of Mysticism	Yale University Press New Haven, Conn.	1923
Binns, H.	Abraham Lincoln	J. M. Dent & Co. London, Eng.	1907
Beard, Paul	Survival of Death	Hodder & Stoughton London, Eng.	1966
Bishop, Jim	The Day Lincoln Was Shot	Harper Bros. New York, N. Y.	1953
Bissett, C. P.	Lincoln, Universal Man	Howell & Co. New York, N. Y.	1923
Blackwell, H.	Abraham Lincoln and His Unseen Helpers (Reprint from Light Magazine)	Dugon, Ltd. London, Eng.	1910
Bradford, G.	The Haunted Biographer	University of Washington Press, Seattle, Wn.	1927
Brockett, L. P.	Life and Times of Lincoln	Bradley & Co. Philadelphia, Penn.	1865
Brooks, Noah	Abraham Lincoln	J. M. Dent & Co. London, Eng.	1907
Browne, Francis	Every Day Life of Lincoln	John Murray London, Eng.	1914
Butler, Nicholas M.	"Across the Years"	Scribner's New York, N. Y.	1940
Butler, Nicholas M.	"Lincoln & Son"	Saturday Evening Post Curtis Publishing Co. New York, N. Y.	2/11/39
Carnegie, Dale	Lincoln the Unkown	Appleton Century New York, N. Y.	1939
Carpenter, F. B.	Six Months in the White House (Inner Life of Lincoln)	Hurd & Houghton New York, N. Y.	1866 1877
Carrel, Alexis	Man The Unknown	Harper Bros. New York, N. Y.	1939
Chapman, Ervin	Religious Expression, Bishop Hamilton	Fleming Revell & Co. Westwood, N. J.	1967
Charnwood, Lord	Abraham Lincoln	Pocket Books, Inc. New York, N. Y.	1939

AUTHOR	TITLE	PUBLISHER	DATE
Chase, Warren	Forty Years on the Spiritual Rostrum	Colby Rich Publishing Co. Boston, Mass.	1888
Chesney, Dr. W. D.		Argos Magazine Popular Publishing Co. New York, N. Y.	2/1/1962
Chesney, Dr. W. D.	"Lincoln Still a Spiritualist"	Chimes Newpaper Encinada, Calif.	2/1957
Chesney, Dr. W. D.	Personal Letter Notations	Personal Letter	1959
Chicago Tribune (Ed.)	"Lincoln the Mystic"	Chicago Tribune Chicago, Ill.	2/7/1909
Christian Science Monitor (Editor)	"DisCerning"	Christian Science Monitor Boston, Mass.	11/25/1969
Christian Science Monitor (Editor)	"A Plea for Support"	Christian Science Monitor Boston, Mass.	11/5/1969
Churches Fellowship	Manual, Churches Fellowship for Psychical and Spiritual Studies	Churches Fellowship for Psychical and Spiritual Studies, London, Eng.	1968
Clark, Leon P.	A Psychoanalytical Biography of Lincoln		1933
Clerical Paper	Doors of Revelation	Psychic News London, Eng.	
Conant, A. J.	"Reminiscences of Abraham Lincoln"	McClure's Magazine McClure & Co. Chicago, Illinois Vol. 32, No. 5	1909
Constad	News Release	United Press New York, N. Y.	1863
Cook, Roy J.	One Hundred One Famous Poems	Cable Co. Chicago, Ill.	1929
Cornell, George W.	"Charismatic Spirit Seen Spreading"	Long Beach Independent, Press-Telegram Long Beach, Calif.	5/16/1970
Crenshaw, James	Telephone Between Two Worlds	DeVorss & Co. Los Angeles, Calif.	1950
Current, Richard N.	The Lincoln Nobody Knew	McGraw Hill Co. New York, N. Y.	1959
Current, Richard N.	Personal Letter	University of North Carolina Greensboro, N. C.	1968
Curtis, E.	The True Abraham Lincoln	Lippincott & Co. Philadelphia, Pa.	1902
D'Albe	Life of Sir Wm. Crooks	D. Appleton & Co. New York, New York	1926
Daley, John	Personal Letter	Philadelphia, Pa.	1968
Dannett, Sylvia	Noble Women of the North	Thomas Yoseleff London, Eng.	1959
Dart, John	"U. S. Spiritualism on New Course as Appeal Grows"	Los Angeles Times Los Angeles, Calif.	11/19/1969 (Front page)
de Chambrun, Adolphe	Impressions of Lincoln and the Civil War	Random House New York, N. Y.	1952

AUTHOR	TITLE	PUBLISHER	DATE
Donald, David	Lincoln Reconsidered	Alfred Knopf & Co. New York, N. Y.	1956
Donovan, F.	Mr. Lincoln's Proclamation	Dodd Meade & Co. New York, N. Y.	1904
Dooley, A.	Dialectical Materialism (Rhine)	Psychic News London, Eng.	
Dowding, Lord Air Chief Marshal	God's Magic	Spiritualist Asst. Great Britain	
Doyle, Arthur C.	History of Spiritualism	Cassel & Co. (now Funk & Wagnall Co.) New York, N. Y.	
Doyle, Arthur C.	Our American Adventure	George H. Doran & Co. (formerly Doubleday Doran) New York, N. Y.	1923
Drinkwater, J.	Lincoln, World Emancipator	Houghton Mifflin Co. New York, N. Y.	1920
Eccles, Sir John C.	One Hundred Most Important People	Esquire Magazine Vol. LXXIII (whole no. 437) New York, N. Y.	4/1970
Eddy, Sherwood	You Will Survive Death	Omega Press Reigate Surrey, Eng.	1954
Eisenschmil, Otto	Why Was Lincoln Murdered?	Little, Brown & Co. Boston, Mass.	1937
Eres, George	"Put On or Real?"	Long Beach Independent Press-Telegram Long Beach, Calif.	7/17/1969
Evans, Louis H.	This Is America's Hour	Fleming Revell & Co. Westwood, N. J.	1957
Evans, W. A.	Mrs. Lincoln, Study of Personality	Alfred Knopf & Co. New York, N. Y.	1932
Fitzgerrell, J. J.	Lincoln was a Spiritualist	Austin Publishing Co. Los Angeles, Calif.	1924
Fodor, Nandor	Between Two Worlds	Parker Publishing Co. New York, N. Y.	1964
Fodor, Nandor	Encyclopedia of Psychic Science	Arthur's Press London, Eng.	
Ford, Arthur	Unknown But Known	Harper Brothers New York, N. Y.	1968
Fornell, Earl	Unhappy Medium	Texas University Press Austin, Tex.	1964
Fox, George	Lincoln's Religion	Exposition Press New York, N. Y.	1959
Franklin, John H.	Emancipation Proclamation	Doubleday & Co. New York, N. Y.	1963
Franklin, John H.	From Slavery to Freedom	Life Magazine Chicago, Ill.	11/22/1968
Franklin, John H.	From Slavery to Freedom	Alfred A. Knopf & Co. New York, N. Y.	

AUTHOR	TITLE	PUBLISHER	DATE
Garrett, Eileen	My Life as a Search for Meaning of Mediumship	Ridder & Co. London, Eng.	1939
Graebner, Norman	The Enduring Lincoln	Sesquicentennial Commission	2/12/1959
Greenbie, M. S.	Anna Ella Carroll and Lincoln	University of Tampa Press Tampa, Fla.	1952
Grierson, Francis	Lincoln, Practical Mystic	John Lane Co. New York, N. Y.	1918
Gross, Anthony	Lincoln's Own Stories	Garden City Publishing Co. Garden City, N. Y.	1926
Hall, Dr. Fayette	Civil War Unveiled	Fayette Hall New Haven, Conn.	1902
Hanaford, P.	(Quotation Excerpts)	B. B. Russell & Co. New York, N. Y.	1865
Hapgood, Norman	The Man of The People	McMillan & Co. London, Eng.	1899
Hardinge, Emma	Report on Spiritualism	Longmans Green Reader & Dyer London, Eng.	1871
Harnsberger, C.	The Lincoln Treasury	Wilcox & Pollett Chicago, Ill.	
Harold, Preston	Shining Stranger (Quotation by Marcus Bach)	S.F.F. News Letter	5/1/1970
Harris, Paul	Personal Letters	Los Angeles, Calif.	6/1/1863 2/3/1864 5/19/1868
Harris, Sydney	"ESP, Poker, Anyone?"	Long Beach Independent, Press-Telegram Long Beach, Calif.	10/2/1969
Harris, Sydney	"Which Lincoln Do You Want To Hear?"	Long Beach Independent, Press-Telegram Long Beach, Calif.	3/21/1969
Hart, F.	"Lincoln, The Great Commoner"	Pasadena Star-News Pasadena, Calif.	1927
Hartranft, Rufus	Last Will and Testament	Philadelphia, Pa.	1897
Haven, Gilbert	Heavenly Messenger of Immortality	S. M. Baldwin Washington, D. C.	1890
Hay, L.	Lincoln Association Papers	(Long Beach, Calif. Library)	
Helm, K.	Mary, Wife of Lincoln	Harper Bros. New York, N. Y.	1928
Herndon and Weik	Life of Lincoln	Albert & Chas. Boni New York, N. Y.	1930
Herndon, William	Lincoln History and Personal Recollections	Herndon's Publishing Co. Springfield, Ill.	
Hertz, Emanuel	The Hidden Lincoln	Blue Ribbon Books Garden City, N. Y.	1938
Hertz, Emanuel	Lincoln Table Talk	Viking Press New York, N. Y.	1939
Hertz, Emanuel	Lincoln Talks	Halcyon House New York, N. Y.	1941

AUTHOR	TITLE	PUBLISHER	DATE
Higgins, J. Pearce	"Survival After Death"	Psychic News London, Eng.	6/19/1965
Higgins, Paul	John Wesley, Spiritual Witness	Dennison & Co. Framingham, Mass.	1960
Hill, Wesley	Lincoln, Man of God	G. P. Putnam & Son New York, N. Y.	1922
Hollis, Chris.	The American Heresy	Minton Balch & Co. New York, N. Y.	1930
Holzer, Hans	Window of the Past	Doubleday & Co. New York, N. Y.	1969
Horner, Harlan	Growth of Lincoln's Faith	Abingdon Press Nashville, Tenn.	1939
Houser, M. L.	Lincoln Group Papers, Second Series	J. Henri Ripstra Chicago, Ill.	1945
Hubbard, E. W.	Little Justin	E. W. Hubbard Descanso, Calif.	1909
Hurkos, Peter	News Letter	Hurkos Associates Foundation Waukesha, Wisc.	1961
Hyslop, James	Contact with the Other World	The Century Co. New York, N. Y.	1919
Ingersoll, Robert	Works of Robert Ingersoll, Vol. I	Ingersoll League New York, N. Y.	1900
James, William	Psychical Research (Ed. Murphy Ballou)	Chatts & Windus London, Eng.	
James, William	Varieties of Religious Experience	Longmans Green & Co. New York, N. Y.	1902
Johnson, Allen (Editor)	Dictionary of American Biography	Chas. Scribner New York, N. Y.	1928
Johnson, George L.	Does Man Survive	Harper Bros. New York, N. Y.	1936
Johnson, Raynor C.	Mysticism	Two Worlds London, Eng.	10/17/1959
Johnson, Raynor C.	Psychical Research	English University Press (Hazell Watson & Viney) Aylesbury, Eng.	1955
Johnson, Dr. Raynor C.	The Spiritual Path	Journal of the Research and Enlightenment Assn., Inc. Vol. IV, No. 3 (reprint) Virginia Beach, Va.	1969
Johnson, Dr. Raynor C.	Watcher on the Hills	Hodder & Stoughton London, Eng.	1959
Jones, DeWitt	Lincoln and the Preachers	Harper Bros. New York, N. Y.	1948
Jones, Judy	"Lincoln Canes Gift 1863"	San Diego News San Diego, Calif.	8/11/1969
Jones, Dr. Ernest	Life and Work of Sigmund Freud, Vol. 3	Basic Books New York, N. Y.	1957

AUTHOR	TITLE	PUBLISHER	DATE
Jordan, Fred	Personal Letter	International General Assembly of Spiritualists Milwaukee, Wis.	
Jung, Carl	Psychological Reflections	Pantheon Books New York, N. Y.	1953
Jung, Carl	"Seances"	Two Worlds Magazine London, Eng.	10/17/1959
Karagulla, Shafica, M. D.	Breakthrough to Creativity	DeVorss & Co. Los Angeles, Calif.	1967
Kase, Col. Simon	Emancipation Proclamation	International Press New York, N. Y.	1861
Kase, Col. Simon	"New Light on Lincoln Seance End of Slavery"	Two Worlds Magazine London, Eng.	9/19/1959 10/2/1959
Keckley, Elizabeth	Behind the Scenes	Carleton & Co. New York, N. Y.	1868
Kelsey, Rev. Morton	Tongue Speaking	Doubleday & Co. New York, N. Y.	1968
Kempf, Ed. J., M.D.	Lincoln Emotional Neurosis Organic	American Medical Assn. (Archives of Neurology) Chicago, Ill.	4/1952
Kempf, Ed. J., M.D.	Philosophy of Common Sense	New York Academy of Science New York, N. Y.	
Kennedy and Lincoln	Comparable Study of Their Lives	Private Printing	1969
Kerner, Fred.	Treasury of Lincoln Quotations	Doubleday & Co. Garden City, N. Y.	1965
Knight, G. Wilson	Byron and Spiritualism	Light Magazine, Summer Issue, College of Psychical Science London, Eng.	1966
Kranz, Henry B.	Abraham Lincoln, New Portrait		
Krueger, Lillian	Mary Todd Lincoln, Two Summers In Wisconsin	Journal of the Illinois State Historical Society, Vol. XXXIV, No. 2	1941 (June)
Kuznetsov, Anatoly	"Kremlin Cosmonaught"	Christian Science Monitor Boston, Mass.	8/9/1969
Lamon, Ward B.	Recollections	A. C. McClure & Co. Chicago, Ill.	1895
Lamon, Ward B.	Life of Lincoln	Osgood & Co. Boston, Mass.	1872
Laney, James T.	Death and Ethical Reflections	Yale Divinity School New Haven, Conn.	3/1969
Lang, Jack	The Wit and Wisdom of Abraham Lincoln	Greenberg Publishing Co. H. Wolff, Printer New York, N. Y.	1941
Lang, Jack	Lincoln Fireside Chat	World Publishing Co. Cleveland, O.	

AUTHOR	TITLE	PUBLISHER	DATE
Lapsley, Arthur	Replay to Commission from Religious Denomination Asking Lincoln To Issue the Emancipation Proclamation Sept. 13, 1862	Knickerbocker Press G. P. Putnam Sons New York, N. Y.	1923
Leiper, Henry S.	Personal Letter	Chautauqua Conference Chautauqua Lake, N. Y.	1968
Lemmon, George	"Feminine Element in Lincoln"	The Delineator Magazine Butterick Publishing Co. New York, N. Y.	3/1909
Lester, Reginald	Church and Survival	Psychic News London, Eng.	
Lester, Sen. James	107th Anniversary	Lincoln Centennial State Armory Springfield, Ill.	2/12/1916
Lewis, Lloyd	Myths After Lincoln	Grosset and Dunlap New York, N. Y.	1929
Lewis, Montgomery	Legends that Libel Lincoln	Rinehart & Co. (now Holt Rinehart & Winston) New York, N. Y.	1946
Life Magazine Editor	Commentary	Life Magazine Chicago, Ill.	1/24/1969
Life Magazine Editor	"The Quest for Spiritual Survival"	Life Magazine Chicago, Ill.	1/9/1970 Vol. 68, No. 1
Lincoln, A.	Great Moments with Lincoln	Walt Disney Productions Anaheim, Calif.	
Lincoln, A.	Quotations from Lincoln Lincoln Encyclopedia		
Lincoln, A.	Lincoln Words and Wisdom	Lincoln Savings & Loan Assn. Sherman Oaks, Calif.	
Lincoln, A.	Quotes from Lincoln	Black Cat Press Chicago, Ill.	
Lincoln, David	Personal Letter	Jamestown, N. Y.	1968
Lincoln, Mary	Personal Letter to Mrs. Orne	Franklin Marshall College Library Lancaster, Pa.	11/20/1969
Lincoln — Unknown Author	Essay On Lincoln	Unknown	

LINCOLN LORE BULLETINS

Editor R. Gerald McMurty	Baker Spirit Message	Lincoln Life Foundation Fort Wayne, Ind.	11/1962
Editor Louis Warren	Burnt Book Myth	Lincoln Life Foundation Fort Wayne, Ind.	9/27/1954
Editor Louis Warren	Herndon As Contemporary	Lincoln Life Foundation Fort Wayne, Ind.	10/13/1941
Editor Louis Warren	Hidden Herndon	Lincoln Life Foundation Fort Wayne, Ind.	3/7/1938

AUTHOR	TITLE	PUBLISHER	DATE
Editor R. Gerald McMurty	Lincoln at Seances, Part I	Lincoln Life Foundation Fort Wayne, Ind.	1/1963
Editor R. Gerald McMurty	Lincoln at Seances, Part II	Lincoln Life Foundation Fort Wayne, Ind.	2/1963
Editor R. Gerald McMurty	Lincoln Cartoons	Lincoln Life Foundation Fort Wayne, Ind.	6/1969
Editor R. Gerald McMurty	Most Significant Lincoln Cartoons—Feb. 1969	Lincoln Life Foundation Fort Wayne, Ind.	6/1969
Editor Louis Warren	Lincoln and Spiritualism	Lincoln Life Foundation Fort Wayne, Ind.	4/1946
Editor Louis Warren	Lincoln Papers, Library of Congress	Lincoln Life Foundation Fort Wayne, Ind.	8/11/1947
Editor Louis Warren	Lincoln Papers, Supplemental	Lincoln Life Foundation Fort Wayne, Ind.	8/25/1947
Editor R. Gerald McMurty	Lincoln's Attendance at Seances, Part I	Lincoln Life Foundation Fort Wayne, Ind.	1/1963
Editor R. Gerald McMurty	Lincoln's Attendance at Seances, Part II	Lincoln Life Foundation Fort Wayne, Ind.	2/1963
Editor R. Gerald McMurty	Painting of the Proclamation	Lincoln Life Foundation Fort Wayne, Ind.	3/1969
Editor R. Gerald McMurty	Personal Letter	Lincoln Life Foundation Fort Wayne, Ind.	7/10/1967
Editor R. Gerald McMurty	The Presidents Eulogize Lincoln	Lincoln Life Foundation Fort Wayne, Ind.	11/1965
Lindbergh, Charles	Letter in Life Magazine	Life Magazine Chicago, Ill.	9/27/1969 pp. 60a-c
Lindsey, Elizabeth	Lincoln Centennial Review	Chicago Tribune Chicago, Ill.	1909
Lindstrom, Ralph	Lincoln Finds God	Longmans Green Co. New York, N. Y.	1958
Lodge, Sir Oliver	Phantom Walls	Hodder & Stoughton London, Eng.	1929
Logan, John	The Great Conspiracy	A. R. Hart & Co. New York, N. Y.	1886
Lorant, Stefan	Lincoln, Ten Guidelines	Private Printing	
Lorant, Stefan	Lincoln Picture Story of Life	Harper Bros. New York, N. Y.	1957
Lorant, Stefan	Preview, Secret Lincoln Papers	Look Magazine Des Moines, Ia.	7/22/1947 pp. 86-9
Lorant, Stefan	Two New Lincoln Finds	Look Magazine Des Moines, Ia.	10/21/1969 Vol. 33, No. 21
Lorant, Stefan	Where Are the Lincoln Papers?	Life Magazine Chicago, Ill.	8/25/1947
Long Beach Independent, Press-Telegram Editor	"Letter Auctioned"	Long Beach Independent Press-Telegram Long Beach, Calif.	11/9/1969
Luthin, R. H.	The Real Abraham Lincoln	Prentice-Hall Englewood Cliffs, N. J.	

AUTHOR	TITLE	PUBLISHER	DATE
Lyne, Cassie	A Quaker Document		
Lytton, Lord	Poem	The Witness Rev. Geo. Daisley Santa Barbara, Calif.	1863
Martin, Dr. A. B.	Abraham Lincoln, Spiritualist	National Spiritualist Magazine Milwaukee, Wisc.	2/1/1927
Masters, Edgar	Lincoln, The Man	Dodd, Meade & Co. New York, N. Y.	1931
Maynard, Mrs. Nettie	Was Lincoln a Spiritualist?	R. C. Hartranft Philadelphia, Pa.	1891
McArthur, Charles	Message (Medium) Lincoln	McArthur, Bergen St. Brooklyn, N. Y.	10/15/1910
McCabe, Joseph	Spiritualists' Comments	Dodd Meade & Co. New York, N. Y.	1920
McElroy	Soul Growth of Lincoln		1943
McMurty, R. Gerald	Ben Hardin Helm, Rebel Brother-in-Law of Lincoln	Dept. of Lincolniana Lincoln Memorial University Harrogate, Tenn. (Civil War Round Table, Chicago Printers)	
McMurty, R. Gerald	What Spiritualism Is and Does	National Spiritualist Churches Milwaukee, Wisc.	
McMurty, R. Gerald	Why You Should Investigate Spiritualism	NATIONAL Spiritualist Churches Milwaukee, Wisc.	
Mearns, David	The Lincoln Papers	Doubleday & Co. New York, N. Y.	1948
Meyers, Fred. W. H.	Human Personality and Its Survival of Bodily Death	Longmans Green & Co. New York, N. Y.	1907
Miers, Carl	Lincoln Day by Day	Lincoln Centennial Washington, D. C.	1960
Mitgang, Herbert	Lincoln as They Saw Him	Collier Books New York, N. Y.	
Miller, Francis I.	Portrait, Life of Lincoln	Portrait Publishing Co. Chicago, Ill.	1910
Monaghan, Jay	Diplomat in Carpet Slippers	Bobbs Merrill & Co. Indianapolis, Ind.	1945
Monaghan, Jay	Was Lincoln Really a Spiritualist?	Journal of the Illinois State Historical Society Springfield, Ill.	6/1941 Vol. 32 No. 2
Montgelbar, Albrecht	Abraham Lincoln	Dreiturme Hamburg, Germany	1949
Morris, E. Joy (Editor)	Speech, House of Representatives	Congressional Record Washington, D. C.	2/12/1956
Moser, Margaret	Personal Letter	Cleveland Public Library Cleveland, O.	10/17/1966

AUTHOR	TITLE	PUBLISHER	DATE
Mugridge, Donald R.	Personal Letter	Library of Congress Washington, D. C.	2/24/1961
Muldoon, Sylvan	Sensational Experiences, Vol. I	New Horizon Publishi,o. Darlington, Wisc.	1941
Mumler, William	Psychic Photography	Two Worlds London, Eng.	9/26/1959
Nathan, Adele G.	Lincoln's America	Grosset & Dunlap New York, N. Y.	1961
Newkirk, Garrett	Lincoln Lessons for Today	Duffield & Co. New York, N. Y.	1921
Newman, Ralph	Libraries Out To Be Fun	Christian Science Monitor Boston, Mass.	1967
Newman, Ralph	Lincoln for The Ages	Pyramid Books Doubleday Co. New York, N. Y.	1960
Newman, Ralph	Personal Letter	Lincoln Book Shop Chicago, Ill.	2/12/1968
Newton, Dr. Joseph	Lincoln and Herndon	Torch Press Cedar Rapids, Ia.	1910
Newton, Dr. Joseph	Spiritual Life of Lincoln	Lincoln's papers Springfield, Ill.	1933
Nicolay, John	Lincoln's Secretary	Longmans Green & Co. New York, N. Y.	1949
Nicolay, Helen	Personal Traits of Lincoln	Century Co. Chicago, Ill.	1912
Niggs, Walter	The Heretics		
Oberholtzer, Ellis P.	Emancipation	George Jacob Co. Philadelphia, Pa.	1904
Oldroyd, Osborn H.	Words of Abraham Lincoln	Oldroyd Washington, D. C.	1895
Packard, R. D.	Riddle of Lincoln's Religion	G. F. Putnam Co. New York, N. Y.	1916
Pardue, Rev. Austin	Parapsychology		
Peale, Dr. Norman V.	Is Peace of Mind Possible Today?	Foundation for Xtn Living	1966 Vol. 18, No. 1
Pennell, Orrin	Religious Views of Lincoln	R. M. Scranton Printing Co. Alliance, O.	1909
Peters, Madison	Lincoln's Religion	Gorham Press, Boston, Mass.	1909
Peterson, William	Lincoln and Douglas	Chas. Thomas Publishing Co., Springfield, Ill.	1943
Phillips, Isaac	Lincoln	A. C. McClure Co. Chicago, Ill.	1910
Phillips, J. B.	Ring of Truth	MacMillan Co. New York, N. Y.	1967
Pike, James	If This Be Heresy	Harper Bros. New York, N. Y.	1967
Pike, James	The Other Side	A. Dell Books New York, N. Y.	1969

AUTHOR	TITLE	PUBLISHER	DATE
Pole, J. R.	Clarendon Biography of Lincoln	University Press New Hyde Park, N. Y.	1964
Prince, Walter	Noted Witnesses of Psychic Occurrences	University Books, Inc. Boston, Mass.	1963
Quinn, D.	Interior Causes of War		
Radio Editor	"Astronomers"	Christian Science Monitor Boston, Mass.	7/12/1969
Randall, J. C.	The Liberal Statesman	Dodd Meade & Co. New York, N. Y.	1947
Randall, J. C.	Lincoln, The President	Dodd Meade & Co. New York, N. Y.	1953
Randall & Current	Mr. Lincoln	Dodd Meade & Co. New York, N. Y.	1957
Randall, Ruth	Lincoln's Sons	Little Brown & Co. Boston, Mass.	1955
Randall, Ruth	Mary Lincoln, Biography of a Marriage	Little Brown & Co. Boston, Mass.	1953
Rankin, Henry B.	Personal Recollections of Lincoln	G. P. Putman & Co. New York, N. Y.	1916
Reader's Digest	"Lincoln Lives in Anecdotes"	Reader's Digest Pleasantville, N. Y.	2/1959
Reeve, Bryant & Helen	Flying Saucers Pilgrimage	Amherst Press Amherst, Wisc.	1967
Reston, James	Lincoln and Johnson	Long Beach Independent, Press-Telegram Long Beach, Calif.	2/14/1968
Rice, Allen	Reminiscences of A. Lincoln	North American Review New York, N. Y.	1888
Richardson, Robert D.	Lincoln Autobiography	Beacon Press Boston, Mass.	1948
Richmond, Thomas	Spirit Message	Religious Philosophy Publishing Co., Chicago, Ill.	1870
Ridder, H. H.	"Poem to Mother"	Long Beach Independent, Press-Telegram Long Beach, Calif.	9/19/1969
Righter, Carroll	Astrological Guide	Bantam Books G. P. Putnam New York, N. Y.	1967
Rodney, Les	"Apollo Scientific Moon Flight"	Long Beach Independent, Press-Telegram Long Beach, Calif.	1/15/1970
Roll, W. G. (Editor)	Theta Magazine	Psychical Research Foun. Durham N. C.	No. 20 Winter/63
Russell, Beatrice K.	The Lincoln Way	Lincoln Research Foundation	
Sandburg, Carl	Lincoln Devotional	Channel Press, Inc. New York, N. Y.	1957
Sandburg, Carl	Mary Lincoln, Wife and Widow	Harcourt Brace & Co. New York, N. Y.	1932

AUTHOR	TITLE	PUBLISHER	DATE
Sandburg, Carl	The Prairie Years, Vols. I & II	Harcourt Brace & Co. New York, N. Y.	1926
Sandburg, Carl	The War Years, Vol. II	Harcourt Brace & Co. New York, N. Y.	1926
Sandburg, Carl	The War Years, Vol. III	Harcourt Brace & Co. New York, N. Y.	1926
Sandburg, Carl	Living Words of Lincoln	Hall Mark Co. Kansas City, Mo.	1967
Sanderlin, Walter	Image of Lincoln	Doubleday & Co. New York, N. Y.	1962
Schauffler, R. H.	Lincoln's Birthday	Dodd Mead & Co. New York, N. Y.	1924
Schurz, Carl	Abraham Lincoln	Chautauqua Press Chautauqua, N. Y.	1924
Schurz, Carl	The Reminiscences	McClure Co. New York, N. Y.	
Scott, Walter (Editor)	"Personal Parade" Sunday Section	Long Beach Independent, Press-Telegram Long Beach, Calif.	
Schwartz, Harold	Lincoln and the Marfan Syndrome	Journal of the American Medical Assn. Chicago, Ill.	2/15/1964
Segal, Charles M.	Conversations with Lincoln	G. P. Putnam & Sons New York, N. Y.	1909
Sharp, Alfred	Conversations with Lincoln	Epworth Press London, Eng.	1919
Sharp, Mary (Editor)	Florissant Valley Community Course in Psychic Phenomena	Spiritual Frontiers Fellowship Evanston, Ill.	2/1970 Vol. 4, No. 2
Shelton, Harriet	Abraham Lincoln Returns	Evans Publishing Co. New York, N. Y.	1957
Shelton, Harriet	Personal Letter	Alrar Hotel New York, N. Y.	3/12/1960
Sherman, Harold	How To Make ESP Work	Faucett Publishing Co. Greenwich, Conn.	1964
Shirley, Ralph	A Short Life of Lincoln	Wm. Rider & Son London, Eng.	1920
Shook, Chester	The Lincoln Story	Krebble & Co. Cincinnati, O.	1950
Shutes, Milton (M.D.)	Lincoln's Emotional Life	Dorrance & Co. Philadelphia, Pa.	1957
Sinclair, Upton	Mental Radio	Chas. Thomas Springfield, Ill.	1930
Sinnott, Edward W.	The Biology of the Spirit	Viking Press New York, N. Y.	1935
Smith, A. J.	Spiritualism Creed		
Smith, T. V.	Lincoln and Spiritual Life	Beacon Press Boston, Mass.	1931

AUTHOR	TITLE	PUBLISHER	DATE
Snider, Denton J.	Abraham Lincoln, An Interpretation	Sigma Publishing Co. St. Louis, Mo.	1908
Snell, Tee L.	(Map) The City as Lincoln Knew It. A Stranger's Guide to Washington, D. C.	U. S. Department of the Interior, Washington, D. C.	1967
Snell, Tee L.	Explanation of the Map Guide	U. S. Department of the Interior, Washington, D. C.	1967
Spiritual Frontiers Fellowship	Manual, Principles and Purposes of the Spiritual Frontiers Fellowship	Spiritual Frontiers Fellowship Evanston, Ill.	1967
Stanford, Neal	Lincoln Letter	Christian Science Monitor	
Starr, J. W., Jr.	Lincoln's Dual Personality	Boston, Mass., Boston Library (Privately printed) Boston, Mass.	1928
Stearn and Fried	The Essential Lincoln	Collier Books, Inc. New York, N. Y.	1962
Stephenson, Nathaniel	Lincoln	Hutchinson & Co. London, Eng.	1924
Stern, Philip V.	Life of Lincoln	Random House New York, N. Y.	1940
Stobart, St. Clair	Torchbearer of Spiritualism	Allen & Unwin, London, Eng.	
Stoddard, William	Lincoln's Third Secretary	Barnes Book Co. Cranbury, N. J.	1955
Stoddard, William	The Table of Lincoln	Collier Books, Inc. New York, N. Y.	1962
Stone, Irving	Love Is Eternal	Doubleday & Co. New York, N. Y.	1954
Stowe, Harriet B.	Men of Our Time	Hartford Publishing Co. Hartford, Conn.	1869
Strout, Richard	"Seeing History and Participating In It."	Christian Science Monitor Boston, Mass.	2/16/1968
Sweeney, Louise	Ford's Theatre and Lincoln	Christian Science Monitor	2/2/1968
Taggart, Raymond	Faith of A. Lincoln	Service Print Shop Topeka, Kansas	1943
Talbot, Hugh	Meet The President	S. C. M. Press London, Eng.	
Tarbell, Ida W.	He Knew Lincoln	Doubleday & Co. New York, N. Y.	1907
Terrell, J'Nevelyn	Shelton Book Review	Mental Book Shop Hollywood, Calif.	
Thomas, B. P.	Abraham Lincoln	Alfred Knopf New York, N. Y.	1952
Thomas, B. P.	Portrait of Posterity	Rutgers University Press New Brunswick, N. J.	1947
Thompson, D. A.	Lincoln First American	Curtis & Jennings New York, N. Y.	1894

AUTHOR	TITLE	PUBLISHER	DATE
Tweedale, C. L.	Man's Survival After Death	Grant Richards, Ltd. London, Eng.	1909
United Nations	We Can Be Delegates Through Thought	M.G.N.A. Greenwich, Conn.	
Van Dellen	"Mental Disorders"	Cincinnati Enquirer Cincinnati, O.	5/16/1969
Walsh, Wm. J.	Lincoln and London Punch	Moffat, Yard & Co. London, Eng.	1909
Ward, D. D.	Tributes from Associates	Crowell & Co. New York, N. Y.	1895
Warren, Louis A.	Herndon's Contribution to Mythology	Indiana Magazine of History	9/1945 XLI pp. 221-4
Weatherhead, Leslie	Christian Agnostic	Hodder & Stoughton London, Eng.	1965
Webster	American College Dictionary	Random House New York, N. Y.	1960
Wiegers, Mary	"Expert Satisfied with Lincoln Works"	San Jose Mercury San Jose, Calif.	1/25/1970
Weiss, Margaret R.	"The Man Who Knows Lincoln"	Saturday Review of Literature New York, N. Y.	2/14/1970
Wham, Joseph	The Other Side of Lincoln	Harper's Weekly New York, N. Y.	1906 Vol. 50, Pt. 2
Wheare, K. C.	Lincoln, U.S.A.	Hodder & Stoughton London, Eng.	1945
Whipple, Wayne	The Heart of Lincoln	Geo. W. Jacobs & Co. Philadelphia, Pa.	1915
Whitlock, Frank	Abraham Lincoln	T. Nelson & Sons New York, N. Y.	1908
William, Tom	"Love Visits a Ship"	Long Beach Independent, Press-Telegram Long Beach, Calif.	11/3/1969
Williams, Dallas	Praise of Lincoln	Bobbs Merrill & Sons Indianapolis, Ind.	1911 & 1925
Williams, Mrs. M. E.	Lincoln, A Spiritualist	Private Printing New York, N. Y.	
Wilson, Rufus R.	Lincoln Among Friends	Caxton Printers Caldwell, Idaho	1942
Wolf, William	The Almost Chosen People	Doubleday & Co. New York, N. Y.	1959
Wright, Gilbert	Psychic Phenomena	General Elecrtic Schenectady, N. Y.	

FOOTNOTES

INTRODUCTION

1. Dowding, *God's Magic*, 4
1a. *Independent, Press-Telegram*, Long Beach, Calif., 5/20/73
2. Murray, *Matters of Life & Death*, 195
3. Schauffler, *Lincoln's Birthday*, 149, 151

PROLOGUE

1. Fox, *Lincoln's Religion*, 16, 9
2. Randall, *The Liberal Statesman*, 175
3. Current, *The Lincoln Nobody Knows*, 18
4. *Ibid.*, 19
5. Harris, "Lincoln Fake Quotations," *Long Beach Independent, Press-Telegram*, 2/21/69. Mr. Harris is a noted columnist.
6. Starr, *Lincoln's Dual Personality*, 21
7. Current, *The Lincoln Nobody Knows*, 18
8. Fox, *Lincoln's Religion*, 19
9. Meyers, *Human Personality and Its Survival of Bodily Death*, 344. This book is considered a classic in the field.

CHAPTER I
ME, MY DEATH AND MY FAMILY

1. My Gift of Words

1. Browne, *Every Day Life of Lincoln*, iii. The author was a friend of Lincoln.
2. Randall, Ruth, *Mary Lincoln, Biography of a Marriage*, 231
3. Evans, W. A., *Mrs. Lincoln, Study of a Personality*, 55. The author is a physician and Lincoln student.
4. *Ibid.*, 56
5. Newman, *Lincoln for the Ages*, 211. This chapter was written by Margaret Flint, Assistant State Historian of Illinois.
6. Keckley, *Behind the Scenes*, 98. Elizabeth Keckley was Mrs. Lincoln's caretaker.
7. *Ibid.*, 99
8. Randall, *Lincoln's Sons*, 93
9. Barton, *The Life of Lincoln, Vol. I*, 171
10. Randall, Ruth, *Mary Lincoln, Biography of a Marriage*, 234
11. Wilson, *Lincoln Among Friends*, 85. The author writes of Lincoln's contemporaries.
12. Randall, Ruth, *Mary Lincoln, Biography of a Marriage*, 272-274
13. Randall, Ruth, *Lincoln Sons*, 92. Mrs. Randall is the wife of the noted Lincoln historian.
14. Randall and Current, *Mr. Lincoln*, 181

2. My Love of Animals

1. Randall and Current, *Mr. Lincoln*, 97
2. Stanford, *A Lincoln Letter*, Christian Science Monitor
3. Keckley, *Behind the Scenes*, 98
4. Stanford, *A Lincoln Letter*, Christian Science Monitor
5. Monaghan, *Diplomat in Carpet Slippers*, 153
6. Hertz, *Lincoln Table Talks*, 663
7. Carpenter, *Inner Life of Lincoln*, 44. The author, an artist, became a personal friend of Lincoln.

3. Spoiled, Yet Unspoiled

1. Nicolay, Helen, *Personal Traits of Lincoln,* 201
2. Lewis, *Myths after Lincoln,* 265
3. Herndon, *Life of Lincoln,* 344
4. Shutes, *Lincoln's Emotional Life,* 141. The author writes as a physician and a Lincoln Student.
5. Randall, Ruth, *Mary Lincoln, Biography of a Marriage,* 146
6. Keckley, *Behind the Scenes,* 107
7. *Ibid.*
8. Randall, Ruth, *Mary Lincoln, Biography of a Marriage,* 155
9. Keckley, *Behind the Scenes,* 107
10. Herndon, *Life of Lincoln,* 381
11. Randall and Current, *Mr. Lincoln,* 381
12. *Ibid.*
13. Randall, Ruth, *Mary Lincoln, Biography of a Marriage,* 151
14. Allport, *Abraham Lincoln,* 32

4. My Illness

1. Hill, *Lincoln, Man of God,* 321
2. Randall, Ruth, *Mary Lincoln, a Biography of a Marriage,* 282
3. *Ibid.*, 284
4. Randall, Ruth, *Lincoln Sons,* 99
5. Randall and Current, *Mr. Lincoln,* 178
6. Snell, *Explanation of The Strangers' Guide Map to Washington, D. C., 1865,* 3, 13
7. Snell, *Guide Map to Washington, D.C., 1865.* This material by Mr. Snell is available at the Ford Theatre, Washington, D.C., which is operated by the United States Department of the Interior.
8. Keckley, *Behind the Scenes,* 98
9. Randall, Ruth, *Mary Lincoln, Biography of a Marriage,* 225
10. Angle, *Abraham Lincoln,* 346
11. Bayne, *Tad Lincoln's Father,* 8. The author, as a young girl, helped in the training of the Lincoln children.
12. Randall, Ruth, *Mary Lincoln, Biography of a Marriage,* 289
13. Baxter, Orville H. Browning, *Lincoln's Friend and Critic,* 176
14. Nicolay, John, *Lincoln's Secretary,* 132

5. Pa Overwhelmed

1. Randall, Ruth, *Mary Lincoln, the Biography of a Marriage,* 285
2. Stoddard, *Lincoln's Third Secretary,* 148
3. Hill, *Lincoln, Man of God,* 321
4. Randall, Ruth, *Mary Lincoln, the Biography of a Marriage,* 286
5. Whitlock, *Abraham Lincoln,* 128
6. Thomas, *Abraham Lincoln,* 478
7. Nicolay, *Lincoln's Secretary,* 133
8. Whipple, *The Heart of Lincoln,* 75
9. Stoddard, *Lincoln's Third Secretary,* 149
10. Monaghan, *Diplomat in Carpet Slippers,* 219
11. Sandburg, *Mary Lincoln, Wife and Widow,* 102
12. Starr, *Lincoln, Dual Personality,* 8
13. Binns, *Lincoln,* 254
14. Randall, Ruth, *Mary Lincoln, the Biography of a Marriage,* 284

15. Jones, *Lincoln and the Preachers,* 37, 38
16. Evans, Louis R., *This Is America's Hour,* 121
17. Jones, *Lincoln and the Preachers,* 35
18. Lewis, *Myths After Lincoln,* 105
19. Stern, *Life and Writings of Abraham Lincoln,* 137
20. *Ibid.,* 143
21. Miller, *Portrait, Life of Lincoln,* 68
22. Lewis, *Myths After Lincoln,* 301

6. My Psychical Pa

1. Hertz, *Lincoln Table Talk,* 662
2. Gross, *Lincoln's Own Stories,* VII
3. Karagulla, *Breakthrough to Creativity,* 210
4. Randall, *The Liberal Statesman,* 190
5. Grierson, *Abraham Lincoln, The Practical Mystic,* 14
6. Stone, *Love Is Eternal*
7. The American Japanese Society, *Fourth Annual Contest,* 23
8. Hyslop, *Contact with the Other World,* 27. The author was a former professor of Philosophy and Logic at Columbia University.
9. Barret, *On the Threshold of the Unseen,* 408. Mr. Barrett was an outstanding British physicist.
10. Editor, *Lincolniana,* 172, *(Journal of the Illinois State Historical Society,* Vol XLI, 1948)
11. Warren, *Lincoln and Spiritualism,* 4/46, 888. This is an issue of *Lincoln Lore,* purchased by the Lincoln Foundation, Fort Wayne, Indiana.
12. Martin, "Abraham Lincoln, Spiritualist." This is an article which appears in *The National Spiritualist Magazine,* 2/1/27.
13. Sharp, *Abraham Lincoln,* 57
14. Helm, *Mary, Wife of Lincoln,* 117
15. Evans, W. A., *Mrs. Lincoln, Study of a Personality,* 264
16. Editor, *Writing Greatest Invention.* This suggestive passage appears in the *Lincoln Encyclopedia,* 391.
17. Karagulla, *Breakthrough to Creativity,* 207, 208
18. Maynard, *Was Lincoln a Spiritualist?,* IX. A complete commentary on this book appears in a later chapter.
19. Randall, *Lincoln, the President,* 342

7. Ma's Affliction

1. Monaghan, *Was Lincoln Really a Spiritualist?,* 251. This author is a recognized historian.
2. Helm, *Mary, Wife of Lincoln,* 143. Mrs. Helm was a sister of Mrs. Lincoln.
3. Randall, Ruth, *Mary Lincoln, a Biography of a Marriage,* 289
4. Monaghan, *A Diplomat in Carpet Slippers,* 235
5. Bayne, *Tad Lincoln's Father,* 200
6. Sharp, *Abraham Lincoln,* 50
7. Edited by Stern, *The Life and Writings of Abraham Lincoln,* 29
8. Editor, *Long Beach Independent, Press-Telegram,* 8/19/69
9. Randall, Ruth, *Lincoln's Sons,* 104
10. *Ibid.,* 98
11. Randall, Ruth, *Mary Lincoln, a Biography of a Marriage,* 100
12. *Ibid.,* 282

13. Keckley, *Behind the Scenes,* 116
14. Bishop, *The Day Lincoln Was Shot,* 24
15. Gross, *Lincoln's Own Stories,* 94
16. Randall, Ruth, *Mary Lincoln, a Biography of a Marriage,* 289

8. Ma and the Mediums

1. Lincoln, Mary, Personal Letter to Mrs. Orne. The original of this letter, signed 'M. L. is referred to in Chapter II and described in detail.
2. Fornell, *Unhappy Medium,* 131
3. Bishop, *The Day Lincoln Was Shot,* 23
4. Randall, Ruth, *Mary Lincoln, a Biography of a Marriage,* 292
5. Carnegie, *Lincoln, the Unknown,* 166-167
6. Randall, Ruth, *Mary Lincoln, a Biography of a Marriage,* 292
7. Sandburg, *The Prairie Years, Vol. II,* 355
8. Hyslop, *Contact with the Other World,* 14
9. Barrett, *On the Threshold of the Unseen,* XIX
10. Sandburg, *Mary Lincoln, Wife and Widow,* 103

10a. Monaghan, *Was Lincoln Really a Spiritualist?* 216

11. Warren, *Lincoln and Spiritualism,* 888. Warren was an editor of *Lincoln Lore.*
12. Randall, Ruth, *Mary Lincoln, a Biography of a Marriage,* 293

12a. Chase, *Forty Years on the Spiritual Rostrum,* 97. This author is an authority on Spiritualism.

13. Randall, Ruth, *Mary Lincoln, a Biography of a Marriage,* 292
14.. Fornell, *Unhappy Medium,* 129. The author is a Professor of Government at the University of Texas.
15. Helm, *Mary, Wife of Lincoln,* 107
16. Holzer, *Widow of the Past,* 15. This is written by a trained psychic researcher. The subtitle is: *Exploring History through ESP.*
17. Thomas, *Portrait of Posterity,* 130
18. Evans, W. A., *Mrs. Lincoln, Study of Personality,* 54
19. Thomas, *Abraham Lincoln,* 299
20. Thomas, *Portrait of Posterity,* 51
21. Editor, *Lincolniana,* 172. This article appears in the *Illinois State Historical Society Journal,* Vol. XLI, 4/46.
22. Current, *The Lincoln Nobody Knows,* 68
23. Randall and Current, *Mr. Lincoln,* 387
24. Lincoln, David, Personal Letter. The author, a Lincoln student, is no relation to Abraham Lincoln. This letter is dated Jamestown, New York, 11/14/68.
25. Sandburg, *Mary Lincoln, Wife and Widow,* 103
26. Lewis, Montgomery, *Legends that Libel Lincoln,* 180
27. Current, *The Lincoln Nobody Knows,* 66
28. Thomas, *Portrait of Posterity,* 58
29. Luthin, *The Real Abraham Lincoln,* 115
30. Thomas, *Abraham Lincoln,* 299
31. Helm, *Mary, Wife of Lincoln,* 195
32. Lewis, Montgomery, *Legends that Libel Lincoln,* 4
33. *Ibid.,* 164
34. Donald, *Lincoln Reconsidered,* 153
35. Hertz, *The Hidden Lincoln,* 64
36. Ward, *Tributes to Associates,* 204

37. de Chambrun, *Impressions of Abraham Lincoln*, 37. This author is a Lincoln student of foreign descent.
38. Randall and Current, *Mr. Lincoln and the Civil War*, 193
39. *Ibid.*, VI
40. Monaghan, *Was Lincoln Really a Spiritualist?*, 214
41. Hall, *The Civil War Unveiled*, 44, 51. The author is a news correspondent, and a severe critic of the President and the White House seances.
42. *Ibid.*, 32
43. Randall, *Lincoln, the President*, 39
44. Jones, *Lincoln and the Preachers*, 28
45. Shook, *The Lincoln Story*, 38
46. Shirley, *A Short Life of Abraham Lincoln*, 33
47. Lorant, *Lincoln, Pictorial Story of His Life*, 182

9. "He Comes To Me"

1. Randall, Ruth, *Mary Lincoln, a Biography of a Marriage*, 333
2. Lewis, Montgomery, *Legends That Libel Lincoln*, 180
3. Fornell, *The Unhappy Medium*, 131
4. Lincoln, Mary, Personal Letter to Mrs. Orne
5. *Ibid.*
6. Hyslop, *Contact with The Other World*, 445
7. *Ibid.*, 448

CHAPTER II
SURVIVAL AND COMMUNICATION

1. A Changed Person

1. Conant, *Reminiscences of Abraham Lincoln*, 516
2. Gross, *Lincoln's Own Story*, 55
3. *Ibid.*, 85
4. Current, *The Lincoln Nobody Knows*, 64, 65
5. Donald, *Lincoln Reconsidered*, 151
6. Stowe, *Men of Our Time*, 16
7. Thomas, *Abraham Lincoln*, 304.
8. Carpenter, *Inner Life of Lincoln*, 188

8a. Wiegers, *Experts Satisfied with Lincoln's Works.* (This is part of a news item as noted in the Bibliography.)

9. Baxter, O. H. Brown, *Lincoln's Friend and Critic*, 60
10. Randall, Ruth, *Mary Lincoln, a Biography of a Marriage*, 292
11. Randall and Current, *Mr. Lincoln*, 388
12. Taggart, *Faith of A Lincoln*, 301
13. Thomas, *Portrait of Posterity*, 58
14. Kranz, *Abraham Lincoln, New Portrait*, 107
15. Bishop, *The Day Lincoln Was Shot*, 176
16. Wolf, *The Almost Chosen People*, 115
17. Binns, *Abraham Lincoln*, 255
18. Stephenson, *Lincoln*, 199
19. Hertz, *Table Talks*, 575
20. Lorant, *Lincoln, a Pictorial Study of His Life*, 135. Lorant has done a thorough piece of research into the life of Lincoln in the process of producing a pictorial biography.

21. Jones, *Lincoln and the Preachers*, 37
22. Sharp, *Conversations with Lincoln*, 57
23. Carpenter, *Inner Life of Lincoln*, 119
24. Browne, *Every Day Life of Lincoln*, 351
25. Bach, *Spiritual Breakthrough for Our Time*, 140
26. Lodge, *Phantom Walls*, 22, 23
27. Carnegie, *Lincoln The Unknown*, 344
28. Kempf, *Abraham Lincoln's Philosophy of Common Sense, Part I*, 49
29. *Ibid.*, 415
30. Baringer, *Philosophy of Lincoln*, 121
31. Kranz, *Abraham Lincoln*, New Portrait, 107
32. Hyslop, *Contact with the Other World*, 328
33. *Ibid.*, 480
34. Current and Randall, *Mr. Lincoln*, 183
35. *Ibid.*, 182
36. Randall, Ruth, *Lincoln's Sons*, 105
37. Hill, *Abraham Lincoln, Man of God*, 149
38. Newton, *Spiritual Life of Lincoln*, 36
39. Barrett, *On the Threshold of the Unseen*, 161
39a. Jung, *Psychological Reflections*, 38
40. Starr, *Lincoln Dual Personality*, 5, 21
41. Hyslop, *Contact with the Other World*, 468
42. *Ibid.*, 476
43. Thomas, *Portrait of Posterity*, 61
44. Lodge, *Phantom Walls*, 290
45. *Life Magazine*, 1/24/69 Article by editor.
46. Hertz, *The Hidden Lincoln*, 110
47. Knight, *Byron and Spiritualism*, 48. This is an article from the publication by the College of Psychical Science in London, England.
48. *Ibid.*, 131
49. Stephenson, *Lincoln*, 270
50. Edited by Rice, *Reminiscences of Abraham Lincoln*, 412. This is an article by Hugh McCulloch. He was appointed Controller of the Currency by Abraham Lincoln.
51. Lodge, *Phantom Walls*, 108
52. Drinkwater, *Lincoln, World Emancipator*, 111
53. *Ibid.*, 115
54. Starr, *Dual Personality*, 11
55. Hill, *Abraham Lincoln, Man of God*, 325
55a. Stern and Fried, *The Essential Lincoln*, 210
56. Lang, *Lincoln Fireside Chat*, 88
57. Hill, *Abraham Lincoln, Man of God*, 325
58. Browne, *Every Day Life of Lincoln*, 478
59. Randall and Current, *Mr. Lincoln*, 385
60. Schurz, *Abraham Lincoln*, 24. As previously noted, this page number appears in the second part of the book.
61. Wilson, *Lincoln Among Friends*, 92
62. Lang, *Lincoln Fireside Chat*, 63
63. Kempf, *Philosophy of Common Sense*, 419. This gentleman is a member of the New York Academy of Science, a physician who has devoted his life to a study of Lincoln.
64. Bach, *Spiritual Breakthrough for Our Time*, 138, 139

65. Appleman, *Abraham Lincoln from His Own Words and Contemporary Account*, 48. This is a yellow paper cover (book size), Reprint, 1961.
66. Smith, *Lincoln and the Spiritual Life*, 10
67. Kempf, *Philosophy of Common Sense*, 274
68. Lorant, *Preveiw Secret Lincoln Papers*, 86
69. Lorant, *Two New Lincoln Finds*, 118
70. Thompson, *Lincoln, the First American*, 173
71. Angle and Meirs, *The Living Lincoln*, 87
72. Whitlock, *Abraham Lincoln*, 39
73. Smith, *Lincoln and His Spiritual Life*, 10
74. Angle, *The Lincoln Reader*, 438
75. Constad. This is a news release, United Press, reported by Constad during 1863. Copy on file in Lincoln Life Foundation, Fort Wayne, Indiana.
76. Blackwell, *Abraham Lincoln's Unseen Helpers*, 8
77. Angle and Meirs, *The Living Lincoln*, 437
78. Current, *The Lincoln Nobody Knows*, 69
79. Shelton, *Abraham Lincoln Returns*, 233
80. Stobart, *Torchbearer of Spritualism*, 174
81. Binns, *Lincoln*, 348
82. *Ibid.*, 349
83. Ford, *Unknown but Known*, 26
84. Angle and Meirs, *The Living Lincoln*, 469
85. Richardson, *Lincoln Autobiography*, 19
86. Newman, *Lincoln for the Ages*, 41. Chapter by Louis Warren, former Director, Lincoln Life Foundation, Fort Wayne, Indiana.
87. Lyne, *A Quaker Document*, 17, 18. This material comes from the rare book section in the Library of Congress; as indicated in my manuscript, it appears to be original material from an old Quaker scrapbook, or album.
88. Newkirk, *Lincoln Lessons for Today*, 79
89. Taggart, *Faith of A Lincoln*, 335
90. Lang, *Abraham Lincoln*, 240
91. Stephanson, *Lincoln*, 78
92. Editor, *Independent, Press-Telegram*, Sunday Magazine section known as *Parade*, 3/2/69, 3
93. Carpenter, *Inner Life of Lincoln*, or *Six Months in the White House*, 186

2. Discerning the Spirits

1. European Center Nuclear Research — Editorial "Discerning" *(Christian Science Monitor* 11/25/69)

1a. Lodge, *Phantom Walls*, 95

2. Sinclair, *Mental Radio*
3. Crenshaw, *Telephone Between Two Worlds*, IX
4. Barrett, *On the Threshhold of the Unseen*, 35
5. Sherman, *How To Make ESP Work for You*, 41
6. Lindbergh, Personal Letter to *Life Magazine*, 60. This noted aviator wrote to *Life* in response to a request for comments on the astronauts' trip or walk on the moon, 7/4/69.
7. Pike, *If This Be Heresy*, 118
8. Kelsey, *Tongue Speaking*

9. Editor, Title, "You Can Be a Delegate to the United Nations through Thought." Publisher, M.G.N.A., 633 Steamboat Road, Greenwich, Conn.
10. Fodor, *Encyclopaedia of Psychic Science*
11. Richmond, *Spirit Messages*, 219
12. Monaghan, *Was Lincoln Really a Spiritualist?*, 212. This historian is writing for the Illinois State Historical Society.
13. Russell, *The Lincoln Way*, 27
14. Haven, *Heavenly Messenger or Immortality*, 12. This is considered by the Library of Congress sufficiently valuable to be filed among their rare books on Lincoln.
15. Schurz, *The Reminiscences*, 155, 156
16. Haven, *Heavenly Messages on Immortality*, 34
16a. Blackwell, *Abraham Lincoln — Unseen Helpers*, 9, 10
17. Warren, the Editor, *Lincoln and Spirtualism*. This constitutes an issue of the Lincoln Lore, as previously described in the footnotes.
18. Shelton, *Abraham Lincoln Returns*, 152. Special reference to this author will be found in a later note.
19. Hyslop, *Contact with the Other World*, 453
20. Shirley, *Abraham Lincoln*, 176
21. Barrett, *On the Threshold of the Unseen*, XIX
22. Current, *The Lincoln Nobody Knows*, 68
23. Sandburg, *The War Years, Vol. III*, 345
24. Warren, Editor, *Lincoln and Spiritualism*, an issue of Lincoln Lore, 4/46
25. Shirley, *Abraham Lincoln*, 175
26. Hill, *Abraham Lincoln, Man of God*, 103
27. Graebner, *The Enduring Lincoln*, 119
28. Sharp, *Abraham Lincoln*, 137
29. Wolf, *The Almost Chosen People*, 156
30. Gross, *Lincoln's Own Stories*, 73
31. Fodor, *Between Two Worlds*, 10
32. Wolf, *The Almost Chosen People*, 22
33. Thomas, *Portrait of Posterity*, 61
34. Barrett, *On the Threshold of the Unseen*, 36

3. Sensitives and Séances

1. Monaghan, *Was Lincoln Really a Spiritualist?*, 215, 216
2. Ford, *Unknown but Known*, 25
3. Maynard, *Was Lincoln a Spiritualist?*, 165. Much of the controversy over Lincoln and Spiritualism centers around this book. It is in fact the story concerning Nettie Colburn and Lincoln.
4. Barton, *The Soul of Lincoln*, 232
5. Barton, *A. Lincoln and Walt Whitman*, Foreword
6. Hartranft, *Last Will and Testament*. This document is related to the publisher of the Maynard book.
7. Maynard, *Was Lincoln a Spiritualist?*, X, XI
8. *Ibid.*, XVIII
9. *Ibid.*, XIII
10. *Ibid.*, XIV
11. Williams, *Lincoln, a Spiritualist*, 10-14
12. Monaghan, *Was Lincoln Really A Spiritualist?*, 207
13. *Ibid.*, 212
14. Sandburg, *The War Years Vol. III*, 343

15. Editor *Lincolniana*, 172, Journal Illinois State Historical Society
16. Maynard, *Was Lincoln a Spiritualist?* XI
17. Daley, Personal Letter, Dept. of Records Philadelphia, Pa. 5/3/68
18. Monaghan, *Was Lincoln Really a Spiritualist?*, 218
19. Maynard, *Was Lincoln a Spiritualist?*, 91
20. Monaghan, *Was Lincoln Really a Spiritualist?*, 222
21. Williams, *Abraham Lincoln A Spiritualist*, 10-14. Reprint for New York Sun, April 5, 1891
22. Johnson, *Psychical Research*, 90. Noted British Physicist.
23. Williams, *Abraham Lincoln a Spiritualist*, 10-14
24. *Ibid.*, 10-14
25. Maynard, *Was Lincoln a Spiritualist?*, 85. 1891 edition
26. Monaghan, *Was Lincoln Really a Spiritualist?*, 219
27. Editor, *New Light On Lincoln*, 3. From British News entitled Two Worlds, 9/19/59
28. McMurty, Editor, Lincoln Lore, 1, Nov. 1962. Article *Baker Spirit Message.*
29. Fitzgerrell, *Lincoln Was a Spiritualist*, 70-71. Author although an avowed Spiritualist provides substantial cross references in support of the attendance of Lincoln and official staff members at certain séances.
30. *Ibid.*, 67
31. Terrell, *Shelton Book Review*, 8. The author operates Book Shop. This is a review of *Abraham Lincoln Returns.*
32. Monaghan, *Was Lincoln Really a Spiritualist?*, 210, 215
33. Ford, *Unknown but Known*, 40, 58, 60
34. *Ibid.*, 57
35. *Ibid.*, 68
36. *Ibid.*, 143
37. Monaghan, *Was Lincoln Really A Spiritualist?*, 215
38. Fornell, *Unhappy Medium*, 118

4. Guilt by Association

1. Ford, *Unknown But Known*, 16

1a. Van Dellen, *Mental Disorder*, 7

2. Higgins, John Wesley, *Spiritual Witness*, 96, 99
3. Beard, *Survival of Death*, 158
4. Ford, *Unknown But Known*, 21
5. Hyslop, *Contact with the Other World*, 484
6. Barrett, *On the Threshold of the Unseen*, 26
7. *Ibid.*, 287

7a. Sandburg, *The Prairie Years, Vol. I*, 473

8. *Webster's Collegiate Dictionary*, 1227

8a. Hertz, *Lincoln Talks*, 152

8b. Johnson, *Does Man Survive*, 178

9. Hyslop, *Contact with the Other World*, 453
10. *Ibid.*, 486
11. Hollis, *The American Heresy*, 149
12. Quinn, *Interior Causes of War.* Historians are inclined to discredit this book as highly prejudicial to Lincoln. It nevertheless provides some insights.
13. Lodge, *Phantom Walls*, 147
14. Hyslop, *Contact with the Other World*, 478
15. Barrett, *On the Threshold of the Unseen*, 22
16. Lodge, *Phantom Walls*, 88

17. *Ibid.*, 68
18. Barrett, *On the Threshold of the Unseen*, 286
19. Maynard, *Was Lincoln a Spiritualist?*, IX
20. Beard, *Survival of Death*, 156
21. Hyslop, *Contact with the Other World*, 30.
22. Lodge, *Phantom Walls*, 80
23. *Ibid.*, 82
24. Current, *The Lincoln Nobody Knows*, 55
25. Chase, *Forty Years on the Spiritual Rostrum*, 96
26. Current, *The Lincoln Nobody Knows*, 57
27. Lewis, *Myths after Lincoln*, 388
28. Chesney, Personal Letter with notations. Milton Junction, Wisc., 2/25/59.
29. Constad, news release by the United Press dated 1863, New York City.
30. McMurty, *Baker Spirit Message*. This is an issue of the *Lincoln Lore*, dated 11/92. The reference appears on page 3.

CHAPTER III
HONEST ABE A WITNESS TO TRUTH

1. Watch Your Language

1. Grierson, *Lincoln, The Practical Mystic*, 30
2. Schauffler, *Lincoln's Birthday*, 312
3. Angle, *The Lincoln Reader*, 245
4. Wright, *Statement of Psychic Phenomena*. Mr. Wright is an engineer at the General Electric Company, Schenectady, New York.
5. Smith, *Lincoln and the Spiritual Life*, 10
6. Lincoln, *Maxims, Observations and Comments*, 10. This is a small anthology of quotations from Mr. Lincoln. Reference has been made to this quotation as it appeared in *The Lincoln Encyclopaedia*.
7. Karagulla, *Breakthrough to Creativity*, 204. See Note 19 for background of Dr. Karagulla.
8. Murray, *Matters of Life and Death*, 195
9. *Ibid.*, 100
10. Crenshaw, *Telephone Between Two Worlds*.
    Sinclair, *Mental Radio*.
11. D'Albe, *Life of Crooks*, 215. Professor Crooks was a recognized British scholar and scientist who devoted much of his time to psychical research.
12. Ford, *Unknown but Known*, 16, 21
13. Karagulla, *Breakthrough to Creativity*, 230
14. Lincoln, *The Lincoln Encyclopaedia*, 77
15. Current, *The Lincoln Nobody Knows*, 18, 19
16. Auder, *Lincoln Images, Part I*, 105
17. Harris, *Lincoln Fake Quotations, Long Beach Independent, Press-Telegram*, 2/21/69
18. Lewis, *Legends that Libel Lincoln*, 4
19. Karagulla, *Breakthrough to Creativity*, 21. Dr. Karagulla is a physician born in Turkey, had her medical training at several universities in Canada and on the research staff at hospitals in the United States. She has recently turned her attention to psychical research. A number of references have been made to her recent book.
20. Hyslop, *Contact with the Other World*, 478

21. Sandburg, *The War Years, Vol. III*, 344, 345
22. *Ibid.*, 343
23. *Ibid.*, 345
23a. Schauffler, *Lincoln's Birthday*, 313
24. Horner, *Growth of Lincoln's Faith*, 123
25. Newkirk, *Lincoln's Lessons for Today*, 71
26. Kelsey, *Tongue Speaking*
26a. Bach, Circular Letter signed by Bach. It contains testimonial on his latest book, *Inner Ecstasy*. This is a quotation from Harold Sherman, ESP authority.
27. Packard, R. D., *Riddle of Lincoln's Religion*, 12
28. McElroy, *Soul Growth of Lincoln*, 8
29. Newkirk, *Lincoln's Lessons for Today*, 74
30. Hyslop, *Contact with the Other World*, 39
31. Jones, *Life Work of Sigmund Freud, Vol. III*, 392. Ernest Jones, a physician and analyst, has provided us with some of the most intimate and authorative insights concerning the life of Sigmund Freud.
32. Webster, *American Collegiate Dictionary*, 1153, 773
33. Bach, *News Letter No. 20*, 7. This is a publication by the Fellowship for Spiritual Understanding, of which Marcus Bach is the founder.
34. Jung, News Article on Séances in the British publication, *Two Worlds*, 10/17/59, London, England

2. Silence of Eternity

1. Newman, *Lincoln for the Ages*, 413. This chapter is written by Richard Paul Graebel. He is a member of the Illinois State Historical Society, and also a member of the Abraham Lincoln Association.
2. Carpenter, *Inner Life of Lincoln*, 188, 189
3. Newman, *Lincoln for the Ages*, 414. As mentioned previously, this chapter was written by Paul Graebel.
4. Binns, *Abraham Lincoln*, 345
4a. Lorant, *Lincoln, a Pictorial Story of His Life*, 107
5. Fornell, *An Unhappy Medium*, 109
6. Hyslop, *Contact with the Other World*, 326
7. McMurty, *Lincoln's Attendance at Séances*, 1. This is an issue of *Lincoln Lore* dated 1/1963.
8. Baxter, *Orville H. Browning, Lincoln's Friend and Critic*, 59
9. Sharp, *Abraham Lincoln*, 50
10. Browne, *Evrery Day Life of Abraham Lincoln*, 448
11. Ward, *Abraham Lincoln, Tributes from his Associates*, 24. This collection of tributes was made by Dr. Ward, who provides the Introduction to the book.
12. Stephenson, *Lincoln*, 209
13. Herndon and Weik, *Life of Lincoln*, 473
14. Richardson, *Lincoln's Autobiography*, 32
15. Lorant, *Lincoln, a Pictorial Story of His Life*, 98
16. Garrett, *My Life as a Search for the Meaning of Mediumship*, 9. This is a British publication by the founder of the Parapsychology School of Thought, and herself a celebrated international medium.
17. Karagulla, *A Breakthrough to Creativity*, 79
18. Editor, *Lincolnia*, 72. This article appears in the *Journal of the Illinois State Historical Society*.
19. McMurty, *Baker's Spirit Message*. This is a *Lincoln Lore* article, dated 11/1962.

20. Hyslop, *Contact with the Other World*, 29
21. Basler, *Collected Works of Lincoln, Vol. VII*, 133
21a. Fodor, *Encyclopedia of Psychic Science*, 203
22. Hardinge, *Report on Spiritualism*, 112
23. Hill, *Abraham Lincoln, Man of God*, 233
24. Grierson, *Abraham Lincoln, the Practical Mystic*, 29
25. Goldsmith, *Beyond Word and Thoughts*, 177
26. Garrett, *My Life as a Search for the Meaning of Mediumship*, 10
27. McLuhan, Marshall, *Independent Press-Telegram*, Long Beach, Calif., *Sunday Parade*

3. Burn This

1. Holzer, *Window of the Past*, 14. This author has a number of his books published in the field of psychical research.
2. Randall, *Mary Lincoln, a Biography of a Marriage*, 270
3. Barton, *The Life of Abraham Lincoln, Vol. I*, 409
4. Nicolay, *Lincoln's Secretary*, 312
5. Current, *The Lincoln Nobody Knows*, 19
6. Warren, *The Burnt Book Myth*, another *Lincoln Lore* publication, dated 10/27/54.
7. Greenbie, *Anna Ella Carroll and Lincoln*, VIII. The author claims to have done considerable research concerning Carroll. She was a confidante to Lincoln.
8. Lincoln, Mary, Personal Letter to Mrs. Horne, dated 11/20/69. As stated before, the original of this letter is with the Franklin Marshall Library, Franklin Marshall College.
9. Holzer, *Window of the Past*, 15
10. Butler, *Across the Years*, 375, 376. A special reference to this author appears in the book.
11. Butler, *Lincoln & Son*, 23
12. Lorant, *Preview of Secret Lincoln Papers*, 86
13. Warren, *Lincoln Papers Supplemental* from *Lincoln Lore*, 8/25/47
14. Editor, Article on E. Joy Morris, *American Biographical Encyclopaedia*, 206. Basler, Article on E. Joy Morris, *Collected Works of Abraham Lincoln, Vol. V*, 176
15. Harris, Personal Letter 5/19/68. Paul Harris, formerly of Great Britain, has written a number of books, including *Science and the Séances* His writings appear under the name of Miller. He is a careful student of the psychical and genuinely interested in Lincoln.
16. Basler, *Collected Works of Abraham Lincoln, Vol. IV*
17. Thomas, *Abraham Lincoln*, 479
18. Monaghan, *Was Lincoln Really a Spiritualist?*, 210
19. *Ibid.*
20. Sandburg, *The War Years, Vol. II*, 306
21. Whitlock, *Abraham Lincoln*, 35

4. Careful Historians

1. Wolf, *The Almost Chosen People*, 51
2. Shirley, *Abraham Lincoln*, 176
3. Stephenson, *Lincoln*, 197, 198
4. Shelton, *Abraham Lincoln Returns*, 206
5. McDonald, *Lincoln Reconsidered*, 39
6. Hyslop, *Contact with the Other World*, 24
7. Jung, Article entitled "Séances," from the British publication, *Two Worlds*, 9/17/59

8. Karagulla, *Breakthrough to Creativity,* 204
9. Doyle, *Our American Adventure,* 148. Sir Arthur Coynan Doyle. one of the most distinguished Spiritualists of his time.
10. Hyslop, *Contact with the Other World,* 28
10a. Barrett, *On the Threshold of the Unseen,* 99
11. Current, *The Lincoln Nobody Knows,* 69
12. Randall, *Mary Lincoln, a Biography of a Marriage,* 294
13. Webster, *The American Collegiate Dictionary,* 1285
14. Longfellow, "Spiritual World," source unknown. This is the American poet, Henry Wordsworth Longfellow.
15. Donald, *Lincoln Reconsidered,* 163
16. Harris, Article on ESP, *Long Beach Independent, Press-Telegram,* 7/22/69
16a. Fodor, *Encyclopaedia Psychic Science,* 203
17. Monaghan, *Was Lincoln Really a Spiritualist?,* 218
18. Miers, *Lincoln Day by Day,* 181
19. Newman, Personal Letter. Mr. Newman is the proprietor of the Lincoln bookshop in Chicago. He also served on the Board of the Chicago Public Library.
20. McMurty, Editor, *Lincoln's Attendance at Séances, Part II, Lincoln Lore,* 2/63
21. Thomas, *Portrait of Posterity,* 81
22. Snider, *Abraham Lincoln, an Interpretation,* 574
23. Randall & Current, *Mr. Lincoln,* 387
24. Current, Personal Letter, 5/31/68. Mr. Current is Professor of History and Political Science at the University of North Carolina
25. Randall & Current, *Mr. Lincoln,* VI
26. Donald, *Lincoln Reconsidered,* 161
27. Muldoon, *Sensational Psychic Experiences,* 141. The author has selected some psychic experiences among noted people in various fields of endeavor.
28. Monaghan, *Was Lincoln Really a Spiritualist?,* 207
29. Hyslop, *Contact with the Other World,* 326
30. Thomas, *Portrait of Posterity,* 84
31. Barton, *The Soul of Lincoln,* 33
32. Thomas, *Portrait of Posterity,* 284
33. Mugridge, Personal Letter from the Library of Congress, 2/24/61. Dr. Mugridge, a specialist in American History at the Library of Congress.
34. Auder, *Lincoln Images, Part I,* 100. This is a publication put out by the Augustine Public Library, Rock Island, Illinois.
35. Grierson, *Abraham Lincoln, The Practical Mystic,* 85
36. Garrett, *My Life as a Search for the Meaning of Mediumship,* 11

5. Free Press

1. Schurz, *The Reminiscences,* 155, 156
2. Schurz, *Abraham Lincoln,* 69
3. *Ibid.,* 60, 61
4. *Ibid.,* 19
5. Whitlock, *Abraham Lincoln,* 126, 127
6. Woldman, *Lincoln and the Russians,* 61
7. Sandburg, *The War Years, Vol. III,* 345
8. Constad, News Release, dated 1863, with the New York Head Line, "by the United Press."
9. Walsh, *Lincoln and the London Punch.* This is from a cartoon which appeared in *The London Punch,* a satirical publication, 64, 65

10. Monaghan, *Was Lincoln Really a Spiritualist?*, 213
11. Quinn, *Interior Causes of War*, 6
12. Hall, *Civil War Unveiled*, 14
13. Monaghan, *Was Lincoln Really a Spiritualist?*, 214-215
14. Helm, *Mary, Wife of Lincoln*, 160
15. Fornell, *The Unhappy Medium*, VII
16. Shelton, *Abraham Lincoln Returns*, 154
17. Moser, Personal Letter, Margaret Moser was Head of the Department of History and Biography at the Cleveland Public Library.
18. Editor, Warren, *Burnt Book Myth*, another *Lincoln Lore* publication, 9/27/54
19. Sunday Editor, *Chicago Tribune*, "Lincoln, the Mystic," Sec. D, 2/7/09
20. Stearn & Fried, *The Essential Lincoln*, 470
21. Donald, *Lincoln Reconsidered*, 60
22. *Ibid.*, 74

6. Religious Crisis

1. Donald, *Lincoln Reconsidered*, 133
2. Randall, *Mary Lincoln, A Biography of a Marriage*, 292
3. Shelton, *Abraham Lincoln's Return*, 52
4. Lewis, *Myths After Lincoln*, 298, 299
5. *Ibid.*, 336
6. Current, *The Lincoln Nobody Knows*, 69
7. Ford, *Known but Unknown*, 26
8. Current, *The Lincoln Nobody Knows*, 71
8a. Houser, *Lincoln Group Papers*, the second series, 19
8b. Jones, *Lincoln and the Preachers*, 142, 143
9. Ford, *Unknown but Known*, 25-27
10. Morris, Speech at the House of Representatives, Washington, D. C., 2/12/1856
11. Fornell, *The Unhappy Medium*, 109
12. *Ibid.*, 118
13. Cook, Roy J. (compiler), *101 Famous Poems*, 35
14. Editor, *Journal of the Illinois Historical Society*, 172
15. McCabe, *Spiritualism*, 82
16. Ford, *Unknown but Known*, 60
17. Franklin, *Emancipation Proclamation*, 265
18. Hall, *The Civil War Unveiled*, 36, 37
19. Fornell, *The Unhappy Medium*, 130
20. *Ibid.*, 131
21. Chesney, *Argos Magazine*, 2/1/1962
22. Randall, *Mary Lincoln, a Biography of a Marriage*, 294
23. Peters, *Abraham Lincoln and Religion*, 20
24. Pennell, *Religious Views of Lincoln* (Preface)
25. Barrett, *On the Threshold of the Unseen*, 13
26. Fodor, *Between Two Worlds*, 10
27. Current, *The Lincoln Nobody Knows*, 68
28. Murray, *Matters of Life and Death*, 187
29. Ford, *Unknown but Known*, 26, 38
30. Barrett, *On the Threshold of the Unseen*, 21
31. *Ibid.*, 34
32. Herndon, *Life of Lincoln*, 351

CHAPTER IV
MY PRIMITIVE PIONEER PA

1. Uninhibited-Untutored

1. Smith, *Spiritualism Creed.* This is a card explaining the principles of Spiritualism.
2. Ford, *Unknown but Known,* 24
3. Peterson, *Lincoln and Douglas,* Chapter entitled "Review"
4. Bissett, *Lincoln,* The Universal Man, 183
5. Bach, *Spiritual Breakthrough for Our Time,* 141
6. *Ibid.,* 137
7. Schauffler, *Lincoln's Birthday,* 114
8. Hyslop, *Contact with the Other World,* 484
9. Wolf, *The Almost Chosen People,* 29
10. Jung, *Psychological Reflections,* 286
11. Stephenson, *Lincoln,* 26
12. Rice, *"Reminiscences of Abraham Lincoln,"* 110. This is an article by George S. Boutwell. Mr. Boutwell was a delegate to the convention that nominated Mr. Lincoln for the office of President. Mr. Boutwell was later to become a member of the House of Representatives.
13. Knight, "Byron and Spiritualism, " 120. This is part of an article which appeared in the summer issue of a magazine published by the College of Psychical Science in London. The title of the magazine is *Light.*
14. Hertz, *Lincoln Talks,* 307, 585
15. Karagulla, *Breakthrough to Creativity,* 120. Reference has been made to the background of this author.
16. Nathan, *Lincoln's America,* 19
17. Sandburg, Editor, *The Living Words of Abraham Lincoln,* 55
18. Lorant, *Lincoln, a Pictorial Story of His Life,* 46
19. Hertz, *Lincoln Talks,* 110
20. Randall and Current, *Mr. Lincoln,* 150
21. Stern, *The Life and Writings of Abraham Lincoln,* 25
22. Jung, *Psychological Reflections,* 287
23. Fox, *Lincoln's Religion,* 65
24. Randall, *Mary Lincoln, a Biography of a Marriage,* 231
25. Rice, *Reminiscences of Abraham Lincoln,* 412. This is an Article by Hugh McCulloch, to whom reference has been made in a previous footnote.
26. Thompson, *Abraham Lincoln,* 107
27. Schauffler, *Lincoln's Birthday,* 95
28. *Ibid.*
29. Randall, *The Liberal Statesman,* 54
30. Shirley, *Abraham Lincoln,* 21
31. *Ibid.,* 178
32. Appleman, *Lincoln's Own Words and Contemporary Accounnt,* 23
33. Jung, *Psychological Reflections,* 294
34. Hertz, *Lincoln's Talk,* 165
35. Schauffler, *Lincoln's Birthday,* 3
36. Schurz, *Abraham Lincoln,* 7. This page number appears in the second half of the book, from a speech by Henry Watterson.
37. Whitlock, *Abraham Lincoln,* 154
38. Sharp, *Abraham Lincoln,* 123
39. Hill, *Abraham Lincoln, Man of God,* 250, 251

40. Gross, *Lincoln's Own Stories*, 114
41. Schauffler, *Lincoln's Birthday*, 42
42. Williams, *Praise of Lincoln*, 39
43. James, *Varieties of Religious Experience*, 7
44. Knight, *Byron and Spiritualism*, 121. A description of this particular reference has been previously made.
45. Hyslop, *Contacts with the Other World*, 28
46. Author unknown. Essay on Lincoln. This is a one-page excerpt which may have appeared in one of the sevice clubs' business magazines.
47. Bissett, *Lincoln, The Universal Man*, 229
48. Preston, *The Shining Stranger* (news letter), Foundation for Spiritual Understanding, Palos Verdes, Calif.
49. Jung, *Psychological Reflections*, 289
50. Barton, *The Life of Abraham Lincoln, Vol. I*, 210
51. *Ibid.*, 238
52. Hall, *The Civil War Unveiled*, 32

2. A Mystic-Agnostic

1. Newton, *Lincoln and Herndon*, 351
2. McElroy, *Soul Growth of Lincoln*, 8
3. Constad, News Release, New York City, date line 1863, United Press, 2
4. Bates, *Religious Life of Lincoln*, 56
5. Bellman, *Architects of a New Age*, 76

5a. Peale, *Is Peace of Mind Possible Today?* Foundation for Xtn Living, Vol. 18, No. 1, 5

6. Barton, *Abraham Lincoln and Walt Whitman*, 87
7. Bradford, *The Haunted Biographer*, 16-17
8. Pike, *If This Be Heresy*, 119
9. Smith, *Lincoln and the Spiritual Life*, 28

10 Herndon, *Life of Lincoln*, 475. This is a reprint of the original book by Herdon and Weik.

11. Whitlock, *Abraham Lincoln*, 29
12. Carpenter, *Six Months in the White House* or *the Inner Life of Lincoln*, 119
13. *Ibid.*, 337
14. Current, *The Lincoln Nobody Knows*, 65
15. Starr, *Lincoln's Dual Personality*, 10
16. *Ibid.*, 11
17. Bennett, Charles A., *Philosophical Study of Mysticism*, 158
18. Lemmon, "Feminine Element in Lincoln." This article appears in *The Delineator Magazine*, 3/1909
19. Stephenson, *Lincoln*, 19
20. Abbott, *Magazine of History, Extra No. 85.* This is a private publication dated 1922, Tarrytown, New York.
21. Ford, *Unkown but Known*, 130
22. Current, *Lincoln, the Man Nobody Knows*, 69
23. Weatherhead, *The Christian Agnostic, XIII.* Dr. Leslie Weatherhead, former pastor of London's Temple and one of the patrons of the Churches' Fellowship for Spiritual and Psychical Study is the author of many books, including a large volume, Religion, Psychology and Health.
24. Bayne, *Tad Lincoln's Father*, 20, 175. Previous descriptive reference has been made to this author who was at one time a member of the Lincoln White House family.

25. Harris, *ESP, Poker, Anyone?*, Editorial. *Long Beach Independent, Press-Telegram*, 7/22/69
26. Barrett, *Life of Abraham Lincoln*, 19. The publication date of this book is 1860. It also contains a sketch of the life of Hannibal Hamlin, Vice President during the Lincoln administration.
27. Shutz, *Lincoln's Emotional Life*, 119
28. Bennett, *A Philosophical Study of Mysticism*, 174. Comment has been made concerning the author of this book.
29. Grierson, *Abraham Lincoln, The Practical Mystic*, 14
30. Thomas, *Portrait of Posterity*, 81
31. Grierson, *Abraham, Lincoln, The Practical Statesman*, 16
32. Editor, Churches' Fellowship for Psychical and Spiritual Studies. This is a manual published by the Fellowship in London, England.
33. *Ibid.*
34. Weatherhead, *The Christian Agnostic*, XII
35. Editor, churches' Fellowship for Psychical and Spiritual Studies.
36. *Ibid.*
37. Fox, *Lincoln's Religion*, 61
38. Weatherhead, *The Christian Agnostic*, XV
39. Ford, *Unknown but Known*, 152
40. *Ibid.*, 152
41. Righter, *Astrological Guide*, 90-93
42. Editor, *Life Magazine*. Article on astrology, 61, 9/27/69

42a. Weiss, *The Man Who Knows Lincoln*, 25, article Saturday Review of Literature, Feb. 14, 1970

43. Johnson, *Watcher on the Hills*, 177. The author is the Professor of Physics at Queen's College, Melbourne, Australia.
44. Hyslop, *Contacts with the Other World*, 473
45. Bissett, *Lincoln, the Universal Man*, 182
46. Editor, "Lincoln Who Lives in Anecdote," *Reader's Digest*, 2/59
47. Graebner, *The Enduring Lincoln*, 105. This article appeared on Feb. 12, 1959, sponsored by the Sequi-centennial Commission.
48. Schurz, *Abraham Lincoln*, 23. This page number appears in the second part of the book in an article by Henry Watterson.
49. Packard, *The Riddle of Lincoln's Religion*, 12
50. Aked, *Lincoln and Gladstone*, 236. This is a part of a publication by the Lincoln Club in Los Angeles, written in 1925.
51. *Ibid.*, 1
52. McElroy, *Soul Growth of Lincoln*, 8, 9,
53. Barton, *Abraham Lincoln and Walt Whitman* (Foreword)
54. Bradford, *the Haunted Biographer* (Preface)
55. Goldsmith, *Beyond Words and Thoughts*, 151. Goldsmith is a teacher and author in the field of practical mysticism through meditation in depth. He has written some 30 books and pamphlets on the subject, translated in numerous languages.

3. A Rebel-Heretic

1. Wheare, *Abraham Lincoln and the United States*, 219. This book was printed for the Great Britain University. The first printing of this book by a British author appeared in May, 1948.

2. Sharp, *Abraham Lincoln*, 22
3. Reeve, *A Flying Saucer Pilgrimage*, 262. Mr. Reeve is an engineer, graduate of the Yale School of Engineering. Mr. Reeve has made a careful study, not so much of flying saucers as such, but rather of communications in outer space.
4. Shirley, *Abraham Lincoln*, 176
5. *Ibid.*, 4
6. Stephenson, *Lincoln*, 200
7. Lorant, *Lincoln, a Pictorial Story of His Life*, 169
8. Curtis, *The True Abraham Lincoln*, 377
9. Karagulla, *Breakthrough to Creativity*, 17, 18
10. Stephenson, *Lincoln*, 200
11. Appleman, *Abraham Lincoln, from His Own Words and Contemporary Account*, 8. Mr. Appleman edited this work for the National Park Service of Richmond, Virginia, 2/23/42. A reprint of this publication was made in 1961. Previous references have been taken from the reprint.
12. Curtis, *The True Abraham Lincoln*, 375
13. Ford, *A Force or a Farce*, 17. This is a publication of the Spiritual Frontiers Fellowship based on a lecture by Rev. Arthur Ford at the 11th Annual Conference 5/13/67.
14. Ford, *Unknown but Known*, 11

14a. Lincoln, "Great Movements with Lincoln," No. 2. Address to Young Men's Lyceum, Springfield, Illinois, 1/27/1838.

15. Starr, *Lincoln's Dual Personality*, 7
16. Randall, J. C., *The Liberal Statesman*, 190
17. Bach, Letter No. 20, Page 7, from the Foundation of Spiritual Understanding. This foundation is one of the projects founded by Marcus Bach.
18. McMurty, Editor, *The Presidents Eulogize Lincoln*, 3. This is another Lincoln Lore publication.
19. Ford, *Force or a Farce*, 22

19a. Smith, *Lincoln and His Spiritual Life*, 13

19b. Nigg, *The Heretics*, 133

20. Jones, *Lincoln and the Preachers*, VIII
21. Richardson, *Lincoln Autobiography*, 3
22. Hyslop, *Contacts with the Other World*, 450
23. Newkirk, *Lincoln Lessons for Today*, 179
24. Masters, *Lincoln, The Man*, 149
25. Starr, *Lincoln's Dual Personality*, 8
26. Lindsey, "Lincoln's Centennial Review." This appeared in the *Chicago Tribune*, 1909. (*Chicago Tribune* was the publisher.)
27. Donald, *Lincoln Reconsidered*, 153
28. Pennell, *Religious Views of Lincoln*, 6 and The Preface
29. Kranz, *Abraham Lincoln, New Portrait*, 107
30. Current, *The Lincoln Nobody Knows*, 66
31. Herndon, *The Hidden Lincoln*, 111
32. Current, *The Lincoln Nobody Knows*, 57
33. *Ibid.*, 57
34. Carpenter, *Six Months at the White House*, 349
35. Hyslop, *Contact with the Other World*, 39
36. Barrett, *On the Threshold of the Unseen*, 119
37. Rodney, *Long Beach Independent, Press-Telegram*, 1/15/69
38. Karagulla, *Breakthrough to Creativity*, 248

39. Barrett, *On the Threshold of the Unseen*, 3
40. Kempf, *Philosophy of Common Sense*, 415
41. *Ibid.*, 413
42. *Ibid.*, 49
43. Maynard, *Was Lincoln A Spiritualist?*, XIV
44. Kase, *Emancipation Proclamation*, 5. This is a booklet found in the rare book collection at the Brown University Library. This is the first of several references to this material. A brief analysis of the booklet appears later in the book.
45. Leiper, Personal Letter, dated Lake Chautauqua, New York, 1968, 8. Dr. Leiper has the highest credentials as a world churchman.
46. Rice, Editor, "Reminiscences of Abraham Lincoln.", 590. This is an article by John C. Alley, Member of Congress during the Lincoln administration; also member of his home state Legislature, Massachusetts.
47. Fodor, *Between Two Worlds*, 11
47a. Peale, *Is Peace of Mind Possible Today?* Foundation of Xtn. Living Vol. 18, No. 1, 4
48. Hertz, *Lincoln Talks*, 5
49. Sandburg, *The Prairie Years, Vol. I*, 227
50. Herndon, *The Hidden Lincoln*, 229
51. Lorant, *Preview of the Secret Lincoln Papers*, 87
52. *Ibid.*, 87
53. *Ibid.*, 87
54. Herndon, *The Hidden Lincoln*, 211
55. Herndon, *The Life of Lincoln*, 3
56. Herndon, *The Hidden Lincoln*, 59
57. Ford, *A Force or A Farce*, 15
58. Hyslop, *Contact with the Other World*, 146
59. Maynard, *Was Lincoln a Spiritualist?* IX
60. Reeve, *A Flying Saucer Pilgrimage*, 230. A description of this work as made by Yale University School of Engineering has previously been given.
61. Editor, *Long Beach Independent, Press-Telegram*, 8/14/69
62. Jung, *Psychological Reflections*, 38

4. The Inquirer-Explorer

1. Bach, *Spiritual Breakthrough for Our Time*, 141
2. Newton, *Spiritual Life of Lincoln*, 36
3. Masters, *Lincoln, The Man*, 148
4. Jung, *Psychological Reflections*, VII
5. Lamon, *Life of Lincoln*, 110
6. Carpenter, *Inner Life of Lincoln*, 263. This book appears under two titles. It also carries the title, *Six Months at the White House*. The author, an artist at the White House, became famous for his painting of the ceremony at the signing of the Emancipation Proclamation.
7. Karagulla, *Breakthrough to Creativity*, 194
8. Hill, *Abraham Lincoln, Man of God*, 52
9. Schurz, *Abraham Lincoln*, 45. This is an essay by General Schurz, one of Lincoln's favorites.
10. Lodge, *Phantom Walls*, 203
11. Newman, *Lincoln for the Ages*, 414. This is a chapter by Graebel. A description of the author is given in a previous reference.

12. *Ibid.*, 104. This chapter is written by Alexander Woldman, a president of Abraham Lincoln associations of Ohio and Vice Chairman of the Ohio Abraham Lincoln Sesqui-Centennial Committee. Mr. Woldman is a Judge in the Juvenile Court of Cleveland, Ohio.
13. Oldroyd, *Words of Lincoln*, 138. The author fought on the Union side during the Civil War, from 1861 to 1865. For some ten years after the death of Lincoln, the author had charge of a collection in the Lincoln homestead in Springfield, Illinois.
14. Karagulla, *Breakthrough to Creativity*
15. Lindberg, Personal Letter to *Life Magazine*, 9/27/69, 60c. A previous reference has been made to this unusual letter in response to a request from *Life Magazine*, concerning the astronauts' wılk on the Moon.
16. Starr, *Lincoln's Dual Personality*, 12
17. Snider, *Abraham Lincoln*, An Interpretation, 574. This page number appears in the third part of the book.
18. Hill, *Abraham Lincoln, Man of God*, 99
19. Stephenson, *Lincoln*, 138
20. *Ibid.*, 237
21. Karagulla, *Breakthrough to Creativity*, 115
22. Editor, Ward, *Abraham Lincoln*, subtitle, Tributes from His Associates, 6. This particular tribute comes from Honorable Henry L. Dawes, former United States Senator from Massachusetts.
23. Hill, *Abraham Lincoln, Man of God*, 101, 102
24. Karagulla, *Breakthrough to Creativity*, 253
25. Current, *The Lincoln Nobody Knows*, 69
26. Luthin, *The Real Abraham Lincoln*, 116
27. Editor, Warren, *Herndon As Contemporary*. This is a *Lincoln Lore* publication.
28. Herndon and Weik, *Life of Lincoln*, 352. The name Weik does not appear on the front cover, but rather on the title page of this particular edition.
29. Barton, *The Soul of Lincoln*, 236
30. Kempf, *Lincoln's Philosophy of Common Sense*, 861. This work appears in two volumes. This is Volume II.
31. *Ibid.*, 870
32. Higgins, J. Pearce, *Survival After Death*. This is Canon Higgins of the Anglican Church of Great Britain and a leader in the Churches' Fellowship for Psychical Study. This is an excerpt from one of his lectures which appeared in the London Psychic News of 6/19/65. Canon Higgins is not to be confused with Paul Higgins., The latter was for many years President of the Spiritual Frontiers Fellowship in the United States.
33. Hapgood, *The Man of the People*, 15
34. Ward, Editor, *Abraham Lincoln, Tribute from His Associates*, 204. This is part of a talk by John H. Littlefield, entitled "Personal Recollections of Abraham Lincoln."
35. Lodge, *Phantom Walls*, 199. Sir Oliver Lodge is one of Great Britain's outstanding scientists in physics.

35a. Gross, *Lincoln's Own Stories*, 117

36. Stern, *The Life and Writings of Abraham Lincoln*, 176
37. Stephenson, *Lincoln*, 202
38. Schurz, *Abraham Lincoln*, 28. This is the first section of this book.
39. Smith, *Lincoln and His Spiritual Life*, 33
40. Randall and Current, *Mr. Lincoln*, 382
41. *Ibid.*, 385
42. *Ibid.*, 387

43. Kempf, *Philosophy of Common Sense*, 415, 421
44. Chesney, *Lincoln Still a Spiritualist*, 186. This gentleman is a medical physician and an avowed Spiritualist. His father was a friend of Lincoln.
45. Bradford, *The Haunted Biographer*, 15
46. Taggart, *Faith of Lincoln*, 281
47. *Ibid.*, 335
48. Thomas, *Portrait of Posterity*, 61
49. Current, *The Lincoln Nobody Knows*, 70
50. Sandburg, *The Prairie Years, Vol. II*, 155
51. Pett, *Long Beach Independent, Press-Telegram*, 2/17/70, C9
52. Shutes, *Lincoln's Emotional Life*, 118
53. Hill, *Abraham Lincoln, Man of God*, 24
54. Rice, Editor, "Reminiscences of Abraham Lincoln," 607. This is an article by Thomas Hicks. Mr. Hicks was a contemporary of Abraham Lincoln. As an artist, he painted a portrait of both Secretary of State Seward and President Lincoln.
55. Lorant, *Lincoln, a Pictorial Story of His Life*, 48
56. Schurz, *Abraham Lincoln*. This article appears in the first section of the book.
57. Wheare, *Abraham Lincoln and the United States*, 1. Mention has been made of this British publication, written for youth in the English universities.
58. Shirley, *Abraham Lincoln*, 23
59. Whitlock, *Abraham Lincoln*, 40
60. *Ibid.*, 40
61. Stern, *The Life and Writings of Abraham Lincoln*, 13
62. Kempf, "Abraham Lincoln's Organic and Emotional Neurosis," 419, 424. This article appears in the archives of neurology and psychiatry of the American Medical Association, 4/19/52.

62a. Schwartz, "Lincoln and the Marfan Syndrome," 478. Also a personal letter from the author. The article, as written by the author, appeared in the *Journal of the American Medical Association*, Vol. 187, 2/15/64.

63. *Ibid.*, 478. Also Personal Letter, 11/19/66.
64. Luthin, *The Real Abraham Lincoln*, 115
65. Herndon and Weik, *Life of Lincoln*, 473. This is a reprint with an introduction and notes by Paul M. Angle.
66. Kempf, *Lincoln's Emotional Organic Neurosis*, 430
67. Hurkos, Peter, *News Letter*. This was published in 1961 by the Hurkos Associates Foundation. The work of Peter Hurkos is described in this chapter and section of the book.
68. Sinclair, *Mental Radio*, 227
69. *Ibid.*
70. Herndon, *The Hidden Lincoln*, 410
71. Starr, *Lincoln's Dual Personality*, Foreword
72. Shutes, *Lincoln's Emotional Life*, 119
73. Luthin, *The Real Abraham Lincoln*, 116
74. Taggart, *Faith of A Lincoln*, 301
75. Shelton, *Abraham Lincoln Returns*, 189
76. Stephenson, *Lincoln*, 24
77. *Ibid.*, 200
78. Whitlock, *Abraham Lincoln*, 123
79. Ward, Editor, *Abraham Lincoln, Tributes from His Associates*, 49. This tribute, entitled "Lincoln's Vigil," was by his private secretary, William O. Stoddard.
80. Wolf, *The Almost Chosen People*, 194

81. Jones, *Lincoln and the Preachers*, 36
82. Hertz, *Lincoln's Talks*, 518
83. Bishop, *The Day Lincoln Was Shot*, 55
84. Bayne, *Tad Lincolns's Father*, 164
85. Brockett, *Life and Times of Lincoln* 338
86. Starr, *Lincoln's Dual Personality*, 22, 23
87. Fox, *Lincoln's Religion*, 60
88. Strout, *Seeing History and Participating In It*, 13. This is from an article from the *Christian Science Monitor*, dated 2/16/1968.
89. Kranz, *Abraham Lincoln, New Portarait*, 106
90. Stoddard, *The Table of Lincoln*, 132
91. Prince, *Noted Witnesses for Psychic Occurrances*, VII
92. Pennell, *Religious Views of Lincoln*, Preface
93. Peters, *Lincoln's Religion*, 48
94. Newman, *Lincoln for the Ages*, 414. This chapter is by Graebel, member of the Abraham Lincoln Association.
95. Thomas, *Portrait of Posterity*, 81
96. Sandburg, *The Prairie Years, Vol. I*, 137
97. Hay, *Lincoln Association Papers*, 122
98. Peters, *Séances*, 20
99. Karagulla, *Breakthrough to Creativity*, 260
100. Oldroyd, *Words of Lincoln*, 138. Reference has been made to the background of this author.
101. Karagulla, *Breakthrough to Creativity*, 261
102. Wheare, *Abraham Lincoln and the United States*, 9
103. Reeve, *Flying Saucer Pilgrimage*, 270. The qualifications of authorship have previously been made.
104. Bach, *Inner Ecstasy*. This is a statement contained in *News Item* by the publisher. The statement was made by Professor Bach.
105. Ford, *Unknown but Known*, 11
106. Barrett, *On the Threshold of the Unseen*, 165
107. Hyslop, *Contact with the Other World*, 4
108. Wolf, *The Almost Chosen People*, 29
109. Kelsey, *Tongue Speaking*. This particular quotation appeared in the Psychic News, a British publication. It is an excerpt from Dr. Kelsey's book.
110. Carrel, *Man The Unknown*, 60, 159. This is part of a footnote which appears on the bottom of both of the pages.
111. *Ibid.*
112. Herndon, *The Hidden Lincoln*, 111
113. Ford, *Unknown but Known*, 11
114. Hyslop, *Contact with the Other World*, 443
115. Editor, *Lincolniana*, 173. This article appears in the *Journal of the Illinois State Historical Society*, Vol. XLI
116. Laney, *Death and Ethical Reflections*, 4. This article appeared in the *Yale Divinity School News*.
117. Hyslop, *Contact with the Other World*, 10
118. *Ibid.*, 484
119. Sandburg, *The Prairie Years, Vol. I*, 473
120. Browne, *Every Day Life of Lincoln*, 351
121. Hardinge, *Report on Spiritualism*, 269
122. Whipple, *The Heart of Lincoln*, 63

123. Lang, *Wit and Wisdom of Abraham Lincoln*, 12
124. Hyslop, *Contact with the Other World*, 446
125. Ford, *Unknown But Known*, 15
126. As in this case, Bible references in the context of the book are noted. In one previous instance a special note number was given.
127. Hyslop, *Contact with the Other World*, 416
128. Fodor, *Between Two Worlds*, 177, 178
129. Editor, Dr. Roll, article entitled "Research in Survival," as it appears in *Theta Magazine*. This is a publication of the Psychical Research Foundation at the University of North Carolina. This issue is dated Winter, 1968.
130. Lewis, *Legends that Libel Lincoln*, 164
131. Wheare, *Abraham Lincoln and the United States*, 156
132. Randall, J. C., *The Liberal Statesman*, 31
133. Editor, McMurty, *Lincoln's Attendances at Séances, Part I*, 1/1963. This is a *Lincoln Lore* publication.
134. Lang, *The Wit and Wisdom of Abraham Lincoln*, 202
135. Thompson, *Lincoln, First American*, 205
136. Editor, Ward, *Abraham Lincoln, Tributes from His Associates*, 99. This is from an article entitled, "President Lincoln's Knowledge of Human Nature," a critical study by Hon. Thomas L. James, a Postmaster General under Abraham Lincoln.
137. Smith, *Lincoln and His Spiritual Life*, 5
138. Sharp, *Abraham Lincoln*, 147
139. Gross, *Lincoln's Own Stories*, 9
140. *Ibid.*, 130
141. Hill, *Abraham Lincoln, Man of God*, 295
142. Hyslop, *Contact with the Other World*, 449
143. Barton, *The Life of Abraham Lincoln*, Vol. I, 262
144. Herndon, *The Hidden Lincoln*, 174
145. Stephenson, *Lincoln*, 114
146. Lorant, *Lincoln, a Pictorial Study of His Life*, 117
147. Karagulla, *Breakthrough to Creativity*, 34
148. *Spiritual Frontiers Manual*, entitled "Principle and purposes of the Spiritual Frontiers Fellowship."
149. Hill, *Abraham Lincoln, Man of God*, 290
150. Hyslop, *Contact with the Other World*, 421
151. Hertz, *Lincoln Talks*, 577
152. *Spiritual Frontiers Fellowship Manual*, entitled "Principle and Purposes of the Spiritual Frontiers Fellowship."

152a. Dart, *U. S. Spiritualism on New Course As Appeal Grows*. This is from a front page article by the Los Angeles Times Religion Writer, Los Angeles dateline 11/19/69.

153. Eddy, *You Will Survive Death*, 7. Sherwood Eddy, as indicated, was one of the founders of the Spiritual Frontiers Fellowship. He is widely known as a world churchman and statesman.

CHAPTER V
THE EMANCIPATION OF THE EMANCIPATOR

1. Mission Impossible

1. Helm, *Mary, Wife of Lincoln*, 236
2. Shirley, *Abraham Lincoln*, 114
3. Wheare, *Abraham Lincoln and the United States*, 191

4. Editor, Letter Auctioned, *Long Beach Independent, Press-Telegram,* A3, 11/9/69. This quotation was contained in a letter dated 8/16/1864, signed by Abraham Lincoln and addressed to John J. Meier; at an auction sale the letter sold for $3,600.
4a. Hertz, *Lincoln Talks,* 353
4b. Hill, *Abraham Lincoln, Man of God,* 46
5. Lorant, *Lincoln, a Pictorial Story of His Life,* 177, 178
6. McMurty, *Lincoln Cartoons,* 6/69, 1. This is one of the *Lincoln Lore* publications.
7. McMurty, *Most Significant Lincoln Cartoons,* 2/68. This is another *Lincoln Lore* issue dated 6/19/68.
8. Randall, J. C., *The Liberal Statesman,* 191
9. Shirley, *Abraham Lincoln,* 176
10. *Ibid.,* 110
11. *Ibid.,* 135
12. Franklin, *From Slavery to Freedom,* 279, 290
12a. Lincoln, *Great Moments in the Life of Lincoln,* 2
13. Sandburg, *The War Years, Vol. II,* 344
14. Barton, *The Life of Lincoln,* Vol. I, 432
15. Schurz, *Abraham Lincoln,* 27, Part I
16. Shirley, *Abraham Lincoln,* 175
17. *Ibid.,* 176
18. Prince, *Noted Witnesses for Psychic Occurrences, Introduction,* VII. Gardiner Murphy was a former Chairman of the Department of Psychology at the College of the City of New York.
19. Martin, "Abraham Lincoln." This is a copy of an article which appeared in the *National Spiritualist Magazine,* 2/1/27.
20. Stephenson, *Abraham Lincoln,* 265
21. Reston, *Long Beach Independent, Press-Telegram,* article on Lincoln and Johnson, 2/14/68. Mr. Reston is the Editor of the *New York Times.*
22. Greenbie, *Anna Ella Carroll and Lincoln,* 348
22a. Sandburg, *Living Words of Lincoln,* 44. Sandburg served as the editorial sponsor of this book.
23. Randall and Current, *Mr. Lincoln,* 348
24. *Ibid.,* 349
25. Quinn, *Interior Causes of War,* 8
26. Franklin, *Emancipation Proclamation,* 20
27. Basler, *Collected Works of Lincoln,* 278, 279. Here we have a list of the names of the progressive friends, presumably Quakers. However, the context in which Lincoln used the term "progressive friends" covered not only the Quakers but a wide range of those who sympathized with his anti-slavery policy. This included the Spiritualists.
27a. Shook, *The Lincoln Story,* 171, 172
27b. Hertz, *Lincoln Talks,* 349
28. Editor Warren, *Lincoln and Spiritualism,* 4/46
29. Shelton, *Abraham Lincoln Returns,* 197. The author discovered her gifts of the spirit late in life; much of her mediumship has been related to Lincoln. In additon she has carried on extensive research projects in relation to Lincoln's psychic activities.
30. Latsley, Proclamation, Title "Reply to Commissions from Religious Denominations Asking Lincoln To Issue the Emancipation Proclamation as of 9/13/1862," 136
31. *Ibid.,* 137
32. *Ibid.,* 137
33. Stephenson, *Lincoln,* 266
34. Franklin, *From Slavery to Freedom,*" article in *Life Magazine,* 1968. The complete date is 11/22/68, 120.
35. Stearn and Fried, *The Essential Lincoln,* 468
36. Franklin, *From Slavery to Freedom, Life Magazine,* 11/22/68, 103

37. Wheare, *Abraham Lincoln and the United States,* 245
38. Nathan, *Lincoln's America,* 15
38a. Hertz, *Lincoln Talks,* 284
39. Wheare, *Abraham Lincoln and the United States,* 233
40. Lewis, *Legends that Libel Lincoln,* 164
40a. Hertz, *Lincoln Talks,* 536
41. Stern, *The Life and Writings of Abraham Lincoln,* 173
41a. Sandburg, Editor, *The Living Words of Abraham Lincoln,* 58
42. Hill, *Abraham Lincoln, Man of God,* 194
43. Lorant, "Two New Lincoln Finds," 118, *Look Magazine,* 10/21/69, Vol. 33, No. 21
44. Miller, *Portrait of Lincoln,* 70
45. Lorant, *Lincoln, a Pictorial Story of His Life,* 169
46. "Reminiscences of Abraham Lincoln," 535. This article is by James C. Welling, a Princeton College graduate in 1844. In 1871 he became President of Columbia University and was appointed Chairman of the Executive Committee of the Smithsonian Institute. During Lincoln's day he was Literary Editor of the National Intelligensia in Washington.
47. *Ibid.*
48. Wheare, *Abraham Lincoln and the United States,* 231
49. Abbott, *Magazine of History,* Extra No. 19 on page 13 as numbered at the top of the page.
50. Sharp, *Abraham Lincoln,* 141
51. Shirley, *Abraham Lincoln,* 311, 312
52. Lewis, *The 107th Lincoln Anniversary,* published by the Lincoln Centennial at Springfield, Illinois, 2/12/16, 22
53. Lang, *Wit and Wisdom of Abraham Lincoln,* 221
54. Smith, *Lincoln and His Spiritual Life,* 55
55. Stephenson, *Lincoln,* 296
56. Contstad, News Release of the United Press, 1863, New York City dateline.
57. Carpenter, *Six Months in the White House* or *The Inner Life of Lincoln,* 292

2. Emancipated Guidance

1. Lorant, *Lincoln, A Pictorial Story of His Life,* 79
2. Monaghan, *Was Abraham Lincoln Really a Spiritualist?,* 215
3. Gross, *Lincoln's Own Stories,* 348
3a. Fodor, *Encylopedia Psychic Science* 203
4. Shelton, *Abraham Lincoln Returns,* 203
4a. News Letter, Mt. Toby Friends Mtg. N. Amherst Mass. 9/73
5. Pike, *If This Be Heresy,* 119
6. Hyslop, *Contact with the Other World,* 328
7. Kase, *Emancipation Proclamation,* 16. Mention has been made of this original source material.
8. Monaghan, *Was Abraham Lincoln Really a Spiritualist?,* 215
9. Kase, *Emancipation Proclamation,* 23
10. Tweedale, *Man's Survival After Death,* 450
11. Hyslop, *Contact with the Other World,* 345
12. Kase, *Emancipation Proclamation,* 24
12. *Ibid.*, 24
14. *Ibid.*, 25
15. *Ibid.*, 16
16. *Ibid.*, 26
17. Fox, *Lincoln's Religion,* 60

18. McMurty, *Lincoln's Attendance at Séances, Part I,* 1/19/63, *Lincoln Lore,* 2
19. Wolf, *The Almost Chosen People,* 156
20. Chase, *Forty Years on the Spiritual Rostrum,* 149
21. Fitzgerrell, *Lincoln Was a Spiritualist,* 22

3. Binding Up the Wounds

1. Hertz, *Lincoln Talks,* 559
1a. Bates, *Religious Life of Lincoln,* 57
2. Thompson, *Abraham Lincoln,* 102
3. Ward Editor, *Abraham Lincoln, Tribute from His Associates,* 23. This was written by General James Rusling, after the Battle of Gettysburg.
4. Monaghan, *Was Lincoln Really a Spiritualist?,* 226-227
5. Gross, *Lincoln's Own Stories,* 154
5a. Hertz, *Lincoln Talks,* 455
6. Karagulla, *Breakthrough to Creativity,* 79
7. Grierson, *Abraham Lincoln, The Practical Mystic,* 30
8. Smith, *Lincoln and His Spiritual Life,* 67
9. Hyslop, *Contact with the Other World,* 453
10. *Ibid.,* 56
11. Maynard, *Was Lincoln a Spiritualist?,* 180
12. Stephenson, *Lincoln,* 111
13. Gross, *Lincoln's Own Stories,* 157
14. *Ibid.,* 117, 118
14a. Mitgang Herbert, Writer and Editor New York Times
15. Stephenson, *Lincoln,* 245
16. *Ibid.,* 59
16a. de Chambrun, *Impressions of Lincoln and the Civil War,* 84. The author refers in the subtitle to *A Foreigner's Account.* This in itself provides a degree of objectivity.
17. Hill, *Abraham Lincoln, Man of God,* 262
17a. Lincoln, *Great Moments in the Life of Lincoln,* 1
18. Whitlock, *Abraham Lincoln,* 128
19. Shirley, *Abraham Lincoln,* 108
20. *Ibid.,* 155
21. Sharp, *Abraham Lincoln,* 95
22. Editor, Rice, *Reminiscences of Abraham Lincoln,* 526
23. *Ibid.,* 526
24. Stern, *The Life and Writings of Abraham Lincoln,* 167
25. *Ibid.,* 173
26. Appleman, *Lincoln's Own Words and Contemporary Account,* 27
26a. McMurty, *Lincoln Lore No. 888,* 4/15/46, page 1 (The Lincolns and Spiritualism)
27. Lorant, *Lincoln, a Pictorial Story of His Life,* 193
28. *Ibid.,* 237
29. *Ibid.,* 240
30. Jones, Judy, *Lincoln's Cane, Gift of 1863.* Miss Jones is a United Press International correspondent writing for the *San Diego News,* 8/11/69.
30a. Neely, *Lincoln Lore,* Lincoln Life Foundation, 9/73 No. 1627 pg. 1
31. Rankin, *Personal Recollections of Lincoln,* VII
32. Randall and Current, *Mr. Lincoln,* 386
32a. de Chambrun, *Impressions of Lincoln and the Civil War,* 85. Special reference has been made to this author in a previous note.
32b. Chesney, Article in the *Argos Magazine,* 2/1/62, 30

4. The Hour of Decision

1. Cook, Roy J. (compiler) *101 Famous Poems,* 34
2. Ford, *Unknown But Known,* 132
3. Mitgang, *Lincoln as They Saw Him,* 328
4. *Ibid.,* 299
5. Wheare, *Abraham Lincoln and the United States,* 232
6. Stern, *The Life and Writings of Abraham Lincoln,* 130, 131
7. Hyslop, *Contact with the Other World,* 138

7a. Segal, *Conversations with Lincoln,* 133

8. Franklin, *Emancipation Proclamation,* 24

8a. Prince, *Noted Witnesses for Psychic Occurrances,* 81

9. Mitgang, *Lincoln as They Saw Him,* 312
10. Browne, *Every Day Life of Lincoln,* 445
11. Oldroyd, *Words of Lincoln,* 98
12. Peters, *Lincoln's Religion,* 48
13. McMurty, *Painting of the Proclamation,* a *Lincoln Lore* publication 3/19/69, 2-3
14. Stern, *The Life and Writings of Abraham Lincoln,* 144
15. Current and Randall, *Mr. Lincoln,* 352
16. Starr, *Lincoln's Dual Personality,* 9
17. Appleman, *Lincoln's Own Words and Contemporary Account,* 42
18. Shutz, *Lincoln's Emotional Life,* 151

18a. Jung, *Psychological Reflections,* 294

19. Kerner, *Treasury of Lincoln Quotations,* 89
20. Hay, *Lincoln Association Papers,* 246. Hay was one of Lincoln's private secretaries.

20a. Hertz, *Lincoln Talks,* 347-348

21. Bennett, *Ebony Magazine,* 2/68. Commentary in the *Long Beach Independent, Press-Telegram,* 1/24/68, has title, "Lincoln Was a Racist, Says Negro Editor."
22. Editor, Commentary, *Christian Science Monitor,* 2/16/68
23. Rice, *Reminiscences of Abraham Lincoln,* 193. Chapter IX is written by Frederick Douglas.
24. Shirley, *Abraham Lincoln,* 149
25. Sharp, *Abraham Lincoln,* 152
26. Warren, Editor, *Lincoln and Spiritualism.* This is Part I of a *Lincoln Lore* publication, 4/46.
27. Stern, *The Life and Writings of Abraham Lincoln,* 728
28. Talbot, *Meet the President,* 64, 65. This is a British publication.
29. Randall and Current, *Mr. Lincoln,* 353
30. Pole, *Clarendon Biography of Lincoln,* 44
31. Jung, *Psychological Reflections,* 288
32. Rice, Editor, *Reminiscences of Abraham Lincoln,* 531. This chapter was written by James C. Welling. Reference has been made to him in a previous notation.
33. Stephenson, *Lincoln,* 278
34. Wheare, *Abraham Lincoln and the United States,* 158
35. Schurz, *Abraham Lincoln,* 11. This is the second part of the book, written by Mr. Watterson.
36. Sharp, *Abraham Lincoln,* 147
37. Lang, *Wit and Wisdom of Abraham Lincoln,* 132
38. Woldman, *Lincoln and the Russians,* 190
39. *Ibid.,* 190
40. Gross, *Lincoln's Own Stories,* 107
41. Hill, *Abraham Lincoln Man of God,* 173

42. Rice, Editor, *Reminiscences of Abraham Lincoln*, 577. This article is written by John B. Halley, a close friend of Lincoln, to whom mention has been made.
43. *Ibid.*, 245. This article was written by Titian J. Coffey. This gentleman was an Assitant Attorney General in the Lincoln administration.
44. Wheare, *Abraham Lincoln and the United States*, 214
45. Appleman, *Lincoln's Own Words and Contemporary Account*, 24. This particular reprint came out in a large blue-covered paperback.
46. *Ibid.*, 32. This page number appears in the smaller leaflet with a yellow paper cover.
47. Donovan, *Mr. Lincoln's Proclamation*, 110
48. Shurz, *Abraham Lincoln*, 20, 21, which appear in the second section of the book by Mr. Watterson.
49. Wolf, *The Almost Chosen People*, 148
50. Brockett, *Life and Times of Abraham Lincoln*, 339. Mr. Brockett was a contemporary of Lincoln and provides an intimate account.
51. Whitlock, *Abraham Lincoln*, 141
52. Stern, *The Life and Writings of Abraham Lincoln*, 142

5. Liberation in Death

1. Jung, *Psychological Reflections*, 288
2. Bach, *Spiritual Breakthrough for Our Times*, 137
3. Hyslop, *Contact with the Other World*, 328, 329
4. Edited by the Lincoln Savings and Loan Association, *Lincoln's Words and Wisdom*, 1965, 2
5. Bayne, *Tad Lincoln's Father*, 181
6. Wahm, Joseph, *The Other Side of Lincoln*, 203 (Appears in Harper's Weekly, Vol. 50, Part 11, 1906)
7. Cook, Roy J. (compiler) *101 Famous Poems*, 123

7a. Muldoon, *Sensational Psychic Experiences*, 22

8. Ford, *Unknown But Known*, 66
9. Newton, *Spiritual Life of Lincoln*, 37
10. Constad, *News Release*, United Press, New York City dateline, 1863
11. Mearns, *The Lincoln Papers*, 333
12. Hill, *Abraham Lincoln, Man of God*, 325

12a. Hertz, *Lincoln Talks*, 653

13. Logan, *The Great Conspiracy*, 642
14. Sandburg, *The War Years*, Vol. 11,86, 87
15. Lamon, *Recollections*, 110
16. *Ibid.*, 112
17. Helm, *Mary, Wife of Lincoln*, 237
18. Carpenter, *Six Months at the White House* or *Inner Life of Lincoln*, 263
19. Lewis, *Myths After Lincoln*, 298
20. Butler, *Across the Years*, 379
21. Monaghan, *Was Lincoln Really a Spiritualist?*, 231
22. *Ibid.*, 232
23. Wolf, *The Almost Chosen People*, 116
24. Rice, Editor, *Reminiscences of Abraham Lincoln*, 190

24a. Aikman, *Ford's Theatre Reborn*, 397

25. Shirley, *Abraham Lincoln*, 165
26. Stephenson, *Lincoln*, 138
27. Aikman, *Ford's Theatre Reborn*, 307
28. Appleman, *Lincoln's Own Words and Contemporary Account*, 49

28a. *National Geographic Magazine*, Mar. 1970, Vol. 137, No. 3, 397
29. Lewis, *Myths After Lincoln*, 105, 106
30. Holzer, *Window to the Past*, 31
31. Barton, *Abraham Lincoln*, Vol. 11, 339
32. Eisenschmil, *Why Was Lincoln Murdered?* 398, 405
33. Lorant, *Lincoln's Secret Papers*, 86
34. Stern, *The Life and Writings of Abraham Lincoln*, 156
35. Lorant, *A Pictorial Story of Lincoln's Life*, 107
36. Whitlock, *Abraham Lincoln*, 22
37. Muldoon, *Sensational Experiences*, Vol. 1, 54
38. Oldroyd, *Words of Lincoln*, 181
39. Lamon, *Recollections*, 119
40. Whitlock, *Abraham Lincoln*, 179
41. Evans, *This Is American's Hour*, 127
42. Hall, *The Civil War Unveiled*, 45
43. Thomas, *Portrait of Posterity*, 130
44. Bradford, *The Haunted Biographer*, 19
45. Donald, *Lincoln Reconsidered*, 151
46. *Ibid.*, 153
47. Shelton, *Personal Letter to Author*, Mar. 12, 1960
48. Stephanson, *Lincoln*, 138
49. Hill, *Abraham Lincoln, Man of God*, 373
50. *The Witness*, Quarterly Journal Hallowed Grounds Fellowship, Mar. 1969, Series No. 2, No. 13, pg. 2

EPILOGUE

1. Pike, *If This Be Heresy*, 5
2. Prince, *Noted Witnesses for Psychic Occurances*, 8
3. *Ibid.*, 104
4. Barrett, *On the Threshold of the Unseen*, 16, 17
5. *Ibid.*, 17
6. Fodor, *Between Two Worlds*, 2

6a. Lincoln, *Great Moments in the Life of Lincoln*, 2

7. Editor, *Long Beach Independent, Press-Telegram*, 2/16/70
8. *Ibid.*
9. *Long Beach Independent, Press-Telegram*, 2/14/68. Article entitled "Mr. Lincoln and Mr. Johnson," by the Editor of the *New York Times*.
10. Leiper, Personal Letter, datelined Chautauqua, New York, 2/10/68
11. James, "Does Modern Psychical Research Need Another William James?," *London Psychic News*, 7/22/61
12. Harris, Editorial, *Long Beach Independent, Press-Telegram*, 10/2/69
13. Barrett, *On the Threshold of the Unseen*, 17, 18
14. *Ibid.*, 4
15. Dart, "United States Spiritualism on New Course As Appeal Grows," *Los Angeles Times*, 11/19/1969. This was a front page, first column news item of some length.
16. *Ibid.*, 1
17. Karagulla, *Breakthrough to Creativity*, 20, 21
18. *Ibid.*, 20, 21
19. Shutes, *Lincoln's Emotional Life*, 149

20. Dart, "United States Spiritualism on New Course as Appeal Grows," *Los Angeles Times*, 11/19/69, 1
21. Barrett, *On the Threshold of the Unseen*, 14
22. Sharp, *Florissant Valley Community College Course in Psychic Phenomena.* This is a Spiritual Frontiers Fellowship News Letter, 2/1970, Vol. IV, 2
23. Eres, "Put On or Real?" *Long Beach Independent, Press-Telegram.* This editorial appeared in the Radio/TV Section.
24. Hyslop, *Contact with the Other World*, 131
25. Newman, *Lincoln for the Ages*, 414. This chapter was contributed by Richard Paul Graebel. Reference has been made to the work of Mr. Graebel and also to this particular quotation.
26. Murray, *Matters of Life and Death*, 187
27. Ford, *A Force or Farce*, 22. Previous reference has been made to this lecture by Rev. Arthur Ford.
28. *Ibid.*, 22
29. Barrett, *On the Threshold of the Unseen*, X
30. Kase, *The Emancipation Proclamation*, 26
31. Bach, *Spiritual Breakthrough for Our Time*, 33
32. Warren, *Herndon's Contribution to Lincoln Mythology*, 13
33. Karagulla, *Breakthrough to Creativity*, 228
34. Hertz, *Lincoln Talks*, 143-144
34a. Johnson, "Can We Know God?" As indicated, this constitutes notes taken from a lecture at the Unity Church, Santa Ana, California, 4/5/70
35. Maynard, *Was Lincoln a Spiritualist?*, VII, XVIII
36. Doyle, *History of Spiritualism*, 70
37. Maynard, *Was Lincoln a Spiritualist?*, XVIII
38. Johnson, *Psychical Research*, 97. This is a small textbook written by a distinguished scientist and professor of physics at Queen's College, Melbourne, Australia. Several references have been made to this author.
39. Peters, *Lincoln's Religion*, 20, 21. This section of the book deals with séances.
40. Evans, *Mrs. Lincoln, Study of Personality*, 265
41. Schurz, *The Reminiscences*, 156, 157
42. Jung, *Psychological Reflections*, 8, 9
43. Phillips, *Ring of Truth*, 117
44. Herndon, *Life of Lincoln*, 351
45. Myers, *Human Personality and Its Survival of Bodily Death*, 351
46. Doyle, *History of Spiritualism*, 149
47. Dart, *United States Spiritualism on New Course As Appeal Grows, Los Angeles Times*, 11/19/69, 1
48. Hyslop, *Contact with the Other World*, 64
49. Sinnott, *The Biology of the Spirit*, 130
50. Lindsay, *Abraham Walks at Midnight, 101 Famous Poems*, 54 compiled by Roy J. Cook

INDEX

INDEX

'A'

'B'

'C'

'H'

'I'

'J'

'K'

'L'

'M'

'N'

'O'

'P'

'Q'

'R'

'S'

'T'

'V'

'W'